NEGRO SELF-CONCEPT:

implications for school and citizenship

The report of a conference sponsored by the Lincoln Filene Center for Citizenship and Public Affairs

WILLIAM C. KVARACEUS
DIRECTOR OF YOUTH STUDIES
LINCOLN FILENE CENTER

JOHN S. GIBSON
SENIOR ASSOCIATE DIRECTOR
LINCOLN FILENE CENTER

FRANKLIN K. PATTERSON
DIRECTOR
LINCOLN FILENE CENTER

BRADBURY SEASHOLES
DIRECTOR OF POLITICAL STUDIES
LINCOLN FILENE CENTER

JEAN D. GRAMBS
ASSOCIATE PROFESSOR OF EDUCATION
COLLEGE OF EDUCATION
UNIVERSITY OF MARYLAND

McGRAW-HILL BOOK COMPANY
New York • St. Louis • San Francisco

The conference reported herein, entitled "The Relationship of Education to Self-concept in Negro Children and Youth," was supported by the Cooperative Research Program of the Office of Education, United States Department of Health, Education, and Welfare, and the President's Committee on Juvenile Delinquency and Youth Development.

CONFERENCE PARTICIPANTS:

John M. Billman
Max Bogart
Howard L. Bowen
Frank W. Brown
Jerome Cohen
Joanna T. Daly
Martin Deutsch
Joseph Devitt
Frank J. Dressler, Jr.
Philip J. Driscoll
G. Franklin Edwards
Martha M. Eliot
Edgar Z. Friedenberg
John S. Gibson
Grace M. Glynn
Bernard Goldstein
Edmund Gordon
Jean D. Grambs
Harold Haizlip
A. John Holden, Jr.
Wyman Holmes
Norris Hoyt
Dalton Jones
Owen B. Kiernan
Bernard M. Kramer
William C. Kvaraceus
Daniel W. Marshall
Howard E. Mitchell
Merrill F. Norlin
Jean M. Oxley
Franklin Patterson
Thomas F. Pettigrew
Richard V. Rapacz
William M. Phillips, Jr.
Frank Riessman
William P. Robinson, Jr.
Margaret N. Rowley
Karlene V. Russell
Ezra V. Saul
Bradbury Seasholes
Fannie Shaftel
Richard W. Smith
John Steele
Ray M. Stine
Anthony E. Terino
Kimball Wiles
Chester E. Willette
James N. Williams
Deborah Partridge Wolfe
Nathan Wright

NEGRO SELF-CONCEPT

Library of Congress Catalog Card Number: 64-66193

DEDICATION

To John J. Mahoney, distinguished educator, cofounder of the Civic Education Project which became the Lincoln Filene Center, and cherished friend of the authors.

ACKNOWLEDGMENTS

The authors and the Lincoln Filene Center for Citizenship and Public Affairs gratefully acknowledge the cooperation of the holders of copyrights who have permitted use of their materials, as follows:

Addison-Wesley Publishing Company, Inc., for brief passages from *The Volunteer Work Camp* by Henry W. Riecken and *The Nature of Prejudice* by Gordon W. Allport (quoted by permission of Addison-Wesley Publishing Company, Inc.). American Council on Education for the passage from Robert S. Sutherland's *Color, Class and Personality. The American Scholar* for quotations from Joseph Adelson's "The Teacher as a Model" (reprinted from *The American Scholar,* Summer, 1961, Vol. 30, No. 3; copyright © 1961 by the United Chapters of Phi Beta Kappa; by permission of the publishers). Anti-Defamation League of B'nai B'rith for a paragraph from *Time to Act* by John F. Kennedy, published by the Anti-Defamation League of B'nai B'rith, and two brief quotations from *The Desegregation of Southern Schools: A Psychiatric Study* by Robert Coles, published by the Anti-Defamation League of B'nai B'rith and the Southern Regional Council. Mr. James Baldwin and the *Saturday Review* for several excerpts from his "A Talk to Teachers." The Bobbs-Merrill Company, Inc., for the privilege of drawing freely on an article, "The Status and Function of Personnel Services," by William C. Kvaraceus, published originally in *Education,* December, 1960, pp. 202–209. The Bobbs-Merrill Company, Inc., and the author for a quotation from *On Being Negro in America* (copyright 1951 by J. Saunders Redding, reprinted by special permission of the publishers, The Bobbs-Merrill Company, Inc.). *Childhood Education* and the author for a quotation from an article (reprinted by permission of the Association for Childhood Education International, 3615 Wisconsin Avenue, N.W., Washington, D. C., from "Reactions of Children from Crowded Areas" by Mary A. Sarvis; from *Childhood Education,* May, 1963, Vol. 39, No. 9). Columbia University Press for a brief passage from *The Optimistic Tradition and American Youth* by Eli Ginzburg, James K. Anderson, and John L. Herma. *Confluence: An International Forum* for two passages from an article (reprinted from *Confluence,* 1957, Robert J. Havighurst, "How Education Changes Society," President and Fellows of Harvard College). The Council for Exceptional Children for a quotation from "The Culturally Disadvantaged: Educational Implications of Certain Social-Cultural Phenomena" by Delmo Della-Dora. Professor Helen H. Davidson and her coauthors for two paragraphs from their study of "Characteristics of Successful School Achievers from a Severely Deprived Environment." The Dial Press, Inc., for brief passages from *Nobody Knows My Name* and *The Fire Next Time* by James Baldwin (copyright © 1963 by James Baldwin; reprinted by permission of the publishers, The Dial Press, Inc.). *Dissent* for two passages from "The Image of Adolescent Maturity" by Edgar Z. Friedenberg (© *Dissent,* Spring, 1963). Miss Victorine Day Dollard for part of a paragraph from *Caste and Class in a Southern Town* by John Dollard. Educational Policies Commission for two paragraphs from *Education and the Disadvantaged American.* Emerson Books, Inc., and George Allen & Unwin Ltd. for a brief passage from *Psychoanalysis for Teachers and Parents* by Anna Freud (Emerson Books, Inc.); reprinted by permission of the publishers. The Free Press of Glencoe for part of a paragraph from Easton and Hess's "Problems in Political Socialization," in Lipset and Lowenthal's *Culture and Social Character.* Harper & Row, Inc., for quotations from *Individual Behavior* (rev. ed.) by Combs and Snygg and *The Culturally Deprived Child* by Riessman. Holt, Rinehart and Winston, Inc., for two short quotations from *Negro and White Youth* by Albert J. Lott and Bernice E. Lott (copyright © 1963). Houghton Mifflin Company for a paragraph from Kirkpatrick's *High School Social Studies Perspectives. Integrated* for a paragraph from "School Integration in New York City" by Ellen Lurie, from Vol. II, February-March, 1964. *The Journal of Educational Sociology* for two quotations from an article by Lukoff, Patterson, and Winick. Meridian Books (The World Publishing Company) for three excerpts from *The Mark of Oppression: Explorations in the Personality of the American Negro* by Abram Kardiner and Lionel Ovesey. Oxford University Press, Inc., for Murray's definition of "press" and for the quotation from Horace Mann. *Science Education* for the quotations from Fletcher Watson's "The Hero Image in Education." *Show* and Miss Lena Horne for two quotations from "I Just Want to Be Myself" (reprinted from *Show,* the Magazine of the Arts, September, 1963). Society for Applied Anthropology for a brief quotation by Martin Deutsch. Syracuse University Press for the privilege of borrowing the substance of Dr. Kvaraceus's study of "The Behavioral Deviate in the Culture of the Secondary Schools" for use in his section of this book. Bureau of Publications, Teachers College, for four quotations: Arthur T. Jersild, *In Search of Self* (New York: Bureau of Publications, Teachers College, Columbia University, 1960), pp. 9f., 13; A. Harry Passow, *Education in Depressed Areas* (New York: Bureau of Publications, Teachers College, Columbia University, 1963), pp. 128, 177. University of California Press for a quotation from "The Language of Our Time" by Dorothy B. Jones, in *Quarterly of Film, Radio, and Television.* The Bureau of Educational Research of the University of Illinois and the author for the use of two quotations from an unpublished paper by David P. Ausubel. University of North Carolina Press for part of a sentence by Park and Burgess. Educational Television Station WGBH, Boston, for an excerpt from its broadcast, "Conversation with James Baldwin." John Wiley & Sons, Inc., for brief quotations from Hollingshead's *Elmtown's Youth* and *Manual of Child Psychology* (2nd ed.), edited by Carmichael.

TABLE OF CONTENTS

introduction THE PURPOSE AND TREND OF THE CONFERENCE

by Franklin Patterson . . . Director, The Lincoln Filene Center for Citizenship and Public Affairs and Lincoln Filene Professor of Citizenship and Public Affairs, Tufts University

The papers gathered in this report were part of a conference entitled "The Relationship of Education to Self-concept in Negro Children and Youth," which was conducted at the Lincoln Filene Center, Tufts University, September 16–19, 1963.

If these materials can suggest to the reader some of the intensity and difficulty that the Conference experienced, I will be grateful. I can speak with some authority on this, since I was chairman of the Conference and well exposed to its tensions. Looking back, I feel that the most instructive thing about it was its difficulty. Thus I hope that the reader, at the beginning, will see these papers in a conference context which included, in addition to a normal quota of goodwill and irreproachable intention, an assortment of such other elements as lack of communication, impatience, anger, and anguish. And I hope the reader will ask, with me, why the concerns that the Conference sought to deal with were so hard to handle.

Conference Theme and Assumptions

It may help if the theme of the Conference is clarified for the reader. The theme itself turned out to be a source of contention within the Conference, and its assumptions may help the reader see why.

Two general assumptions beckoned those who planned the Conference: One was *that, in general, the environmental press of the American color-caste system tends to develop conceptions of self in Negro children and youth which result in defeated behavior, as far as academic and*

***political** development are concerned.* The other general assumption was *that schools, which tend to serve as part of this defeating press, can instead serve to strengthen the self-concept of Negro children and youth, with a consequent strengthening of their performance as students and citizens.*

The term *press* is borrowed from Henry A. Murray, in whose usage it meant a tendency, or "potency," in the environment to facilitate or obstruct an organism. Murray defined press as "a temporal gestalt of stimuli which usually appears in the guise of a *threat of harm* or *promise of benefit* to the organism."[1] The papers in this report view the color-caste system under which American Negroes live as such a press, exercising negative impact on self-concept and behavioral responses of Negro children and youth. It was hard for some of the Conference participants who were school people and whites to face the premises that a color-caste system in America really exists and that it could exercise the kind of negative press which can damage personality and distort or inhibit behavior.

In her paper, Dr. Jean D. Grambs deals with ways in which the negative impact of the color-caste system bears critically on the personal and educational development of individuals. She devotes particular attention to the idea and definition of *self-concept,* a term which some of the Conference participants found uncongenial. That self-concept was not an equally congenial construct to all participants was, among other things, a symptom of the diversity within the group. It was also a sign that a common language with regard to psychosocial phenomena is hard to come by. As a construct, self-concept is drawn from the work of James, Sullivan, Horney, Mead, and others. Jersild has put the meanings of the idea of self together in the following way, calling self "a composite of thoughts and feelings which constitute a person's awareness of his individual existence, his conception of who and what he is."[2] Erikson prefers the term *identity,* saying that "identity *formation* neither begins nor ends with adolescence: it is a lifelong development largely unconscious to the individual and to his society. Its roots go back all the way to the first self-recognition . . ."[3] The term *self-concept* in these papers, then, refers to the process of identity development and maintenance which occupies each human life. We assume, with Harry Stack Sullivan, that the self "can never be isolated from the complex of interpersonal relations in which the person lives and has his being," and that the self is heavily affected by the "reflected appraisals" of the society in which the person lives. We agree with Jersild that, if the reflected appraisals

> . . . of which the self is made up are mainly derogatory, . . . then the growing child's attitudes toward himself will be mainly derogatory. The child toward whom the predominant attitude of significant persons has been one of hostility, disapproval,

> and dissatisfaction will tend to view the world in similar terms. He will have difficulty in seeing or learning anything better, and, although he may not openly express self-depreciatory attitudes, he has a depreciatory attitude toward others and toward himself.[4]

These orientations and viewpoints (i.e., those suggested by Sullivan, Jersild, and others) relate the self primarily to "significant others" in the family and in other close ties. Membership in an allegedly inferior color-caste, it is the judgment of the present papers, further and massively conditions interpersonal relations and self-perception for Negro children and youth. Dr. Grambs examines ways in which Negro caste experience affects self-concept and opens up a discussion of means by which school programs can provide Negro children with a sense of self that is not foreclosed by caste experience.

Dr. Bradbury Seasholes, in his basic paper, deals with problems of citizenship, political development, and political education which are raised for Negroes by the press of a color-caste system. He also assays the impact of the Negro protest movement and other factors upon self-concept among Negro youth and examines the developing political reality to which Negro political education and action should bear relevance. In this connection, we can note that a new sense of power through political and social action is available to many Negroes, and that the present era of change opens new possibilities for the political education of all Negro youth. At the same time, the fact that the Negro electorate, even if fully enfranchised, would still be in a numerical minority (except in certain of the major inner cities and parts of the South) imposes some notable constraints on the choices of effective political behavior for which Negro citizens should be prepared. Skill in coalition politics, for example, will be increasingly valuable to Negro citizens as their electoral power increases.

Dr. William C. Kvaraceus undertakes, as the reader will see, a broad and thorough review of the possibilities and limitations of the school as an agent of change, with particular reference to the needs of Negro youth. While cautioning that there is no one thing that the school alone can do that will make any great difference in the self-concept of Negro youth, Kvaraceus suggests multiple ways that the school can help more than it helps now, through its total program and its potential community relationships.

Conference Objectives

The three basic papers prepared by Grambs, Seasholes, and Kvaraceus were intended as springboards for discussion at the Conference. The papers were conceived against a background in which those of us at the Lincoln Filene Center shared. We saw school failure, early dropouts, unemployment, unwed motherhood, and delinquency as representing a familiar, patterned sequence in the lives of many disadvantaged and culturally deprived youth, Negro and white. We saw that for many Negro young people, this all-too-familiar series of events is typically aggravated by accumulated incidents of discrimination, segregation, and social ostracism. We felt that these experiences tend to reinforce and reflect low self-concept among such youth. We felt that such experiences evoke deeper frustrations that beget aggression. The aggression may be turned inward; it may be sublimated through more positive channels (sports and recreation); it may take more overt and attacking forms of expression, as in delinquent acts or in the joining of extremist movements. In every case, there is a serious waste of human energy that could be harnessed for social and civic betterment and for self-realization.

With others, we have been happily aware that there are fresh signs that low self-esteem is becoming less the rule for more Negro Americans. Sit-ins, freedom rides, and other such demonstrations are indicative of a different mood of aggressiveness—significantly led by younger Negroes—that in turn speaks of a more positive racial image.

As we prepared for the Conference, then, we felt that a twofold challenge presented itself to concerned Americans. First, constructive channels for emergent high self-esteem among the Negro vanguard must be found. Second, the continuing grip of *low* self-esteem among the overwhelming majority of Negro citizens must be recognized and broken.

The *consequences* of self-concept rather than the phenomenon itself have concerned us most. The varieties of pathological behavior that are presumed to follow negative self-concept run from political apathy to suicide and homicide, to juvenile delinquency and sexual deviation. The range of consequences that might be studied was far broader than our interests. Following the primary interests of the Lincoln Filene Center, we proposed to focus on the consequences of self-concept in the educational and citizenship spheres. How do Negro students view the political world? Do they consider themselves or their parents as policitally potent? What kinds of political activity do they consider most effective for achieving their own objectives? What are those objectives? What can be done at the classroom level to enable Negro youth to succeed and to stay in school unto the benefit of self and society?

All self-concepts are significant in understanding individuals. But those that are of greater concern to us as educators and citizens are the negative ones. The child with a negative view of self is a child who will not be able to profit adequately from school. Once a child is convinced he cannot learn in school, the task of educators becomes almost impossible. He may well make trouble for his classmates, his teachers, and himself. A negative self-concept is just as crippling and just as hard to overcome as any physical handicap. In fact, a negative self-image may be even more crippling, because it is often hidden from the view of the naïve or untrained observer. Most children who hate themselves act out this self-hatred by kicking the world around them. They are abusive, aggressive, hard to control, and full of anger and hostility at a world which has told them that they are not valued, are not good, and are not going to be given a chance. Such attitudes often continue to cripple an adult life.

With this background, the Conference to which these papers were directed aimed to achieve the following purposes. We hoped to reexamine the implications of available research relevant to the self-concept of Negro youth, with reference to theoretical conceptualizations, methodological problems, and germinal areas for continuing research effort. We hoped also to secure a delineation of the school's role in developing a realistic and positive self-concept by:

1. Examining negative school forces that downgrade the self-concept,
2. Identifying positive practices that now tend to upgrade the self-concept,
3. Searching for new interventions that might be tested out for their effectiveness in changing and improving the learning behavior of Negro youth in the classroom.

We also hoped to explore the relationship of self-concept to political thinking and behavior. In this connection, we wanted to examine:

1. The extent to which variations (positive and negative) in self-concept are reflected in different degrees of optimism about political potency,
2. The extent to which political pessimism flows from actual ineffectiveness of Negroes in the political processes,
3. The extent to which low self-esteem in relation to politics is an effect rather than a cause of political impotence,
4. The extent to which a sense of political impotence, as one type of low self-esteem, is a part of an overall set of negative images of the self.

These were our objectives in the Conference, both in the papers which were prepared for it and in the discussion which these papers generated.

Conference Procedure

The procedure which the Conference followed was simple. The papers by Grambs, Seasholes, and Kvaraceus had been mimeographed and distributed to the Conference participants in advance of their coming to Tufts University. It was the intention of the Conference to use the three background papers as the nucleus for commentary, criticism, and elaboration. To make this possible, on each of the first three mornings, one of the position papers was carefully reviewed by its author. The author did not read his paper but summarized it informally, supplementing it with additional comments and points of clarification in the process. After each author introduced his paper, he engaged in a panel dialogue with two participant members of the Conference who had prepared oral critiques. Dr. Thomas F. Pettigrew, Laboratory of Social Relations, Harvard University, and Dr. Deborah Partridge Wolfe, Education Director, Staff of the Committee on Education and Labor, U.S. House of Representatives, responded to Dr. Grambs's presentation of her paper. Dr. Bernard Goldstein, Director of Research, Youth Opportunities Project, Urban Study Center, Rutgers University, and Dr. Bernard M. Kramer, School of Medicine, Tufts University, entered into a dialogue with Dr. Seasholes following his presentation of his paper. Professor Edgar Z. Friedenberg of Brooklyn College and Mr. Harold Haizlip, Education Director, Action for Boston Community Development, Inc., commented on Dr. Kvaraceus's paper.

The give-and-take of the panel dialogue was rapid and vigorous. It was followed in the morning sessions by open discussion from the floor on the part of all participants who cared to partake. Thus by noon of each day, the issues raised by the working papers, and issues that might be related to them, were identified. In each of the first three afternoons, Conference participants divided into several smaller groups representing a variety of professional and occupational backgrounds. In these afternoon working sessions, the focus for the most part was on the issues and areas of interest that had been raised in the morning session.

On each of the first three afternoons, at the close of business, the whole Conference reassembled to hear brief reports from the working groups. On the fourth day, a variation in the pattern of work was decided upon, and throughout the morning the Conference was divided into three basic groups according to the general occupational classification of the participants: social scientists, community education and agency personnel, and school people. At the very end of the Conference, reports were heard from these three groups, recommending lines of action and research which were thought to deserve serious consideration.[5]

I have suggested earlier that the Conference was not without its times of intensity and difficulty. This was certainly true, but it should be emphasized that whatever pain the Conference caused to those who participated in it was almost certainly testimony to the seriousness with which participants approached the questions and needs raised by the Conference. Whatever frustration and difficulty welled up in the Conference in the second and part of the third days, the accumulation of seriousness of intention and effort among participants was impressive, too. This accumulation led to a push by all participants in the fourth day to overcome barriers and tensions and to move as well as possible and together toward responsible recommendations.

Conference Participants

The Conference participants included:

Mr. John M. Billman
Pennsylvania Department of Public Instruction

Dr. Max Bogart
New Jersey Department of Education

Dr. Howard L. Bowen
Gorham (Maine) State College

Mr. Frank W. Brown
New Hampshire Department of Education

Mr. Jerome Cohen
Brandeis University

Dr. Joanna T. Daly
Boston Public Schools

Dr. Martin Deutsch
New York Medical College

Dr. Joseph Devitt
Maine Department of Education

Dr. Frank J. Dressler, Jr.
Buffalo Public Schools

Dr. Philip J. Driscoll
Brandeis University

Dr. G. Franklin Edwards
Howard University

Dr. Martha M. Eliot
Massachusetts Committee on Children and Youth

Dr. Edgar Z. Friedenberg
Brooklyn College

Dr. John S. Gibson
The Lincoln Filene Center

Dr. Grace M. Glynn
Rhode Island Associate Commissioner of Education

Dr. Bernard Goldstein
Rutgers University Urban Study Center

Dr. Edmund Gordon
Yeshiva University

Dr. Jean D. Grambs
University of Maryland

Mr. Harold Haizlip
Action for Boston Community Development, Inc.

Dr. A. John Holden, Jr.
Vermont Commissioner of Education

Mr. Wyman Holmes
The Lincoln Filene Center

Mr. Norris Hoyt
Houghton Mifflin Company

Mr. C. Dalton Jones
Tufts University

Dr. Owen B. Kiernan
Massachusetts Commissioner of Education

Dr. Bernard M. Kramer
Tufts University School of Medicine

Dr. William C. Kvaraceus
The Lincoln Filene Center

Dr. Daniel W. Marshall
Tufts University

Dr. Howard E. Mitchell
Philadelphia Council for Community Advancement

Mr. Merrill F. Norlin
The Lincoln Filene Center

Mrs. Jean M. Oxley
Boston Public Schools

Dr. Franklin Patterson
The Lincoln Filene Center

Dr. Thomas F. Pettigrew
Harvard University

Dr. William M. Phillips, Jr.
Rutgers University Urban Study Center

Mr. Richard V. Rapacz
Boston University Law-Medicine Research Institute

Dr. Frank Riessman
Mobilization for Youth, Inc.

Dr. William P. Robinson, Jr.
Rhode Island Commissioner of Education

Dr. Margaret N. Rowley
Morris Brown College

Dr. Karlene V. Russell
Vermont Department of Education

Dr. Ezra V. Saul
Tufts University Institute for Psychological Research

Dr. Bradbury Seasholes
The Lincoln Filene Center

Dr. Fannie Shaftel
Stanford University

Mr. Richard W. Smith
McGraw-Hill Book Company

Dr. John Steele
Massachusetts Education Commission

Dr. Ray M. Stine
Pennsylvania Department of Public Instruction

Mr. Anthony E. Terino
New York State Education Department

Dr. Kimball Wiles
University of Florida

Mr. Chester E. Willette
Maine State Department of Education

Mr. James N. Williams
Urban League of Rhode Island

Dr. Deborah Partridge Wolfe
U.S. House Committee on Education and Labor

Reverend Nathan Wright
Massachusetts Education Commission

We are grateful to all these people for their active interest and vigorous participation in the Conference. Each group—social scientists, school people, community education personnel—came to the September sessions with different backgrounds, concerns, and expectations. Such difficulty as the total group encountered arose largely out of the challenge the Conference presented to communicate across the barrier of such differences. That a degree of communication was achieved and that the discussions ultimately resulted in constructive proposals testifies alike to the urgency of the theme with which the Conference dealt and the personal concern of all of the participants. The Conference tried a hard voyage of exploration, manned by a diverse complement. The explorers were, in fact, nearly as diverse as are the responsible social science–education personnel who must somehow work together to invent a better educational and civic future for Negro youth in America. That the journey of exploration was made *together,* that a certain amount of new terrain was discerned, and that a sense of need for further reconnaissance and action developed made us feel that the Conference was valuable.

I was privileged to serve as the chairman of this Conference. Dr. John S. Gibson, Senior Associate Director of the Lincoln Filene Center and Associate Professor of Government at Tufts University, served as the vice-chairman.

We are grateful to Dr. Ethel C. Dunham of Cambridge, whose initial generosity helped the Conference take form. The Conference was sponsored by the Cooperative Research Branch, U.S. Office of Education (Project G-020-0E-410057) and the President's Committee on Juvenile Delinquency and Youth Crime (Grant No. 64203).

References

1. Henry A. Murray et al., *Explorations in Personality: A Clinical and Experimental Study of Fifty Men of College Age,* Fair Lawn, N.J., Oxford University Press, 1938, pp. 40–41. *See also* p. 115 ff.
2. Arthur J. Jersild, *In Search of Self,* New York, Bureau of Publications, Teachers College, Columbia University, 1960, p. 9 f. *See also* Harry Stack Sullivan, *Conceptions of Modern Psychiatry,* Washington, D.C., The William Alanson White Psychiatric Foundation, 1947; George Herbert Mead, *Mind, Self and Society,* Chicago, The University of Chicago Press, 1934.
3. Erik Homburger Erikson, "The Problem of Ego Identity," in Maurice R. Stein, Arthur J. Vidich, and David Manning White (eds.), *Identity and Anxiety: Survival of the Person in Mass Society,* New York, The Free Press of Glencoe, 1960, p. 47. Reprinted from the *Journal of the American Psychoanalytic Association,* vol. 5, no. 1, 1956, pp. 58-121.
4. Jersild, *op. cit.,* p. 13.
5. The results of the Conference in terms of substantive recommendations and other developments are noted in the last section.

section one THE SELF-CONCEPT: BASIS FOR REEDUCATION OF NEGRO YOUTH

by Jean D. Grambs . . . Associate Professor of Education, College of Education, University of Maryland

The Position Paper

The human personality is a bundle of dynamic forces about which we have many conjectures and few certainties. Like the inner particles of the atom, which are seen only by the shadows they cast, so we have only the shadows of the workings of the human psyche. We are not always sure, and certainly not always in agreement, as to what these shadows represent. But whatever components there may be to personality, in the words of Park and Burgess, "it is an organization of traits and attitudes of which the individual's conception of himself is central."[1]

There are unresolved differences of opinion among psychologists as to the sources of behavior. Whatever it is that impels an individual to act or not to act, a significant role is played in this determination by what the person thinks about himself.[2] He may be able to tell us something about his view of himself, or he may be able to tell us very little. What he tells us may be what he really thinks, or it may be a selective version for a particular public; on what appears to be safer ground, he may reveal a different version of what he thinks he is. Or he may be completely unaware of what his true feelings about himself are. We are assuming, however, that the person acts and can only act in terms of what he thinks about himself in a given situation, and he cannot assess that situation and its action requirements except in terms of his own view of himself.

Contemporary research in child growth and development has highlighted the central significance of the individual's concept of himself.[3] The way a person views himself is the way he will behave. If he sees himself as successful, as someone whom others like, as good-looking, then his behavior will reflect these views. If the person considers himself to be inadequate, as someone whom others probably won't like, as unattractive, then again his behavior will reflect these valuations. The factual truth of any of these statements is irrelevant. A very beautiful girl may consider herself unattractive; children with adequate intellectual endowment may do poorly in school because they perceive themselves as not able.[4]

The source of one's self-image is, of course, not internal; it is learned. The way a mother responds to her newborn baby—with delight or with weary acceptance—will be apparent in the behavior of the baby before very long. A child whose parents trust and love him will be a loving and trustful individual who will tend to go out to greet the world and its many new experiences.

We have some research insights into the differential treatment that parents accord their children from the very beginning.[5] It is true, too, that different cultures produce different personality types. The ways in which children are reared, the things that they are told to do or not to do, the rewards for various kinds of competencies or their lacks, differ from one culture to another.[6] This produces, as Kardiner has pointed out, what might be termed a basic personality type consistent for a given culture.[7]

Venturing outside the family provides the child with additional clues to his self-worth. As he meets teachers, policemen, and storekeepers, he is told what these powerful persons think of people like him. He learns about himself from other children on the block who report to him how they feel on seeing him and playing with him. Out of countless messages, the individual contrives a picture of who he is.[8]

It is obvious that individuals develop different concepts of themselves and that the concept of self is always in terms of degrees of *adequacy*. Everyone must have some sense of adequacy, no matter how minimal, or he cannot cope with his own existence and then must escape into psychosis or suicide. *"We can define man's basic need, then, as a need for adequacy."*[9] Jersild refines this further: "The needs associated with a person's idea and appraisal of himself include both desires for enhancing his self-esteem and also striving to preserve the integrity or consistency of the self."[10]

There is agreement that the contemporary situation of the American Negro is deplorable. A nationwide, continuing debate is concerned with ways of ameliorating this condition. As educators, we need to develop strategies for change which will aid the individual in achieving more adequate adjustment to and control of his environment. The role of the concept of self in achieving this sense of adequacy thus appears to be central. The questions that must be considered are these:

1. How do Negro children and youth now achieve a sense of who and what they are?

2. What is the role of education in the school in developing this sense of self?
3. What is the potential within the educational setting of achieving a desirable shift in self-image?

These questions can only be answered by further research. Our purpose here is a brief review of the relevant research and speculation.

The Question of Differences between Negroes and Whites

One of the clearest differences between Negro and white is that society in the contemporary United States continually tells the groups that they are different. Not only are the groups different, but the Negro group is considered inferior to the white group. This message has been communicated in different ways via different social media ever since the Negro was first brought to America. It is obvious that this kind of differential social communication is going to have a differential impact on the personality. As Allport asks:

> . . . what would happen to your own personality if you heard it said over and over again that you were lazy, a simple child of nature, expected to steal, and had inferior blood. Suppose this opinion were forced on you by the majority of your fellow-citizens. And suppose nothing you could do would change this opinion—because you happen to have black skin.[11]

Or, stated in the words of the late President Kennedy:

> If an American, because his skin is dark, cannot eat lunch in a restaurant open to the public; if he cannot send his children to the best public school available; if, in short, he cannot enjoy the full and free life which all of us want, then who among us would be content to have the color of his skin changed and stand in his place?[12]

The self-concept of the Negro is contaminated by the central fact that it is based on a color-caste complex. The American color-caste system was evolving at the same time that the brave concepts of the American and French revolutions about human equality were also born. It was thus almost inevitable that the racial situation would cause trouble. The first drafts of the Declaration of Independence contained a clause objecting to the imposition of slavery upon the American colonies by the English power. The clause was stricken from the final version for fear of alienating Southern support. Shades of contemporary political maneuverings over civil rights legislation in Congress!

In order to cope with the obvious discrepancy between Christian beliefs about the oneness of the human family, slaveholders had to resort to the idea of the supposed inferiority of the Negro, preaching in some instances that he really was a subhuman breed of animal. Even today there continue to be strenuous efforts to convince those who require scholarly evidence that the Negro is, in fact, inferior.[13]

The social system that emerged out of the need to rationalize the owning of slaves and, following the Civil War, refusal to accord the Negro full citizen status was a clear development of a caste system. Unlike the caste system of India based on religious beliefs, the caste system in the United States was based on color and on the assumption of inferiority due to color. The Brazilian melting pot, unlike that in the United States, classifies anyone with any amount of white ancestry as white; in the United States, the smallest amount of Negro ancestry classifies an individual as Negro.

In the evolution of institutions, those provided for the Negro in the United States, therefore, had to be *separate,* but also *unequal.* It is possible that there are caste systems in which parallel caste-class groups exist without any presumption of superiority or inferiority for one caste over another; this certainly has not been true in America.[14] Of course, the South had to refuse to provide equal educational opportunity for the Negro; the Negro was *not equal.*

The Impact of Inequality in Valuation

It does not take much imagination to understand what generations of being told one is unworthy do to a group's own valuation of its worth. From the first slave revolts, Negro leaders have continually fought against this self-view; but there have been relatively few leaders, a condition also produced by the effect of inferior caste status. Only in recent decades have there been enough Negroes who have overcome these multiple barriers to challenge the general valuation of the Negro.

To quote Dollard, whose original study of caste first focused general attention on this problem:

> Nothing has happened since 1936 [the date of the original study] which has served to unconvince me about what I saw. It seems as real now as then. We are still in the hot water of conflict between our democratic ideals and our personal acceptance of caste status for the Negro. We are still deliberately or unwittingly profiting by, defending, concealing or ignoring the caste system.[15]

Interestingly enough, a recent comprehensive review and evaluation of the research in the area of self-concept does not include any discussion of research that considers race as an aspect of self-concept, though research relating to other factors, such as sex, religious affiliation, social-class status, is discussed.[16] Blindness to, or avoidance of, the implications of the caste system on the self-concept of the Negro, and of the white, which is thus seen to occur at the most- and least-sophisticated levels of society, is symptomatic of the difficulty of dealing with color discrimination in American life and thought.

The Negro personality *cannot* be unmarked by the experience of caste discrimination based upon color.[17] One of the first family learnings of the Negro child has to do with his color. The more white a Negro child is, the more he will be accepted by his family, the greater his opportunity will be to use his talents, the more likely it is that he will be able to make the most of the limited opportunities of his environment. The love that his family will accord him can be calibrated on the same scale as one calibrates color differences. To be most loved as a Negro child, one has to appear least Negro.

In one of their cases, Kardiner and Ovesey describe the reactions of a middle-class Negro woman, herself light, on giving birth to a dark baby. She was sure she had been given the wrong baby; later she tried to bathe it in bleaches of various kinds; she refused to appear in public with it. She reacted almost the same way with a second baby.[18]

In the early drawings and stories and dreams of Negro children appear many wishes to be white. Negro children have a harder time than white children in identifying themselves correctly in terms of race.[19] This identification is also related to color: the darker Negro is able to see himself as a Negro earlier than a light-colored one. In the latter instance, is the nearness to being white such as to make the acceptance of being Negro that much harder?

The self-esteem of the Negro is damaged by the overwhelming fact that the world he lives in says, "White is right; black is bad." The impact on the Negro community is to overvalue all those traits of appearance that are most Caucasian. Evidence is clear that in almost every Negro family, the lighter children are favored by the parents. It is interesting to note that most of the Negro leadership group today are not Negroid in appearance, many being almost completely Caucasian in terms of major physical appearance.

What effect does this have on the child? Of course, his own color becomes extremely important to him. As Dai points out, ". . . the color of one's skin, which does not occupy the consciousness of children of other cultures, is here made an issue of primary importance, and the personality problems thus created are almost as difficult to get rid of as the dark skin itself."[20] The Negro press is replete with advertisements for skin lighteners and hair straighteners. It strikes some Negroes as ironic that, while they strive to become lighter and to make their hair less curly, whites go to great pains to stay out in the sun in order to become darker and spend endless amounts of money on getting their hair to curl! Unfortunately, the efforts of the whites do not assume an acceptance on their part of the features of the Negro which appear to be desirable: darker color and curly hair. But the efforts of the Negro do spring from a deeply ingrained view regarding appearance: it is better to be more white.

One interesting feature of the current Negro revolution has been a small but persistent insistence that the Negro cease trying to make himself white. The Black Muslim group is an almost pure expression of the need to reject all that is white and replace Negro self-hatred with justified hatred of whites, including the dominant white Christian religion.[21] With some Negroes, it is now considered a matter of racial pride to refuse to straighten the hair or to use cosmetics to lighten the skin. It is possible that this movement will reach other Negroes, and with it will come a lessening of the rejection of color and the personal devaluation that this has carried. But unfortunately it hardly seems possible that a reversal of the value system will occur for many, and certainly not for a long time to come.

Thus we see the central ambivalence that makes the world of the Negro so baffling, frustrating, confusing, and demeaning. On the one hand, he is told that white is better, and he relates this to his own social system in which the Negro who is most white, but still a Negro, has highest status. But to *be* white is not good. Whites are not to be trusted; they are, in fact, hated as much as they are feared.

Hatred breeds aggression. Aggression seeks an outlet. A major focus of the hatred of Negroes is the white group, but this group is almost completely protected because of the potency and immediacy of white retaliation.[22] One must remember that the antilynch laws are quite recent. Pictures of burning buses, fire hoses, mounted police with electric cattle prods, and attacking police dogs show only too well that the Negro is still not protected from the quick and vicious reactions of the white group when this power is challenged in any way. Incapable of attacking the white group, the Negro has several psychological alternatives: to hate himself, to act out his aggressive needs within his own group, and to escape into apathy and fantasy. All these paths are utilized, and often by the same individual, depending on the situation. As Combs and Snygg point out, responses to feelings of inadequacy range from the neurotic through perceptual distortions and may result in actual psychosis. The production of "multiple personalities" is, as they see it, one response to feelings of loss of self-esteem.[23] This splitting of the personality in response to the social disvalue placed on being a Negro is graphically stated by Redding:

> From adolescence to death there is something very personal about being a Negro in America. It is like having a second ego which is as much the conscious subject of all experience as the natural self. It is not what the psychologists call dual personality. It is more complex and, I think, more morbid than that. In the state of which I speak, one receives two distinct reactions—the one normal and intrinsic to the natural self; the other, entirely different but of equal force, a prodigy created by the accumulated consciousness of Negroness.[24]

As the gifted Negro writer James Baldwin puts it, in commenting on his own childhood:

> In order for me to live, I decided very early that some mistake had been made somewhere. I was not a "nigger" even though you [whites] called me one. . . . I had to realize when I was very young that I was none of those things I was told I was. I was not, for example, happy. I never touched a watermelon for all kinds of reasons. I had been invented by white people, and I knew enough about life by this time to understand that whatever you invent, whatever you project, that is you! So where we are now is that a whole country of people believe I'm a "nigger" and I *don't.*[25]

It does not escape the Negro observer that Negro crimes against Negroes are considered far less serious by the law in many areas than similar crimes of whites against whites, and certainly not nearly so serious as Negro crimes against whites. And white crimes against Negroes are the least serious of all. Again, these social symptoms report to the Negro that he is not valued as a person; he cannot, against such massive evidence, counter by his own feelings of self-esteem, since in truth he can typically show little factual support for a contrary view.[26]

Crucial Social Forces Creating the Negro Self-image: The Family and Poverty

The potency of the family in producing the culturally approved person has tempted social manipulators since the dawn of history. Sparta intervened at a very early age in the child-rearing functions of the family. Recent attempts to supplant the family have been unsuccessful. The most enduring such contemporary situation, the Kibbutz of Israel, appears to have produced a rather special kind of person whose social potential can be questioned.[27] So far, no adequate substitute for the family has been found, despite Huxley's predictions.[28]

That there are unique stresses and strains in the modern family is agreed; but the stresses in a Negro family are qualitatively different from those in a white family, even when we hold socioeconomic status constant. The poor have never lived in comfort, and the struggle for material survival has certainly made psychologically adequate survival extremely problematical anywhere in the world. The situation of the Negro family today in the United States is qualitatively different on a number of important counts.

The Negro family is much more likely than the white family to be on the lowest economic rung. Furthermore, we could say that no more than a very small percentage of Negroes is more than one generation removed from abject poverty, so that "Negroes have [a] deeply ingrained sense of impoverishment."[29] It is a rather special kind of impoverishment, too; it is almost inescapable. Although we have seen in recent generations the rise of a Negro middle class, and even a few very wealthy Negroes, most Negroes remain in the "last hired, first fired" category of employment—and if not this generation, their parental generation. Most Negro children, then, inherit a family which is economically insecure from the very start. Most of them live at the edge of survival; and those who have moved a little bit away have a constant fear of a future which may reduce them, too, to desperation.

It is almost impossible for one not reared in a slum to understand its awfulness. Middle-class America flees from a true picture of slum degradation.[30] But as Riessman points out, children reared in these environments will soon constitute 50 percent of all children enrolled in schools in large cities.[31] Most of these children will be Negroes, unless something drastically changes the housing situation which exists in urban centers.

The Negro slum child is far more liable than a white slum child to experience also an unstable home.[32] The self that the Negro child learns early in life is one exposed to the most difficult of all situations for the human being to cope with: an inadequate family living on the edge of economic insufficiency. The impact of family disruption is accentuated by the incapacity of those involved in the rearing of the children to do an adequate job of it because they have had few experiences with family stability and adequacy to guide them.

The circle is indeed a vicious one. The case studies reported by Riese provide appalling accounts of generation after generation of defeat in Negro families.[33] Often neither mother nor father is able to provide the minimum of affection and attention that an infant needs in order to grow into a person able to like himself and others, because, of course, his parents do not like themselves. Too many of these marriages are the result of impulsive escape wishes and lack a secure base in personal regard for the marital partner.[34] Poignant testimony to the difficulties facing the Negro wife and husband is given by talented Negro singer Lena Horne.[35]

As she describes it, her marriage was an effort to get away from the miseries of being a Negro singer in a white man's world. Yet she was not able to accept her role as a Negro wife. The needs her husband brought home from his work, mainly with white colleagues, she felt quite unable and unwilling to deal with. Not only had she to cope with the ordinary problems of running a home and rearing children, she had to absorb the anger and hurt her husband bore on his job, the countless humiliations and degradations that he, a Negro, experienced daily in his contact with white people.

What Lena Horne tells us provides a needed window into the inner reality of Negro family life. The normal hazards of the working world are multiplied many times over by the pervasive insecurity attendant on almost all of the Negro's economic activities. Not only is the Negro the last to be hired and the first to be fired, but he pays more for insurance premiums, he has a much harder time obtaining home mortgage money and any kind of bank or credit loans. Even the slum store preys upon the poor with higher prices for shoddier stuff. In such an environment, it is hard indeed for the Negro male to achieve a sense of self-worth as a breadwinner and provider for his family.

The woman typically is aggressive and hostile; the man is hostile and dependent. Because his economic situation is so insecure, the husband-father cannot be sure that he will provide the economic base for a family; and in a majority of cases, he is right. He cannot assure his wife of support or his children of food and shelter. Who can feel pride of self in such circumstances, and who can pass on feelings of adequacy to anyone else?

The economic security of the Negro family rests primarily with the mother. This is one outgrowth of slavery, when at least the mother could keep the children with her until they could be physically independent and able to work, while the father was often not even accorded the recognition of paternity. Certainly the family as the white population knew it was prohibited for slaves. The patterns of employment in today's urban centers have continued to make economic stability more available to the women than to the men. The significance of this family situation appears in study after study.

The home life reported in many case studies of Negro youth is one of constant bickering and fighting. One father leaves; a stepfather or father substitute appears. The family conflict continues. Because of death or illness or desertion, children often are left with grandparents or other relatives. If an attachment occurs, it may not last until adulthood. Thus many Negro children have few experiences with stability, warmth, attention—all of the things that are taken for granted as part of the necessary environment for healthy personality development.

The important point, of course, is that while many of the conditions reported are a result of acute and continued poverty, a major ingredient is also the color-caste of the Negro. One of the child's early racial learnings is that he cannot turn to his parents for help and retaliation if he is hurt.

> A white man yanked me off a streetcar because I got on ahead of a white woman. He shook me good and tore my clothes. I walked home crying, knowing that my father would do something about it. (But his father could do no more than remark, "You should have known better.")[36]

The denial to a parent of his role in protecting his own child is deeply destructive, not only to the parental feeling but to the possibility that the child will look to his parents as adult models. Nor will the growing child be able to internalize the parental feeling without which having children of one's own is a dangerous enterprise.

What the Negro child is likely to learn is that no one is to be trusted. He is given such small ingredients of affection and attention that he has too meager a hoard to share with anyone else. He learns, too, that his family is only partly responsible for the horrors of his existence; it is the whites who have created this situation, and it is they who keep him in abasement. The burden of hatred for the whites is increased because he is also told that he cannot do anything about that hatred; in fact, he must be particularly careful and watchful in all his relations with whites. These persons hold the key to all that is desirable and good. If only one were white, too!

The earliest learnings, then, of the Negro child, particularly one in the rural or urban slums, is that the family is not a source of basic nurture and support. He seeks his gratifications, therefore, on the street and among peers.[37] But as Kardiner and Ovesey point out, at no time are these relationships such as to produce a feeling of comfort and safety. No one can find in the street a substitute for parental and adult guidance and parental affection. If the child does not necessarily become antisocial, he is asocial.[38]

The damage to the child's self-esteem appears greater for Negro boys than for girls.[39] Though it is debatable whether, in general, it is more or less difficult to grow up as a boy or as a girl in our culture,[40] it seems clear from the evidence that during early childhood and school years, the Negro girl accommodates better to the circumstances of existence. Certainly in school performance the Negro girl exceeds the Negro boy. In most measures of social disorganization, the Negro boy appears to be far more vulnerable. This can be accounted for in part by the fact that the male models available for the growing boy are themselves demoralized. A father who feels defeated by the world is not in a good position to give his son a sense of optimism and a feeling that he can achieve something himself. The fact that the father is most likely to be the absent member of the family and often is replaced by a succession of fathers or father substitutes also tends to militate against the establishment of a view of the male as a reliable, responsible individual. If the boy sees around him men who are unable to sustain a consistent and positive social and economic role, it is hard for the youngster to build a different pattern out of his limited experiences.

Recent efforts to equalize educational opportunities for Negroes in the South should not obscure the fact that these efforts are indeed very recent, and still fall far short of providing, even on a segregated basis, an adequate education for all Negro young people. The fact that even today many Negro children and youth have far from adequate schooling, whether they live in the rural South or the urban North, Midwest, West, or Southwest, should not make us forget that, with few exceptions, the story of Negro education to this day has been one of gross lacks.[41] As Horace Mann said over a hundred years ago, "No educated body of men can be permanently poor"[42]; and the obverse is that no uneducated group can expect to rise out of poverty.

Although the Ausubels state that "Negro girls in racially incapsulated areas are less traumatized than boys by the impact of racial discrimination,"[43] further evidence is needed to support such a statement. On the surface, Negro girls seem more able to cope with some of the demands of middle-class society: going to school, behaving in school, keeping out of serious trouble with the law, showing responsibility for child rearing, and keeping a job.[44] It is nevertheless possible that the impact of their situation is just passed on to the men in the household. Certainly a mother is a prime source, as we have stated, of the child's self-concept. It is communicated to Negro boys, somehow, that they are less wanted, less able to deal with their world, bound to fail in their efforts to be men. We cannot lay the major blame for the way Negro boys develop on the lack of adequate male models. It is highly probable that the trauma suffered by Negro females is passed on and displaced upon the males in the situation. Certainly the case material of Kardiner and Ovesey shows much personal trouble experienced by female as well as male Negroes.[45] The fact that so many Negroes become contributing and stable members of society is an extraordinary tribute to the resilience of the human psyche.

Educational Processes and Self-concept

It is clear that the life experiences of the Negro child are not such as to aid him in developing a positive sense of himself or of his place in his world. What does this suggest to us? It would seem that a very compelling hypothesis is that *the Negro child, from earliest school entry through graduation from high school, needs continued opportunities to see himself and his racial group in a realistically positive light. He needs to understand what color and race mean, he needs to learn about those of his race (and other disadvantaged groups) who have succeeded, and he needs to clarify his understanding of his own group history and current group situation.*

At the moment, these are missing ingredients in the American public school classroom. Numerous studies of textbooks have shown them to be lily-white.[46] Pictures do not show Negro and white children together; when Negroes appear they are usually either Booker T. Washington, George Washington Carver, or foreign.[47] Neither whites nor Negroes have an accurate picture of the American Negro and his history.[48] One observer noted that a commonly used contemporary civics book had no index entry for *urban renewal, transportation, transit, or Negro.*[49] The lily-white nature of text materials is true also of other visual aids used in the schools. If Negroes appear in school films, they are in stereotyped roles. One film, for instance, showing "community helpers" illustrated the work of repairing the street with a Negro crew and a white foreman. The educational consultant, incidentally, who worked with the film company to produce the film was surprised at his own blindness. This kind of presentation merely reinforces the many communications to children that Negro work is inferior work.

That these materials can and do have a strong impact on the child's perception of himself and others was well documented in the study by Trager and Yarrow. When a story describing a Negro child as a funny savage *(Little Black Sambo)* was read aloud to young children, white and Negro children's feelings were affected, particularly when the white children pointed this out in the schoolyard.[50] The only thing that is surprising about these findings is that educators and others have consistently ignored them. It is interesting that the Trager–Yarrow research report is probably the only study made of the differences in education (textbook) content that is reported in the literature. As a matter of fact, it is claimed by one of the very knowledgeable experts in the field, that *no* experimental study has been done of differences in textbook content, despite the fact that the textbook is the most consistently and constantly used educational aid in the classroom, other than the teacher.[51]

If teaching materials present a slanted view of him and his place in the world to the Negro child, what does the teacher tell him? It is no very startling piece of news that teachers, too, bear the majority version of the Negro. Studies of their attitudes toward children show that the Negro child is rated lowest in all rankings of groups on a Bogardus-type social-distance scale.[52] The original study was completed thirteen years ago; teachers in training in 1963 give the same responses. Attempts to change teachers' attitudes through human relations workshops and special courses have reached very few. In formulating some guidelines for the education of the culturally disadvantaged, Niemeyer stated:

> Our hypothesis is that the chief cause of the low achievement of the children of alienated groups is the fact that too many teachers and principals honestly believe that these children are educable only to an extremely limited extent. And when teachers have a low expectation level for their children's learning, the children seldom exceed that expectation, which is a self-fulfilling prophecy.[53]

Nor is the situation made easier where Negro teachers are employed. The Negro teacher represents a middle-class position, and there is evidence that virulent anti-Negro feelings are expressed by middle-class Negroes for lower-class Negroes. Unfortunately, most Negro children come from lower-class homes. Dai makes the point that, denied access to other rewards in life, the Negro tends to put an overemphasis upon status.[54] The Negro professional, who may have many contacts with white professionals, must even in these professional relationships maintain an etiquette which prevents showing resentment or rage; but this is not necessarily controlled to the same extent when dealing with fellow Negroes. Children, particularly, are available targets of all the displaced self-hatred of the professional middle-class Negro teacher. If they are lower-class children, they typically will demonstrate everything the middle-class Negro most despises about the race from which he cannot dissociate himself. The warmth, welcome, and support which children should find, particularly in the early elementary school grades, and which the Negro child needs in abundance because of so much deprivation at home, is exactly what teachers, Negro or white, as presently oriented, can least provide.

In this necessarily brief discussion of the factors that enter into the development of the self-concept of the Negro, we have utilized only a small sampling of the wealth of research literature and other documentation which bears on this subject. We have merely tried to suggest some of the crucial situations which help to mold the Negro child. It is these of which educational practitioners must be aware.

Educational Intervention

The child with a negative view of self is a child who will not be able to profit much from school. Once a child is convinced that school is irrelevant to his immediate needs and future goals, the task of education becomes almost impossible. As one junior high student said, after having failed all his subjects for two years:

> I just don't like it. It seems to bore me. It seems silly just going there and sitting. And most of the time it is so hot and they don't do anything about it and the teachers just talk, talk, and you never learn anything.[55]

Deutsch's research points out that the lower-class Negro child probably received about one half to one third less instructional time in the primary grades than did white children from the same slum environment: "our time samples indicated that as much as 80% of the school day was channeled into disciplining, and secondarily, into ordinary organizational details. . . ."[56]

In 1951, it could be said:

> It is difficult to conceive of a more hopeless and dispirited group than a high school class of Negro adolescent girls; nor a more bored and resentful group than a high school class of Negro boys. Both seem equally aimless and befogged. They

do not assume these attitudes through choice. The fault is society's, not theirs.[57]

Recent research indicates that Negro youth are responding to their caste position and selecting lower goals and lower standards for themselves, even when their family, socioeconomic position, and innate capacities would indicate higher achievement motivation: "lower caste and lower class status go hand in hand and . . . even when some lower caste members have achieved a more favorable class position, their caste restrictions continue to be perceived and to influence their behavior, both overt and implicit."[58]

Negro youth are almost totally ignorant of the community in which they live and the vocational and educational opportunities available.[59] They have a very restricted view of their community because their contacts via parents and other Negro adults are also limited by patterns of discrimination and selective reporting. Although many Negroes may today be aware of the outstanding few Negroes in sports, entertainment, and diplomacy, few know of the middle group of Negroes working in skilled trades, businesses, and other ordinary occupations. As Ginzburg and others so eloquently put it, persons of "exceptional accomplishments may not be as helpful a guide to the average Negro youngster as the knowledge that individuals not too different from himself have risen one or two rungs on the ladder."[60]

This point is amply supported by the research by Lott and Lott, who state that "we would predict a real change in the level of academic accomplishment among Negroes would be one of the major consequences of a greater availability of Negro models who could illustrate that such achievement 'pays off' and thereby increase the expectation that the Negro youth, too, might reap tangible benefits from his academic labors."[61]

It is not our purpose here to provide a blueprint for educational innovations which might be the object of experimentation. What is significant, however, is that the school has not as yet been used deliberately to change the self-concept of students. As Combs and Snygg state it: "To be really effective, education will have to accept the task of dealing with the whole phenomenal field of the individual, of producing changes in perception of himself as well as in his perception of his environment."[62]

Some interesting experimentation does indicate that the self-concept of the learner can be affected by deliberate school practices. Brookover and associates[63] explore a number of possible approaches that might be taken with early adolescent youngsters. Significant results were obtained when special methods were introduced for working with the young people and with their parents. There are many comments about the role of self-concept in achievement, but very few deliberate experimental studies aiming toward changing such an image.

Can the self-concept of the Negro child be changed in a positive direction by education? The study by Campbell, Yarrow, and Yarrow suggests that an integrated camp experience did have a significant effect on the self-perceptions of children, in particular of Negro children.[64] The permanence of this change, however, the authors state, would depend in large part on the support for such change on the return home. Studies of school desegregation have shown tendencies toward better school achievement on the part of Negro youth, but so far relatively little has been done to explore either the changes in self-concept that might have occurred or the causes for such change. In fact, some indications are that integration actually lessens the Negro child's view of himself; that is, Negroes growing up in segregated communities and attending segregated schools tend to have a higher appraisal of Negroes in general, according to one study.[65] This supports, too, the finding of Campbell, Yarrow, and Yarrow that in the initial stages of the camp experience, Negro children were highly tentative and withdrawn, expressing most often the fear that the *other* Negro children would not behave properly.

The situation facing the school is exceedingly complex, and the problem is not one that is amenable to easy solutions. A number of approaches have been suggested. The Special Guidance Project in New York City has been described as an effort to change the perception of Negro and other disadvantaged youth regarding their own potential and opportunity.[66] Essentially, most proposals relating to school programs strive toward giving the Negro child more of what the average white child has been having all along—a good school environment.[67] It is our contention that this is not enough. Arguing from the data on self-concept, we would suggest that it is the view of self that has to be the focus of specific attention.

We are suggesting that education *can* make a difference. One difference, so far cited, as far as Negro youth are concerned, is the deliberate provision in guidance procedures to demonstrate to Negro youth that other Negroes have succeeded in moving up and out of the ghetto, becoming skilled and white-collar workers.

Other kinds of educational intervention might be utilized. For instance, in his reports of observations of classroom behavior, Deutsch found that only during Negro History Week did the majority of the students appear to be making a real effort to learn, and in some classrooms this was the only time at which some semblance of order was achieved and maintained for any length of time.[68] Arguing on theoretical grounds, Lewin claims that the child who has insight into his group status, particularly if it is a disadvantaged one, is better equipped to cope with this status in a positive manner, though he was speaking with particular reference to the problem of the Jewish child.[69] In the Campbell, Yarrow, and Yarrow study, one of the most effective counselors was a Negro who dealt forthrightly and frankly with the question of race and did not attempt to evade and avoid it as did other counselors.[70]

As James Baldwin has so eloquently stated it:

> If . . . one managed to change the curriculum in all the schools so that Negroes learned more about themselves and their real contributions to this culture, you would be liberating not only Negroes, you'd be liberating white people who know nothing about their own history.[71]

In the fifth, eighth, and eleventh grades, when schools typically tell the story of American history, supplementary materials could be provided which show accurately the place and role of the American Negro during the historic periods being studied. For the eleventh grade, some fairly sophisticated material might be organized, including some documentary sources. It would be important to draw on such sources as *The Myth of the Negro Past,* by Herskovits,[72] and other recent historical findings. The superb collection of materials from the Federal Writers Project, the Slave Narrative Collection, available in the volume, *Lay My Burden Down,* edited by Botkin,[73] is another example of the kind of material that might well be more widely known by Negro youth. Trueblood suggests[74] that files of the Urban League be perused and actual case reports of successful Negro workers be made available. *Ebony* magazine regularly runs articles about the unusual, and some usual, successes attained by Negroes.

Material for kindergarten and primary grades is more difficult to produce and to define. It is possible that some cartoon-type booklets could be made which would show integrated and nonintegrated real-life situations with opportunities for the youngster to complete the action sequence himself. The sequence would focus in part on normal interaction among children but also would include the typical "race" situation in which children ask questions about differences, respond to racial attack ("nigger"), and so forth. It is possible that some comparative-culture material could be introduced earlier than is usually done, showing vividly contrasting ways of life, including that of the segregated American-Negro community.

It is clear that considerable exploration must be done before any decisions are made regarding what kinds of materials would be most appropriate. It would be useful to gather a panel of Negro and white social scientists knowledgeable in the fields of child psychology, education, history, psychiatry, and sociology to help explore and plan the development of materials.

Pilot materials might then be developed and tried out in several situations: a large northern city, Negro and white schools predominantly; suburban white schools; and southern Negro and white schools (if possible), both city and rural. These trial runs would not only test the materials but would provide evidence as to the impact on self-concept of such materials on the part of Negro youth. It would be highly important also to see if any modification of white students' attitudes could be achieved. Workshops of teachers and administrators would be valuable in helping to understand what it is these adults would need to know in order to use the materials with competence and acceptance. The Campbell and Yarrow research, as well as our own experience, suggests great adult confusion when it comes to dealing directly with the problem of race with an integrated group of children or youth.

The analysis by Riessman regarding the kinds of instructional materials and instructional situations which are educationally effective with culturally deprived children suggests some of the kinds of materials to be developed.[75]

A study of the differences between good and poor achievers from severely deprived areas found some differences with significant educational implications:

> From the findings of this study, the hypothetical good achiever from an underprivileged environment emerges as a child who is relatively controlled and cautious, often stereotyped and constricted, but who still retains a degree of originality and creativity. He seems more willing than his less successful classmates to conform to adult demands, has a more positive view of authority figures and greater self-confidence. In cognitive functioning he excels chiefly in tasks requiring memory, attention and verbal abilities. He is also superior in analytical and organizational abilities and generally in processes that require convergent thinking.
>
> In contrast, the composite picture of the poor achiever is that of a child burdened by anxiety, fearful of the world and authority, and lacking in self-confidence. He is more apt to be impulsive and labile with relatively poor controlling mechanisms. His defenses against anxiety and feelings of inadequacy may be expressed in talking and in uncritically favorable surface attitude toward self and others. Nevertheless, the poor achiever still seems to have sufficient potential for adaptive behavior which the school could build upon. His cognitive activities are often quite similar in content, approach and process to those of the good achiever and in fact, he demonstrates greater facility in divergent production. Many of his reactions give evidence of creative capacity which might be directed and controlled. From his behavior in the testing situations and in tasks requiring social comprehension, the poor achiever seems to possess substantial understanding of the world around him, although he seems less able to act upon this understanding than the good achiever.[76]

As this research indicates and as other studies substantiate, the beginning scholars of any race or socioeconomic condition tend to start school at somewhat the same level.[77] But they soon diverge. Those who are not going to succeed are soon exposed to failure of various kinds. After a few years in school, the culturally deprived child may show an actual decline in tested intelligence.[78] Again, however, it must be noted that what may be tested may not be native endowment, and the test instrument may be measuring success plus knowledge, rather than innate capacity. As Hunnicutt and his associates point out, primary grade teachers may assume an oral vocabulary that just may not exist among the deprived children and thus fail the student for lacks that he cannot help, instead of diagnosing the problem and teaching to fill the gaps.[79]

Diagnosis of learning lacks is essential. These may be restricted oral vocabularies, poor speech habits, or lack of auditory discrimination skills.[80] Beyond that, to meet the requirement of effective education, we would suggest other kinds of educational materials that capitalize on divergent thinking and the immediate environmental experience of the student. These would probably be open-ended, problem-centered, realistic presentations. The use of short films, six minutes or less in length, which defined a problem that would lend itself to role playing as a class sought a solution, should be explored. Semiprojective pictures, such as those used in the "Focus" series of the National Conference of Christians and Jews,[81] might be further developed to stimulate discussion of the problems of racial self-identity. Recordings of stories, poems, or dramatic skits could be used to convey a particular sense of immediacy. Anthologies of stories, biography, and commentary might also be useful, particularly where these focused on the perception of the Negro in society and his ways of coping with his world.

The development of appropriate instructional materials for children with backgrounds which differ substantially from the middle-class norm is urgent; there also exists a need to modify the standard classroom procedure. For example, we do not know what are the real effects of overcrowded living. Recent research on the effect of overcrowding on laboratory animals demonstrates that these kinds of living conditions foster many pathological behaviors. The parallel between the pathology that develops among overcrowded animals and the social pathology of the slum seems obvious.[82] A psychiatrist notes that slum children are exposed to continual overstimulation, which results in behavior not conducive to learning in the standard school situation. This kind of "overloading of the perceptual apparatus," in the words of Sarvis, can be an extremely disorganizing experience—so much so that the children so exposed may, in school,

> . . . often act as if they were under the influence of one of the overstimulating drugs. Their thinking is scattered, their

attention span is short. Frequently they talk in an excited, irrepressible way without regard for whether anyone is listening or not. Conversation may be almost unknown. Distractibility and hyperactivity may be marked. Teachers become frustrated because efforts to calm such a child are transient; moments later he has returned to his previous wild and distractible behavior.[83]

The schools are not prepared to deal with such children. We have suggested that the attention of these children may be attracted by different kinds of instructional materials. We also may suggest that different kinds of learning situations may be required. How large a group, for instance, can such children tolerate and for how long? When does the group become too small? Can these children bear to be alone, and if so, for how long? Sarvis suggests that many small-group activities, carefully scheduled and structured, may be one answer.[84] The work of Reger[85] with hyperactive, distractible children suggests that some of these youngsters need more rather than less stimulation.

It is imperative, however, that one take care in developing both special materials and special procedures to use with the culturally deprived Negro child. He may differ in many ways, as we have noted, but only some of these may be significant to a given child. He may have all the handicaps of massive and continued poverty and defeat, or he may only be struggling with a problem of adequate self-identity. It would be a mistake to assume that because some slum dwellers are particularly rich in some kinds of vocabulary that all are and that all are creative in nonintellectual ways because many are. In fact, the need to meet such individual differences may actually boomerang against programs to speed up school integration, which are probably the best method for ultimate solution to our problem. As one writer observed:

> Teachers talk at length about the "cognitive difficulties" of the economically, socially deprived, disadvantaged child. Whether or not Dr. Frank Riessman, who has written eloquently about different learning styles, realizes it, many parents in my neighborhood use his thesis to "prove" that children must be educated differently. It is so easy to make the erroneous assumption that all poor children have one style of learning and all middle-class children another.[86]

It is hypothecated that no one kind of material nor one kind of program will suffice. Children respond to materials differently; what will produce insight in one child may merely baffle another. A multiple approach using as many media as possible is therefore more promising. Research may be helpful in identifying the approach and the medium which seem to be most effective with most youngsters at a given age and in a given cultural setting. More work, following the lead of Hoban,[87] could be done to find these "bridges" which aid children in understanding and accepting the "message" of a given communications medium.

Conclusion

If today we note a change of tone, a militancy and impatience on the part of Negro youth, it is not because schools are any different. For the first time, the Negro, via TV, is beginning to see that the world of comfort, luxury, and fun is all around him. He wants some of it, too. As Hayakawa pointed out in a speech at a recent American Psychological Association convention in Philadelphia, the ads that beckon one to join the fun on the picnic do *not* add "for whites only."[88]

But the militancy, welcome as it may be, cannot erase the burden of self-hatred that has accumulated through so many generations. And many who most need to hear the call to challenge the racial status quo may already be too deeply sunk in despair and apathy. These feelings are so quickly communicated to the infant and child that intervention by the school even as early as kindergarten or the first grade may be too late. But if many older adolescents can respond to a new concept of their role in the world, then certainly the younger child can be reached, too, by deliberate efforts to change the way in which he views himself. These, then, are the challenges we must meet.

References

1. Bingham Dai, "Minority Group Membership and Personality Development," in Jitsuichi Masuoka and Preston Valien (eds.), *Race Relations: Problems and Theory,* Chapel Hill, N.C., The University of North Carolina Press, 1961, p. 183.
2. Ruth C. Wylie, *The Self-Concept,* Lincoln, Nebr., University of Nebraska Press, 1961, pp. 1–22.
3. Arthur T. Jersild, "Emotional Development," in L. Carmichael (ed.), *Manual of Child Psychology,* 2d ed., New York, John Wiley & Sons, Inc., 1954, p. 837. "Selective Bibliography on Self," *Childhood Education,* vol. 35, October, 1958, pp. 80–81.
4. M. B. Frink, "Self-Concept as it Relates to Academic Underachievement," *California Journal of Educational Research,* vol. 13, March, 1962, pp. 57–62.
5. Robert R. Sears, Eleanor E. Maccoby, and Harry Levin, *Patterns of Child Rearing,* New York, Harper & Row, Publishers, 1957.
6. John W. M. Whiting and Irvin L. Child, *Child Training and Personality: A Cross-Cultural Study,* New Haven, Conn., Yale University Press, 1953.
7. Abram Kardiner et al., *The Psychological Frontiers of Society,* New York, Columbia University Press, 1945.
8. Helen G. Trager and Marian Radke Yarrow, *They Learn What They Live: Prejudice in Young Children,* New York, Harper & Row, Publishers, 1952.
9. Arthur W. Combs and Donald Snygg, *Individual Behavior* (rev. ed.), New York, Harper & Row, Publishers, 1959, p. 46.

10. Jersild, *op. cit.*
11. Gordon W. Allport, *The Nature of Prejudice,* Reading, Mass., Addison-Wesley Publishing Company, Inc., 1954, p. 142.
12. John F. Kennedy, "A Time to Act," an address to the American people, June 11, 1963. Reprinted by Anti-Defamation League of B'nai B'rith, New York.
13. Robert D. North, "The Intelligence of American Negroes," *Research Reports,* Anti-Defamation League of B'nai B'rith, vol. 3, no. 2, November, 1956; Melvin M. Tumin (ed.), *Race and Intelligence: A Scientific Evaluation,* New York, Anti-Defamation League of B'nai B'rith, 1963.
14. John Dollard, *Caste and Class in a Southern Town,* 3d ed., Garden City, N.Y., Doubleday & Company, Inc., 1957.
15. *Ibid,* p. viii.
16. Wylie, *op. cit.*
17. Abram Kardiner and Lionel Ovesey, *The Mark of Oppression: Explorations in the Personality of the American Negro,* Cleveland, The World Publishing Company (a Meridian Book), 1962.
18. Kardiner and Ovesey, *op. cit.,* pp. 252–253.
19. Kenneth Clark and Mamie P. Clark, "Racial Identification and Preference in Negro Children," in Eleanor Maccoby et al. (eds.), *Readings in Social Psychology,* New York, Holt, Rinehart and Winston, Inc., 1958, pp. 602–611.
20. Bingham Dai, "Problems of Personality Development Among Negro Children," in Clyde Kluckhohn and Henry A. Murray (eds.), *Personality in Nature, Society and Culture,* New York, Alfred A. Knopf, Inc., 1953, p. 560.
21. C. Eric Lincoln, *The Black Muslims in America,* Boston, The Beacon Press, 1961; E. U. Essien-Udom, *Black Nationalism,* Chicago, The University of Chicago Press, 1962; James Baldwin, *The Fire Next Time,* New York, The Dial Press, Inc., 1963, pp. 61–120.
22. Baker M. Hindman, "The Emotional Problems of Negro High School Youth Which Are Related to Segregation and Discrimination in a Southern Urban Community," *Journal of Educational Sociology,* vol. 27, November, 1953, pp. 115–127.
23. Combs and Snygg, *op. cit.,* pp. 265–303.
24. J. Saunders Redding, *On Being Negro in America,* Indianapolis, Ind., The Bobbs-Merrill Company, Inc., 1962, p. 12.
25. James Baldwin, "A Talk to Teachers," *Saturday Review,* vol. 46, December 21, 1963, pp. 42–44+.
26. Walter Reckless et al., "Self-concept as Insulator Against Delinquency," *American Sociological Review,* vol. 21, no. 6, 1956.
27. Abram Kardiner, "When the State Brings up the Child," *Saturday Review,* vol. 44, August 26, 1961, pp. 9–11; Albert J. Rabin, "Culture Components as a Significant Factor in Child Development: Kibbutz Adolescents," *American Journal of Orthopsychiatry,* vol. 31, 1961, pp. 493–504.
28. Aldous Huxley, *Brave New World,* New York, Harper & Row, Publishers, 1932.
29. Kardiner and Ovesey, *op. cit.,* p. 366.
30. Michael Harrington, *The Other America: Poverty in the United States,* New York, The Macmillan Company, 1963, Chap. 4, "If You're Black, Stay Black," pp. 61–81.

31. Frank Riessman, *The Culturally Deprived Child,* New York, Harper & Row, Publishers, 1962, p. 1.
32. Martin Deutsch, *Minority Group and Class Status as Related to Social and Personality Factors in Scholastic Achievement,* monograph 2, Ithaca, N.Y., The Society for Applied Anthropology, Cornell University Press, 1960; E. Franklin Frazier, *The Negro Family in the United States* (rev. ed.), New York, The Dryden Press, Inc., 1951; Nathan Glazer and D. P. Moynihan, *Beyond the Melting Pot,* Cambridge, Mass., The M.I.T. Press and Harvard University Press, 1963, pp. 25-85.
33. Bertha Riese, *Heal the Hurt Child,* Chicago, The University of Chicago Press, 1962.
34. Kardiner and Ovesey, *op. cit.,* pp. 345–349.
35. Lena Horne, "I Just Want to be Myself," *Show,* vol. 3, September, 1963, pp. 62–65+.
36. Robert L. Sutherland, *Color, Class and Personality,* Washington, D.C., American Council on Education, 1942, p. 41.
37. David and Pearl Ausubel, "Ego Development Among Segregated Negro Children," in A. Harry Passow (ed.), *Education in Depressed Areas,* New York, Bureau of Publications, Teachers College, Columbia University, 1963, p. 113.
38. Kardiner and Ovesey, *op. cit.,* p. 380.
39. David and Pearl Ausubel, *op. cit.,* pp. 127–128.
40. Walter Waetjen and Jean D. Grambs, "Sex Differences: A Case of Educational Evasion?" *Teachers College Record,* December, 1963.
41. Virgil Clift, Archibald W. Anders, H. Gordon Hullfish (eds.), *Negro Education in America,* New York, Harper & Row, Publishers, 1962.
42. Majorie B. Smiley and John S. Diekoff, *Prologue to Teaching,* Fair Lawn, N.J., Oxford University Press, 1959, p. 286.
43. David and Pearl Ausubel, *op. cit.,* p. 128.
44. Albert J. Lott and Bernice E. Lott, *Negro and White Youth,* New York, Holt, Rinehart and Winston, Inc., 1963.
45. Kardiner and Ovesey, *op. cit.*
46. Abraham Tannenbaum, "Family Living in Textbook Town," *Progressive Education,* vol. 31, no. 5, March, 1954, pp. 133–141; Martin Mayer, "The Trouble with Textbooks," *Harper's Magazine,* vol. 225, July, 1962, pp. 65–71; Otto Klineberg, "Life is Fun in a Smiling, Fair-Skinned World," *Saturday Review,* February 16, 1963; Albert Alexander, "The Gray Flannel Cover on the American History Textbook," *Social Education,* vol. 24, January, 1960, pp. 11–14.
47. Lloyd Marcus, *The Treatment of Minorities in Secondary School Textbooks,* New York, Anti-Defamation League of B'nai B'rith, 1961; Jack Nelson and Gene Roberts, Jr., *The Censors and the Schools,* Boston, Little, Brown & Company, 1963.
48. Melville J. Herskovits, *The Myth of the Negro Past,* Boston, The Beacon Press, 1958.
49. Atlee E. Shidler, "Education for Civic Leadership: The School's Responsibility," an address presented to the 68th National Conference on Government, The National Municipal League, Washington, D.C., November 16, 1962, mimeo.
50. Trager and Yarrow, *op. cit.*

51. A. A. Lumsdaine, "Instruments and Media of Instruction," in N. L. Gage (ed.), *Handbook of Research on Teaching,* Chicago, Rand McNally & Company, 1963, p. 586.
52. Jean D. Grambs, "Are We Training Prejudiced Teachers?" *School and Society,* vol. 71, April 1, 1950, pp. 196–198.
53. John Niemeyer, "Some Guidelines to Desirable Elementary School Reorganization," in *Programs for the Educationally Disadvantaged,* Washington, D.C., U. S. Office of Education Bulletin 1963, no. 17, p. 81.
54. Bingham Dai, "Minority Group Membership and Personality Development," *op. cit.*
55. Kardiner and Ovesey, *op. cit.,* p. 264.
56. Deutsch, *op. cit.,* p. 23.
57. Kardiner and Ovesey, *op. cit.,* p. 72.
58. Lott and Lott, *op. cit.,* p. 163.
59. Dennis L. Trueblood, "The Role of the Counselor in the Guidance of Negro Students," *Harvard Educational Review,* vol. 30, no. 3, Summer, 1960, p. 252–269.
60. Eli Ginzberg, James K. Anderson, and John L. Herma, *The Optimistic Tradition and American Youth,* New York, Columbia University Press, 1962, p. 107.
61. Lott and Lott, *op. cit.,* p. 155.
62. Combs and Snygg, *op. cit.,* p. 374.
63. Wilbur B. Brookover and Associates, "Improving Academic Achievement Through Students' Self-concept Enhancement," Report of Symposium at the 1964 Meeting of the American Research Association, Chicago.
64. John D. Campbell, Leon J. Yarrow, and Marian Radke Yarrow, "A Study of Adaptation to a New Social Situation"; "Acquisition of New Norms: A Study of Racial Desegregation"; "Personal and Situational Variables in Adaptation to Change"; and "Leadership and Interpersonal Change," *The Journal of Social Issues,* vol. 14, no. 1, 1958, pp. 3–59.
65. Joshua A. Fishman, "Childhood Indoctrination for Minority-Group Membership," *Daedalus,* vol. 90, no. 2, Spring, 1961, pp. 329–349.
66. J. Wayne Wrightstone, "Demonstration Guidance Project in New York City," *Harvard Educational Review,* vol. 30, no. 3, Summer, 1960, pp. 237–251.
67. For example, Horace Mann Bond, "Wasted Talent," in Eli Ginzberg (ed.), *The Nation's Children, 2: Development and Education,* New York, Columbia University Press, pp. 116–137; Dorsey Baynham, "The Great Cities Projects," *NEA Journal,* vol. 52, April, 1963, pp. 17–19.
68. Deutsch, *op. cit.*
69. Kurt Lewin, "Bringing Up the Jewish Child," in *Securing Our Children Against Prejudice,* New York, Community Relations Service.
70. Campbell, Yarrow, and Yarrow, *op. cit.*
71. Baldwin, "A Talk to Teachers," *op. cit.,* p. 44.
72. Herskovits, *op. cit.*
73. B. A. Botkin (ed.), *Lay My Burden Down: A Folk History of Slavery,* Chicago, The University of Chicago Press, 1945.
74. Trueblood, *op. cit.*
75. Riessman, *op. cit.;* Frank Riessman, "Cultural Styles of the Disadvantaged," *Integrated Education,* vol. 1, April, 1963.

76. Helen H. Davidson, Judith W. Greenberg, and Joan M. Gerver, "Characteristics of Successful School Achievers from a Severely Deprived Environment," unpublished research report, The School of Education, The City University of New York, October, 1962, p. 18, mimeo.
77. Gordon P. Liddle, "Modifying the School Experience of Culturally Handicapped Children in the Primary Grades," in *Programs for the Educationally Disadvantaged.* Washington, D.C., U.S. Office of Education Bulletin 1963, no. 17, p. 59.
78. C. W. Hunnicutt et al., *Survey of the Croton and Washington Irving Elementary Schools of the City of Syracuse,* Syracuse, N.Y., Syracuse University, Bureau of School Services, June, 1963, pp. 19–21, mimeo.
79. *Ibid.,* pp. 28–34.
80. Joseph M. Wepman, "Auditory Discrimination, Speech, and Reading," *Elementary School Journal,* vol. 60, March, 1960, pp. 325–333.
81. *Focus on Problems Facing Youth* (a picture packet), New York, National Conference of Christians and Jews, 1954.
82. "Sociology: A Self-corrective for the Population Explosion?" *Time,* vol. 83, February 28, 1964, p. 56.
83. Mary A. Sarvis, "Reactions of Children from Crowded Areas," *Childhood Education,* vol. 39, May, 1963, pp. 413–415.
84. Sarvis, *loc. cit.*
85. Roger Reger, "Stimulating the Distractible Child," *Elementary School Journal,* vol. 64, October, 1963, pp. 42–48.
86. Ellen Lurie, "School Integration in New York City," *Integrated,* vol. 2, February-March, 1964, pp. 3–11.
87. Charles F. Hoban, Jr., *Focus on Learning,* Washington, D.C., American Council on Education, 1942.
88. *Washington Post,* September 10, 1963.

Discussion, Comments, and Issues

When the blind men in the famous fable tried to describe an elephant, each one reported on that portion of the anatomy of the animal that he had touched. In our approach to the question of the education of Negro children and youth, we perforce tend to report that part of the problem with which we have had most intimate contact. In this Conference, we were fortunate in having available the insights of a wide variety of specialists from many disciplines and agencies and with experience in many kinds of research and action programs. Hopefully, by putting together all of these insights, we may have a better picture of our particular elephant.

This section is one attempt at such a picture. As the author of the first paper presented to the Conference, it was my privilege to be able to expand somewhat upon my remarks and emphasize some points which seemed crucial, then, with the help of the two respondents, to open up areas of disagreement and identify some of the issues for the total Conference. Further discussion from the floor by all participants followed. In small afternoon discussion groups, participants were further enabled to share their views. A final brief summary session reported back to all of the Conference participants the highlights of each subgroup discussion.

Here I will attempt to pull together the thinking as it was recorded throughout the day. Mention of individual commentators will be omitted, partly because it was not always possible to identify from the recorded remarks who was speaking, but also because similar ideas were often expressed by several different people.

When one has to deal with an abundance of riches, one usually has a difficult time picking and choosing. Out of the richness of ideas which were offered by the Conference participants, I have had of necessity to do some difficult selection. In presenting the issues, I have tried to provide a balanced view of what the Conference participants contributed, since I have had abundant opportunity to express my own biases in the background paper and in the opening part of this section. It is hoped that the issues raised and the comments offered will lead others to even more fruitful exchanges.

Research: The Current and Continuing Need

The contemporary situation of the Negro in America has produced a voluminous new literature. It is as though social scientists of all kinds were making up for years of neglect. There has been in existence for decades a modest research effort to throw light on America's most baffling dilemma. But even the landmark publication of Myrdal's classic,[1] or the penetrating and devastating studies of the American Council on Education of Negro youth during the depression,[2] or the classic study by Dollard[3] did not make a major impression upon the American intellectual audience and certainly did not reach the public in general.

We met in conference because of the new urgency of the problem of the American Negro, but we also met with the realization that much of what we need to know is woefully unavailable. It has been said that psychologists know more about the American college sophomore than any other group of human beings. It is also true that these sophomores have been mostly middle class and white. This is true of the other areas of research into human behavior and motivation. Although we may have begun to develop some insights into human psyche, we must admit that much of what we do know is probably only true for some segments of our population, and we are not always sure which ones. It may be almost too late to make up for the neglect of years. Certainly we must admit that much of what we thought we knew about Negro personality and the Negro community may no longer be true. But again, we lack the breadth of research findings to let us know how far we may be in error.

One rather signficant finding, however, which we can be somewhat sure about is the fact that education has relatively little impact upon attitudes and behaviors. Coleman's study of adolescent society,[4] Jacob's study of college education,[5] and the research reported by Sanford[6] indicate that *most* students enter school, whether it be high school or college, and leave it without any visible change except that they are four years older. Some are changed, true, but only, as Jacob points out, when the total collegiate atmosphere is consistent and pressing or, as Sanford indicates, due to the particular personality of the particular person. In almost any instance, however, the change is to produce more of the same; that is, the intellectual becomes more intellectual, the nonconformist becomes more deviant, the conservative more entrenched in conservatism. The school serves to reinforce what is already present.

Is education to be considered, then, merely a neutral institution which serves society by permitting children and youth to grow up as they would have anyway, except that they now enjoy the patina of literacy and some marketable skills? In effect, this is the situation today. It is our contention that this is not enough. Such a view of the school is particularly inadequate when we consider the situation of the Negro child and youth.

These youngsters are typical of all who go through the schools and emerge feeling worse than when they started; all who have been in classrooms and been found wanting, have been failed and, through such failure, emerge uneducated. Such failures are the experience of millions of young people; the fact that it is likely to be the *typical* experience of all Negro youth is our major concern.

Since, therefore, the standard approach to classroom instruction has produced only neutral or negative response, we would propose a new approach. We would suggest that the utilization of the idea of deliberate efforts to change the self-concept of students will appreciably affect their total education as well as their personal experience.

It is a rather interesting commentary upon the educational lag that, despite our awareness of the role of psychological processes in human behavior, little if any psychology of whatever school is to be found in the average classroom. The education of teachers is only minimally contaminated by psychological instruction. It is probable that today's teachers learn more psychology from Dr. Spock's columns than they do in their formal training. The materials of instruction reflect this singular omission. Deliberate efforts to guide young people toward an understanding of themselves and other human beings as psychological organisms are rare, usually of an experimental nature, and not typical of the American classroom. Probably there is a wider spread of popular "psychology" in America than in most other countries, but little of it is being used in the deliberate guidance of student learning.

We would suggest, therefore, that it is appropriate to put to work in the classrooms the things we now know about human behavior and learning, about conscious and unconscious motivation, and use such insights to establish new educational situations and new educational materials and processes. Furthermore, we would suggest that a good deal more research must be done to see to what extent the educational situation can become an agency for genuine self-realization, to develop what Maslow calls the "self-actualizing personality."[7]

As has been stated, the concept of self appears to be a fruitful focus of attention. It has already been pointed out that the person who sees himself as potentially good is more likely to achieve this goal than the person who sees himself as potentially bad. The status of the minority-group person is often a reflection of how the person perceives the way society perceives *him*. What Allport terms "Traits Due to Victimization" are liable to appear in the behavior and personality structure of those who have a view of self which is that of an outcast, minority person, lacking power and perceived as not as worthy as others. We can see the mechanism operating in many spheres of life, some of them quite familiar to all of us. I am likely to bristle when I hear derogatory remarks about women drivers. Current comments about college teachers of education cause me to become antagonistic and angry. I am always strongly tempted to attack the perpetrators of the remarks, not the validity of the remarks themselves. It is obvious, of course, that women are as competent drivers as men and that college professors of education are an eminent and competent breed—as capable as any of their colleagues. Teachers typically reflect a minority view of self in many of their behaviors.[8]

It was interesting and instructive to observe one's friends during the massive drafting of men into the service during World War II and thereafter. One observed the reaction of young men who, in civilian life, felt relatively successful and also felt themselves to be at a socially approved status level, suddenly finding that, as enlisted men, they were absolutely of no account whatsoever. Or at least so they felt. Here was an authority structure which not only put them at the bottom but put a very visible label on them. Anyone could tell from two blocks away whether a man was an enlisted man or an officer. Some individuals reacted by doing all in their power to go to officer candidate schools. These persons could, in many instances, not tolerate the view of self which said that there were many who were better, who could be seen as better, and who had the power of exclusion and privilege. Others found the life of the enlisted man one of relative freedom from responsibility. Here was a chance to hate a group in authority with freedom and approbation. It was right and proper to think all officers were stupid, incompetent, or worse. By contrast, today's training camps usually permit all personnel to be off camp in civilian clothes.[9] Rank is then hidden from view, and one can escape the feeling of inferiority.

The example above is probably as close as the average middle-class white person can come to understanding the situation of the Negro. The major difference is that the Negro cannot change his clothes when he leaves the "reservation." He is always walking and living behind his label, the label of color.

Some Crucial Issues

Much that is in the preceding statement includes what is obvious and agreed upon. But there are some crucial issues which need further clarification. As discussed by the Conference participants, these focused upon several key questions:

1. Is the concept of self the most fruitful framework for initiating action and research in the amelioration of the situation of the Negro?
2. Is the problem of the Negro one unique to this group, or is it one whose dimensions are shared by all who are at the lowest place in our social scale?
3. To what extent does the protest movement of the last few years change the situation of the Negro, and what may lie ahead?
4. Is it possible to achieve any measurable change for Negro children and youth if only the school is involved and not the total community?
5. What kinds of educational changes are most promising?

1. Self-concept as Focus of Reeducation

There is no general agreement among social scientists that the approach taken by the phenomenological school of psychologists, most typically represented by Combs and Snygg,[10] have the last word to say about the dynamics of human personality. It is clear that much of the research on the role of self-concept is suggestive without being definitive. It is also apparent that many of the research findings are the efforts of middle-class white psychologists who may, by this very fact, be unable to ask the right questions about the Negro world and the lower-class world.

It is possible, too, that unconscious or subconscious motivations are a major force in behavior and personality and that what we have are merely the symptoms, in behavior, of such forces. The very idea of the concept of self is a derived one, since the roots of one's view of self are hidden from conscious view.

But again and again one is reminded of the utility of the idea of identity, or self. It has played a large part in the success of the Black Muslim movement. This movement tells the Negro that it is *good* to be what he is, a black man. It is possible that the success of Dr. Samuel Shepard in raising achievement levels in the primarily Negro schools of St. Louis has been the utilization of antiwhite feelings, which then promote an enhanced view of the self as nonwhite and, therefore, able to succeed.

An alternative approach would be to consider the behavior of the Negro as a function of *role taking*.

A Conference participant commented:

> "I think the worst effects on Negro personality come about not so much from explicit teaching about inferiority to the Negro, but by the forced role adoption of a culturally defined role of inferiority. A person made to act inferior grows into this role. This is where the most devastating damage occurs to the Negro personality, and is thus not the direct result of teaching about inferiority. Forced role adoption is very hard to fight. In the book, *Black Like Me*,[11] a white man brings out very clearly what it means to have to handle the terror of taking the Negro role, without lifetime history of defenses in learning how to take such a role."

The Negro child, youth, or adult behaves according to what he perceives to be the role that he is expected to take. He is expected to be subservient; therefore, he behaves in a subservient fashion. He is expected to be slow in school; therefore, he is slow. He is expected to sit at the back of the bus; therefore, he does so. But when the Negro ceases to take these roles, then he also breaks the expectations of the white group. By refusing to accept the forced role of inferiority, the Negro will cease to behave as an inferior.

The reciprocal nature of this relationship was well expressed:

> "The Negro is forced to play a role, and so is the white, in the whole structure of discrimination. This structure cannot be maintained unless both sides play the role. One of the most valuable functions of the current revolution is that the Negroes find in their revolt that suddenly it really does take two to tango, and if they refuse to dance, the game does not go on; the dance does not occur. The idea of disengagement, which the protest illustrates, is an insight with implications for personality as well as for maintaining the protest."

This concept suggests that education should be focused on helping Negro children and youth to role play behaviors that are the antithesis of the stereotype. Initiative rather than passivity would be tried out in actual *behavior*. It is hypothecated that by acting out these roles, the Negro would in truth *become* a different person. It was noted that:

> "The other important contribution of the protest is that it provides a chance to act out an identity crisis, and this is in terms of the basic values of our nation. It is also a way of acting out aggression, which in this case is very healthy. Certainly much of the motivation of the protest is moving against as well as moving toward the oppressor."

Those young people who have sat-in at drug stores, or sat in the front of a bus, or boycotted a store or a school are acting out a different concept of their role. This in turn would certainly shift their view of their own potential and serve to enhance their feelings about their own adequacy.

Current research in child growth and development appears to be making increased use of the self-concept as a useful organizing principle. The increased sophisticated use of projective devices of all kinds—Rorschach, TAT, sentence-completion tests, and so forth—suggests windows whereby self-processes can be viewed and related not only to observable behavior but to the individual's explicit verbal description of himself. What is needed, it would appear, is a more exact formulation of the theoretical framework within which the self-concept plays a role and further elaboration of research methodologies which will provide an insight into the world of the Negro child and youth.

Yet whatever changes may occur will obviously take place in a larger context.

> "We cannot talk about a changing self-concept of the American Negro without recognizing the broader map in which this is taking place. I mean, we have to understand the meaning to the American Negro of the thirty or more African nations who have joined the United Nations in the past few years. This has had a tremendous impact on the American Negro and his image of himself and of Negroes in American life."

Also,

> "The protest can be used as a hook to change Negro role perception. Remember the famous quotation of the lady who started the Montgomery, Alabama, bus strike, 'My feet is tired, but my soul is rested.' What is needed in the schools, then, is reinforcement for all the kinds of behavior that go counter to the so-called Negro way of acting now."

2. *How Unique Are the Problems of the Negro Lower-Class Individual?*

Individuals who are starving, says the folk view, will respond similarly to food: they will want to eat. Yet we know that culturally induced attitudes toward food may interfere with how hunger is appeased. A hungry Hindu will not eat the cows that roam his fields; in fact, many literally starve to death in the presence of what is to us a prime source of food. Will individuals respond in the same ways to the experience of social deprivation, family disorganization, and economic insecurity?

One position taken is that children who live in the tenement centers of cities, no matter what their backgrounds or group identifications, will have many, if not all, of the same kinds of educational and personal problems. It is further argued that children from the poverty-level rural areas of the country can also be classed with the city-bred "culturally deprived."

Another point of view is that there are similarities among such children, but that one can factor out those responses which are due to poverty and cultural isolation and still find a set of behaviors and attitudes which can only be accounted for by the differential social valuation accorded to color. That is, the Negro and the white slum child may pose educational problems, but a procedure which aids the white child may not necessarily be of help to the Negro child. For instance, a white child may respond with added interest in schoolwork if his white teacher praises him. A Negro child may respond with suspicion and hostility to the praise of a white teacher and become less, rather than more, motivated to work.

The meager research that is available provides evidence of a qualitative difference between the Negro and the white child, even when living conditions are held constant, that is, family income, neighborhood, etc. In fact, as the research of Deutsch[12] and Lott and Lott,[13] among others, points out, no matter how carefully one may seek to equate groups, qualitative differences will emerge. The white and the Negro child, though living on contiguous blocks, do not live in the same world.

As studies of immigrant groups have shown, although many started at the bottom of the economic heap, there were always available models which indicated that, with appropriate energy, an individual could get out of the slum.[14] The Negro, however, has no such assurance. He has few available models demonstrating effective escape from slum living. A few of those who are no longer on the edge of poverty, like the teacher or the minister, are often apt to reject the child who comes to school knowing nothing except slum-conditioned behavior, which is everything the middle-class person most resents and resists. As Riessman has stated, the positive aspects of the environment, the good things that the child comes to school with, are ignored, underestimated, or suppressed.[15]

A participant commented, "The position paper does not develop the psychological resources which Negroes have, even those most deprived in economic terms."

Pettigrew reports unpublished research regarding information Negroes held about the new African nations. In one slum area, it was found that the darker the Negro, the more apt was he to be informed about Africa and its leaders. In other words, since it was evident that a dark color was not an asset in America, it was psychologically useful to identify with remote nations where a dark skin was an asset and an avenue toward power.

Furthermore, there is abundant evidence from the autobiographical material of contemporary successful Negroes, such as James Baldwin,[16] Lena Horne,[17] and others, that the burden of being a Negro is not removed by mere economic success.

It is true, however, that research is needed to identify the significant ways in which deprivation affects all children in our culture and the ways it may affect some groups differently. One assumption, which is not necessarily shared by all students of the subject, is that there is a qualitative difference between Negro children and youth and white children and youth, and it becomes greater with greater social and economic deprivation.

Elaborations of the idea of the significance of the fact of being Negro were provided by a number of Conference participants:

> "When we are talking about the culturally deprived Negro, it seems to me we have to change our terms and talk perhaps more about the emotionally deprived Negro. Persons like me, for instance. I was never culturally deprived. My father was the first Negro graduate of Princeton University in my little town in New Jersey. We had all the books about Negroes there were at that time. I had a good cultural understanding of Negroes and my cultural heritage. Even though I went to school and heard the children chant,
>
> 'Nigger, nigger, never die,
> Black face and shiny eye,
> Crooked nose and crooked toes,
> That's the way the nigger goes,'
>
> I had support from my parents, who pointed out the truth about my background. Yet in a sense I have been very deprived, emotionally deprived. You can't grow up a Negro, even a middle-class Negro, without knowing many defeats and discriminations just because of who you are."

> "The Negro family, as we have heard, is marked very often by the absence of a father, which is more damaging to the boys than the girls. Boys in particular in father-absent families have less ability to postpone gratification. They will accept the small chocolate bar today rather than wait next week for one five times as large. Such boys have low need achievement, but high need power. This high need power is of

considerable significance to us, however, if we are looking for a hook whereby achievement can be raised, too.

"The boys in father-absent families tend to develop sexual role confusion. Only secondarily do such boys adopt a masculine role, since primarily the only adult moralities are feminine as expressed by the mother, the only consistent adult present. But gaining a masculine role and the compensatory toughness and acting out means rejection of everything feminine. The school is a symbol of femininity, with female teachers and the fact that girls do better than boys. Somewhere along the line this problem probably must be faced, perhaps with men teachers in primary grades or through some other device."

3. Is There a New Negro?

We were forcibly reminded by Conference participants that the last few years have produced a revolution in the Negro community. The research, for instance, on the influence of color on personality completed twenty or more years ago[18] may be quite wrong in the context of today's sit-ins, marches, wade-ins, picketings, and so forth. To have a dark skin today may be an asset for a Negro leader rather than the handicap of a bygone day. As a participant pointed out:

> "It is interesting to note that all the major leaders among Negroes today tend to be quite Negroid in appearance. In fact, my black skin has a great value among Negroes today. I do remember a time when being as black as I am did not have much value, but today it is different.
>
> "Who is indeed the New Negro we are talking about? As a matter of fact, as I read the position paper, it seemed to me that you were talking about the American Negro such as I was twenty years ago or ten years ago, or even three or four years ago. But now we have to consider that the Negro about whom we have concern is not the same kind of creature that was the object of research in the 1940's. The Negro of 1963 is certainly not the Negro of 1952 or even of 1959. In February, 1960, the sit-ins began. A whole new kind of way of living and a whole new concept of the Negro began, and reached larger masses and groups of Negroes."

The significance of the hard drive for civil rights is difficult to assess in terms of its impact on average Negro personality and behavior. The Jew, for instance, has been fighting for equality of treatment for generations, yet there is abundant evidence that there is still a "Jewish problem" in terms of the larger community as well as for the individual Jew or ex-Jew. The fact that Jews are more likely to be found in middle- and upper-income brackets than in lower-class brackets, with commensurate rates of education, has not reduced either the evidence of anti-Semitism at some levels or the feelings of probable and expected anti-Semitism on the part of Jews.[19]

Several factors must be weighed: first, a revolution, with its attendant disorders and sacrifices, cannot continue forever. Increasingly, fewer young people may be willing to go to jail in order to sit where they please in a movie theater. Second, while demonstrating that the Negro need not be a passive victim of social cruelties, the fact remains that the world of jobs and housing is still controlled by whites, and entry by Negroes is restricted and difficult. The battle may be won, but the war may be lost. Third, the attitudes of generations are not removed quickly when the factual conditions that created them continue to exist. In other words, apprentice programs may be opened up for more Negroes, but if Negro parents, living as third- or fourth-generation slum dwellers with no experience with job security or continuity of effort or faith in the white man's promises, do not support their children in seeking out and sticking with an apprentice program, the program will reach very few indeed. Fourth, the protest leadership group, which now includes many middle-class and long-time Negro leaders as well as many new ones, may not necessarily continue in power. The results may be too limited, and followers may drift away. The effort of sustaining such leadership may be too much of a drain on the individuals themselves. A different element, desiring immediate returns for the effort right now, may abandon the Christian, passive-resistance approach and prefer more direct and more violent means.[20] The reaction from the white power structure will be immediate and restrictive—even more so than it has been and in spite of the relatively peaceful protest measures now being utilized. Thus the revolution may be squelched, the momentum lost, and the cause returned again to the courts and to negotiation, with resultant continued apathy and lowered motivation for achievement. Negro migration from South to North may be expected to continue for many more years as marginal farms are closed out. The migrant from the South has learned with even greater thoroughness than his Northern-born and -bred relatives the futility of fighting the white world. He has also learned the white man's valuation of him, has incorporated it into his self-system, and will pass it on to his children.

Conference participants also made a point of other forces at work.

> "The protest provides its own motivation once it gets going. Attitude change and personality change come about through behavior, not necessarily through explicit teaching. All of you are familiar with the power of role playing as a technique. But I am not talking about it as a therapeutic technique. If a five-minute role play can have a permanent effect, as we know from some of the research, then continued role taking can

also have a very significant effect. Thus the forced role adoption of the Negro for a whole lifetime can be seen as having a very significant influence on personality. You can see the implications here probably for reeducation."

"The protest, as considered in this paper, assumes that only the vanguard has been touched. I think that's wrong. I think it has gotten down to the Negro lower class, too."

"I think that there is general agreement today, as I see it, that the Negro is willing and anxious to identify with his African heritage, though not always the way the Black Muslims identify it. However, the Muslims do have a point, because they are part of the basic feeling of the American Negro regarding a need to be part of a larger group."

"I do not believe that you can look at the American Negro without recognizing that a large part of his concept of himself comes from the religious orientation of his society. This may sound naïve to many of you who consider that education is the sole avenue to self-expression. But one cannot look at the Negro revolution today without being reminded of the fact that this is a spiritual revolution. The religious basis of the revolution is one of the enduring facts about the Negro in America and one of the most positive aspects of the development of the Negro in a hostile society. If you sing any of the freedom songs, you know they weren't just born in 1960. It was my great-great-grandmother who was singing, 'Before I'll be a slave, I'll be buried in my grave, and go home to my Lord and be free.' This has been the motivating force that led Harriet Tubman and Frederick Douglass and the other great people.

"I resent your putting hatred as one of the major motivating forces that contributes to the Negro revolution. I feel that the religious motivation has been very significant, and one of the reasons why the Negro could pray for those who used spite against them, and to keep a positive tone in spite of the handicaps that have been theirs."

Much of the aggression of the Negro is a very healthy thing. Some or all of these factors may prove out in the times ahead. They may none of them prove to be correct. It is possible that within one generation the Negro group will be assimilated into the total social and economic structure of the country. But few are optimistic enough to believe this will be so. How long it will take before this democratic condition does exist depends, it seems, on the efforts used to make deliberate interventions through the major institution we have at hand for behavioral and attitudinal change: the schools.

4. Can Education Alone Make Any Significant Difference?

> "Since 1954 we have good poll data which show that Negroes are more optimistic than whites as to what will happen in the next five years. No matter what segment of the Negro population you look at, it is still true. In the July 29, 1963, issue of *Newsweek,* the data clearly indicate that the Negro is expressing a brimming optimism. This can lead to two effects: one is that such optimism can produce more rather than less frustration. Despite the social gains of the last twenty years, the Negro is more frustrated rather than less, since his aspirations have gone up faster than his gains. Also the data show that the Negro places incredible faith in education. Many of us tend to run down what the schools can do for the total culture. But in terms of the American Negro, the motivation toward education is incredible. Even at the lowest socio-economic levels, tremendous faith in education is expressed."

We have already pointed out the relative ineffectiveness of the schools to make basic changes in student personality and behavior. Yet we are saying that, if used in a deliberate fashion, education can make, or rather should make, a difference. Research is urgently needed to identify what kinds of education can make what kinds of difference to what kinds of individuals. Now we can only advance as an article of faith that education can be a dramatic tool in the shaping of personality.

But the school does not exist in a social vacuum. The child may spend more time in the school than in any other organized institutional setting, yet he spends even more time with his family and with his peers outside of school, and his total adult life is spent beyond the reach of the school. The influences from these sources are obviously highly important. In a society dominated by TV, the child may be more familiar with a cartoon character he sees repeatedly than with the face of his own father. He may know more about space flight than he may know about the next block.

It is probable that the answer cannot be "either/or." Certainly if education serves to change the motivation and aspirations of Negro youth and is able to endow them with the requisite skills, but the world of work and of adequate housing is closed, then these aspirations and motivations will not last long and may become ugly and perverted from frustration and rejection.[21]

> "One major problem which we must consider is that laws themselves are not the whole answer. I would defy you to

> think of another discrimination law that Massachusetts hasn't got. We have just about exhausted the supply of antidiscrimination laws. Yet our race relations, particularly in Boston, at the moment couldn't be worse. Antidiscrimination laws certainly are needed, but they are only a bitter first step. We need rather basic changes in our economic structure: more jobs are needed; the tax structure needs to be modified to benefit the lower-income groups as well as the upper-income groups; minimum wage laws must be extended to cover service areas where so many Negroes work. Every time Congress meets, they pass legislation to study juvenile delinquency. If the same time and effort were spent to raise the minimum wage rate of service workers to $1.25, it would do more than all the social science research."

Yet it is possible that if we solve the problem of Negro identity, that is, aid the Negro in developing a fully positive sense of self-worth, the economic problem may well take care of itself.

> "Many of us who have been working in human relations a long time recognize how important it is to be a part of a subgroup: to be able to function effectively in a larger group membership. This is one of the things that is happening so definitely to the Negro today."

A person with a secure sense of self-worth does not take rebuff as a way of life: he finds a way out; he finds another door to open. Having achieved a sense of worth, the individual is able to put to work latent abilities so that he will learn skills that are in demand on the labor market. Instead of setting his goal at being an elevator operator, since such persons are rapidly becoming obsolete, he sets his sights on being the skilled mechanic that keeps elevators in safe and efficient electronic operation.

If it were possible, full-scale, community-wide attack on the causes of poverty, on the elimination of slum living conditions, on the creation of stable, integrated communities, along with appropriate and more effective education would, of course, be the ideal. Yet major cities, in which such programs are most urgent, are places where such cooperation and consistency of effort are most difficult to achieve. As the Negro becomes more concentrated in urban centers and achieves more political power, it is even possible that new metropolitan governments will emerge which will widen the community base to include white suburbs. By this device, the power of the Negro to make city government more responsive to his needs may well be negated. The hope of community-wide, sustained, and continuous efforts does not seem feasible for some years to come. America has not yet become convinced it has a problem. Only in experimental pockets do community agencies work toward a common goal. The social welfare shelves are littered with the reports of promising projects proving that good works pay off, only to disappear because of lack of community interest and public money.

It can be argued, as indeed it has been, that society has a stake in poverty and disease and discrimination. There may be some social utility in having the poor with us always, in having some whom we can look down on, distrust, shove around, and to whom we can reach out the gracious hand of charity at Thanksgiving and Christmas. Whatever the social root, it is probable that those concerned social scientists, welfare workers, educators, and Negro protest leaders and their followers are those today who feel the true urgency of the situation. Despite the publicity, the needed large-scale attack on the problems of poverty, discrimination, and the ills they spawn has not been launched.

5. What Kind of Education Can Make a Difference?

We must, then, make maximum effective use of the agency that is within our control, namely, the school. If the true power of education were utilized, it is conceivable that within a few generations the vicious cycle might be stopped. Indeed, if we can effectively solve the key problems of the education of the Negro child and youth in the urban centers of America, we may be able to solve some of the major problems of American education for all, both the favored and the defeated.

The educational potential of the Negro has not been successfully tapped. It is obvious that more research is needed if we are to understand the impact of schools as they exist today upon the Negro child. For instance, we need to inquire into the kind of teacher who is most effective with the Negro child. What makes such a teacher effective? What kinds of training and institutional support help to make this teacher what he or she is? Research is needed to gain insight into the impact of the high school upon all youth as well as upon Negro youth, but particularly the latter, since they contribute more than their share to school dropouts.

If it is true that the Negro revolt may produce a new view of what the Negro can achieve, it is essential to identify at what point in the passage of generations this new view, if it comes into being, is passed on to children. Will today's high school students who participated in the March on Washington in August, 1963, produce children who, when in school, will have a markedly different attitude toward themselves and, therefore, toward their education? While these are research questions, they become crucial whenever we attempt to devise a new approach to education, since what may be appropriate for this generation may be outmoded for the next.

"I talked to many Negroes who participated in the March on Washington on August 28, 1963, but I had not talked to many kids. I said to this young girl of twelve, 'Just tell me, honey, how did you feel when you walked down Constitution Avenue?' And this little girl answered me and said, 'I felt proud.' Now here you see a whole new ingredient in the Negro group."

There is a danger, too, in the explicit labeling of the Negro as "different." The very presence of the label may suggest a lowering of achievement standards or the establishing of different ones. Such a differential will be resisted by Negro leadership. There is a need for educational strategy of a high order if it can actually be shown that qualitative differences in the Negro child's life span make mandatory qualitative differences in his educational experiences, if we are to arrive at the same goal for Negro children as we seek for white children.

> "The reason I am concerned with the lack of Negro images in textbooks, in motion pictures, in every other educational tool that we use in the American school is not just because I want my son, or any other Negro son, to have a better image of himself, but because I want every American to have a sense of value for every other American. I feel this is exceedingly important in the development of the positive self-image within each individual."

One may object, as Henry does, to education of all children for the goal of living in contemporary middle-class society.[22] Unfortunately, this is what the public wants, Negro and white. The evidence at hand, however, seems to indicate that more effective instructional procedures which meet the particular needs of the Negro child, especially in the slum areas of large cities, must be invented. It is probable that if these new devices or procedures are effective with such children, they may well be effective with many children of all groups. The great emphasis in education on "individual differences" and "starting where the child is" has meant, in effect, providing a white-oriented middle-class curriculum to all children, merely modifying the pace at which it has been presented.

The very fact of finding more effective ways of developing competence with the tools of education—reading, writing, speaking, listening, figuring—will produce a better feeling of self and certainly better mental health. The problem we face, obviously, is that present methods are not achieving this end with significant numbers of children, many of whom are Negro.

Summary

The need for a new look at the educational situation of the Negro today has been made abundantly clear. Many promising efforts are being made to find answers that may have validity and utility on a wide base. However, we are struck not only by the energy with which many are working on the problem but by our lack of information and research. So pressing is the problem that one is strongly tempted to act first and find out whether it works later. That this may be the condition for some time to come means that those who are actively engaged in programs right now should, by all means, move full speed ahead. But the social scientist, with his evaluative tools, must also move ahead to provide new insights and point out new and promising directions for further action.

References

1. Gunnar Myrdal, *An American Dilemma,* New York, Harper & Row, Publishers, 1944.
2. Charles S. Johnson, *Growing Up in the Black Belt,* Washington, D.C., American Council on Education, 1941; J. H. Atwood et al., *Thus Be Their Destiny,* Washington, D.C., American Council on Education, 1941; Allison Davis and John Dollard, *Children of Bondage,* Washington, D.C., American Council on Education, 1940.
3. John Dollard, *Caste and Class in a Southern Town,* New Haven, Conn., Yale University Press, 1937.
4. James S. Coleman, *The Adolescent Society,* New York, The Free Press of Glencoe, 1961.
5. P. E. Jacob, *Changing Values in College,* New York, Harper & Row, Publishers, 1937.
6. Nevitt Sanford, *The American College,* New York, John Wiley & Sons, Inc., 1962.
7. Abraham H. Maslow, *Toward a Psychology of Being,* Princeton, N.J., D. Van Nostrand Company, Inc., 1962.
8. Jean D. Grambs, "Teachers as a Minority Group," *Journal of Educational Sociology,* vol. 22, February, 1949, pp. 400-405.
9. David Boroff, "Fort Hood: Sparta Goes Suburban," *Harper's Magazine,* vol. 228, January, 1964, pp. 46-53.
10. Arthur W. Combs and Donald Snygg, *Individual Behavior,* rev. ed., New York, Harper & Row, Publishers, 1959.
11. John H. Griffin, *Black Like Me,* Boston, Houghton Mifflin Company, 1961.
12. Martin Deutsch, *Minority Group and Class Status as Related to Social and Personality Factors in Scholastic Achievement,* monograph 2, Ithaca, N.Y., The Society for Applied Anthropology, Cornell University Press, 1960.
13. Albert J. Lott and Bernice E. Lott, *Negro and White Youth,* New York, Holt, Rinehart and Winston, Inc., 1963.
14. Nathan Glazer and Daniel P. Moynihan, *Beyond the Melting Pot,* Cambridge, Mass., The M.I.T. Press and Harvard University Press, 1963.
15. Frank Riessman, *The Culturally Deprived Child,* New York, Harper & Row, Publishers, 1962.
16. James Baldwin, *Nobody Knows My Name,* New York, The Dial Press, Inc., 1961. ———, *The Fire Next Time,* New York, The Dial Press, Inc., 1963.

17. Lena Horne, "I Just Want to be Myself," *Show,* vol. 3, September, 1963, pp. 62–65+.
18. Regina M. Goff, "Culture and the Personality Development of Minority Peoples" in Virgil A. Clift et al. (eds.), *Negro Education in America,* New York, Harper & Row, Publishers, 1962, pp. 124–152. Interestingly enough, the references in relation to the significance of color are ten years old or older. No recent research on the role of color is cited.
19. Judith R. Kramer and Seymour Leventman, *Children of the Gilded Ghetto,* New Haven, Conn., Yale University Press, 1961.
20. "The Civil Rights Movement," *Current,* October, 1963, pp. 35–42.
21. "The Negro in America," *Newsweek,* vol. 62, July 29, 1963, pp. 15–36.
22. Jules Henry, *Culture Against Man,* New York, Random House, Inc., 1963.

section two POLITICAL SOCIALIZATION OF NEGROES: IMAGE DEVELOPMENT OF SELF AND POLITY

by Bradbury Seasholes . . . Director of Political Studies, The Lincoln Filene Center for Citizenship and Public Affairs, and Assistant Professor of Government, Tufts University

THE POSITION PAPER

Political effectiveness is a major key to social and economic betterment, and improvement in the social and economic spheres in turn further enhances that effectiveness. The union movement demonstrated this to the American laboring class. Political action, in conjunction with strictly economic action, helped win for union members better incomes and working conditions and also greater status and respect in society. And the greater income and respect in turn simply added to the unions' increase in political effectiveness. The use of *politics* as a major tool to stimulate this increase is instructive. It was the CIO, deeply committed to political action as the AFL was not, which was primarily responsible for labor's surge in the 1930's and 1940's.

Political effectiveness is also a key to personal stability. It helps to establish and maintain strong positions of income and respect against what would be, without the element of politics, the shifting winds of market and status. And political effectiveness reinforces an individual's general sense of personal adequacy in the society at large.

Because of these salutary effects on the objective and subjective lives of people, it is of greatest concern that in American society those who perhaps most need these consequences, Negroes, tend to be less involved and less effective as citizens than whites are. Low involvement and low effectiveness in government severely weaken a critical link, politics, between what Negroes want in all major areas of life and the fulfillment of those aspirations.

Low involvement and low effectiveness are not characteristics of Negroes which suddenly appear at adulthood. They are the behavioral consequences of states of mind that begin developing in early childhood. Just as we can speak of a child's gradual adaptation to society as "socialization," so we can speak of his increasing familiarity with his political environment as his "political socialization." Somewhere along the line, the political socialization of too many Negroes goes awry. In an attempt to understand how and why, it may be helpful to consider analytically what is encompassed for any individual, black or white, in the process of becoming socialized politically.

Components of Political Socialization

Becoming politically socialized can be thought of as comprised of at least five component processes:

1. Learning to be *partisan*. Somewhere in one's life span, positions are taken, are to one extent or another made consistent with one another on issues, and are related to candidates running for office.
2. Learning to *participate* in politics. Beyond learning to take sides, a person develops a proclivity to participate in politics in certain ways (voting, wearing buttons, giving money, and so forth) and with a certain frequency or intensity.
3. Learning to be *optimistic* about politics. This refers to one's basic sense of effectiveness in politics. (It does not refer to whether or not one actually is effective.)
4. Learning political *information*. A large part of political socialization, of course, is accumulating facts about the structure of government, the avenues of activity open, the positions candidates and parties take on issues, and so forth.
5. Learning to participate with *skill*. Given a potential effectiveness in politics, how skillfully does a person use his resources to approach the full potential?

Political Socialization in the School Years

Partisanship, participation, optimism, information, and skills are learned (if at all) over a large number of years, and for most of us the process starts quite young. The literature available on political socialization concentrates on school-age children and adolescents, leaving an impression that the process is essentially complete by the early twenties. Although this is not true, certainly a large part of political attitudes and behavior patterns is developed prior to adulthood, that is, prior to the time when individuals are conventionally permitted to be full participants in government. In discussing what is currently known about political socialization of Negroes, it will be necessary to unite on a speculative basis two sets of information, one dealing with Negro adults and one with white political socialization.[1]

Regarding the learning of *partisanship,* we would expect that as a child proceeds toward adulthood and as his information about the world in general, and more particularly about the world of politics, increases, a sharpening of political opinion and ideology would occur. This sharpening would be noticed first through decreasing "no opinion" among school students and then through increasing polarization of political feelings within the growing group that does hold opinions. This hypothesis is pretty well substantiated. Herbert Hyman cites definite evidence that class differentials on political opinions do in fact increase over time as a student proceeds through his school years.[2] The basic reason is increased awareness of class position and class interest, which leads to the finer definitions of interest translated into political stands.

So far, so good. But what do we hypothesize about *participation?* Again one might expect that a growing awareness of one's specific class or other subgroup interest in the activities of a society would be coupled with a growing awareness of how the political process can have some effect on those interests. Consequently, the hypothesis would state that as one proceeds through the school years, greater interest in taking part in politics would accompany greater awareness of one's stake in society. But we run into some counterevidence, or at least counterspeculation, which points to a peaking of interest in participation and optimism about the effectiveness of participating somewhere before the completion of high school and the intervention thereafter of declining *optimism* about political efficacy.[3] Encroaching cynicism in turn is alleged to dampen interest in participation itself. Finally, it needs to be pointed out that, as one would expect, over a period of time during the school years an increased differentiation develops in the amount of political *information* learned. That is, certain subgroups of students—the wealthy, for example—learn political facts at a greater rate than other subgroups.[4]

Among the very young it is difficult to distinguish fact-learning from affective development of optimism about governors. David Easton and Fred Greenstein have both published discussions of relatively young children's political information and feelings about political participants. With Robert Hess, Easton reports, for example, that children in grades two through eight tend to have very favorable images of the President and to have no knowledge or favorable feelings about other governmental officeholders. As children proceed from grades two through eight, their collective image of the President proceeds from being extremely like their feelings and impressions of their fathers to a position where father and President are quite distinct creatures. The increased differentiation comes at the expense of the father. For example, the child remains impressed at how much a President knows but becomes increasingly unimpressed with what his father knows.[5] Greenstein footnotes the Easton study by pointing out that in his quite similar work in New Haven, Conn., the mayor appears quite prominent to young people and also has quite a favorable image. This he attributes to a particular situation, namely, that Mayor Richard C. Lee visits every classroom in the city during the year![6]

Neither study provides any insights into Negro students in these grades. But the findings immediately suggest rather interesting questions. Are Negro children of this age level more likely to have more information about and be more proud of Negro officeholders above and beyond their admiration for the President or possibly instead of admiration for the President? It is very unlikely that many young school children know the names of, or care about, congressmen or city councilors; but are Negro children more likely to be aware of Negro officeholders at this level than white children are of whites? The extent to which Negro youngsters single out Negro athletes for special attention and admiration is well known. Is the same kind of excitement generated in them by Negroes active in politics and government?

Sense of Efficacy, Frustration, and Self-image

Central to the development of all the components constituting political socialization is a feeling that participating, taking stands, accumulating information, and sharpening skills are all worth the effort. A person is not likely to spend much time, energy, or money in politics if he is convinced that no results follow ("You can't fight city hall") or that in some sense no results *should* follow ("I haven't got anything worth saying or being considered"). The first of these attitudes could be labeled "conspiratorial" and the second identified as the political segment of negative self-image. Traditionally, both have been considered under the general heading of a low sense of political efficacy.[7] But for the moment, it may be useful to consider the two separately.

"You Can't Fight City Hall"

That Negroes have experienced severe frustration in political life is hard to dispute. In the South, city hall and especially the county courthouse have proven impenetrable fortresses to the brave few Negroes who have in many instances literally risked their lives in trying to register their political preferences. As a country increasingly absorbed in our own urbanization and in the problems of Negroes in the large cities, we tend to overlook how many Negroes still live on farms in the South and how much their political thought and activity (or lack of it) contributes to the parameters of Negro politics nationally.[8] In the North, the actual frustration experienced by Negroes is much more a function of social and economic disadvantage.

Presumably the experience of political frustration is one of the psychological mechanisms that ultimately account for low involvement of Negroes in politics. But the relationship is not such a simple one. In theory, sense of frustration is designated as a state of mind resulting variously in destructive aggression, constructive aggression, and withdrawal. In short, frustration is unsatisfactory as a predictive or analytical device when taken as a total concept.[9]

Some differentiation among kinds of frustration helps to explain the direction in which resulting behavior is likely to go. Three typical varieties of frustration known to Negroes can be characterized as follows:

1. Achievement drive smothered by paternalism. Negro orientation toward political achievement, or just plain perseverance, has in some instances been consciously or unconsciously undermined through paternalistic guidance and assistance by whites. Examples are not hard to find. The behavior of the big-city machine is one (and suggests that Negroes are not the only ethnic minority that have been "pastoralized" in this fashion). The attitude of "enlightened Southern white leadership" in systematically short-circuiting the growth of Negro leadership through token anticipation of Negro demands is another. And the way some whites behave in racially mixed integration organizations is a third example.
2. Frustration turned to constructive aggressiveness. On rare occasions, political leadership among Negroes has been fostered through encouragement without paternalism in a general context of political frustration.
3. No help, and no help intended. The most typical Southern situation is severe frustration without accompanying encouragement toward self-help: this is frustration designed to perpetuate demoralization.

The first and third forms—and they are by far the most prevalent—both tend to encourage withdrawal. In the first instance, paternalism, the ultimate objective is to maintain Negro passivity, even if substantive concessions in public policy have to be made. In fact, concessions are used as a means of obtaining "behavior control." In the third instance, whether Negroes are passive or aggressive is almost beside the point: the ultimate objective is to maintain a substantive policy status quo in which Negroes are at a disadvantage. (This status quo is indicated by a minus sign below.) Inability of Negroes to change their status by means of switching from aggressive to passive behavior constitutes "fate control" by whites. The two situations are illustrated below. The plus and minus signs refer to public *policy* outcomes only and are assigned from a Negro point of view. Signs in parentheses indicate theoretically possible situations that are not likely to be encountered in the social contexts described.

In the fate-control situation, the policy outcome is the same regardless of what Negroes do. But this does not mean that everything is the

BEHAVIOR CONTROL:

		Whites help	Whites oppose
Negroes are:	passive	+	−
	aggressive	−	(+)

FATE CONTROL:

		Whites help	Whites oppose
Negroes are:	passive	+	−
	aggressive	+	−

same; if Negroes should choose to be aggressive, they might encounter more violence than if they remained passive. When this type of possibility is encompassed, a double minus is required in the lower right-hand cell, and the situation moves toward a behavior-control type. For this reason, we can say that the third form of frustration, no help and no help intended, tends finally to encourage passivity.[10]

The existence of such overwhelming forces pushing the frustrated Negro into political withdrawal does not correspond neatly to fundamental observations of social psychologists about the correlation of frustration with aggressive behavior.[11] Outbreaks of irrational violence in New York City and other northern cities during 1964 followed more closely the traditional model linking frustration to aggression. The overall context of sanctions against aggressive behavior is critical. It is instructive to observe what types of Negroes presently are the most aggressive in pressing for civil rights. They tend, quite naturally, to be relatively safe from economic and social sanctions, and to a lesser extent from physical sanctions, than those who have chosen not to lead. They are also young, relatively unencumbered by decades of repeated rebuff and injury.[12]

Under controlled conditions, frustration can be a constructive goad to achievement.[13] Although this form of frustration is encountered all too rarely, it is a hope upon which to build. Fortunately, the condition need not presuppose conscious white policy of seeking to help Negroes in this matter. The condition may exist without the whites knowing it or wanting it. American Negro leaders today find themselves trying desperately to avoid falling prey to paternalism while in the process of escaping the total frustration of "no help, no help intended"; of the alternatives open, they seem to prefer that of controlled frustration. The wave of Negro demonstrations of summer of 1963, and the Washington

March especially, can be viewed as Negro attempts to operate under controlled frustration and to avert well-meaning white takeover. Malcolm X's claim that the march in fact did fall into the hands of white liberals, whether true or not, undoubtedly raised a sensitive issue for the Negro leaders responsible for the demonstration.

That controlled frustration can be effective in producing demonstrable increases in Negro interest, participation, and accomplishment is perhaps better illustrated in the sports than in the political realm. The disproportionate success of Negro youth in sports must be attributed to greater achievement drive in this area rather than to unusual physical characteristics of the race. (This is certainly the lesson of previous waves of stellar athletes drawn from other oppressed minorities earlier in the century.) There has been no particular white encouragement of Negro athletes—particularly ten to fifteen years ago—but once accomplishment has been made, there has been white admiration and approval.

Why has there not been so spectacular a rise in Negro involvement and success in political life? Except in the South, the frustration level has been about the same as in sports, that is, grudging permission by whites to take part, but no enthusiastic encouragement. On the other end, however, the parallelism sags. Political accomplishment by Negroes is not generally followed by white admiration and approval. The athlete's reward—white acclaim and often increased social and economic well-being—is not lost on the Negro masses. The Negro politician or political activist is not generally so fortunate. To the Negro masses who might be tempted to adopt him as an idol, the rewards from political activity and high achievement are far less obvious than with their Negro sports idols. To be perfectly candid, they are not only less obvious; they may be less substantial in reality. For Negroes eager to improve their images in others' eyes (and their own), political activity is not a clear-cut means to the end. For educators, the rugged job is to demonstrate more clearly the relevance of politics as a means to reach Negro ends. The importance of "city hall" needs to be established if we are to expect anyone to bother with "fighting city hall."

"I Haven't Got Anything Worth Saying"

In the end, the most serious consequence of Negro frustration and noninvolvement in politics is the possibly deleterious effect on the Negro's own evaluation of himself. The Negro who sees politics as a conspiracy against him may or may not have a low political self-image. The Negro who traces his political insignificance to his own shortcomings does: "They don't care *because I am worthless.*" This quotation incorporates a big leap psychologically for the individual as well as theoretically. But empirically, the link between cynicism about government and a low self-image seems to be a strong one. This link can be seen in the lower right corner of the following diagram. The other cells

	RESPONSIVE GOVERNMENT	UNRESPONSIVE GOVERNMENT
POSITIVE SELF-IMAGE	+ + "I am worth a lot, and the government is responsive (so I will participate in politics)."	+ − "I am worth a lot, but the government is not responsive (so I won't participate)."
NEGATIVE SELF-IMAGE	− + "The government is responsive, but I am worthless (so I won't participate)."	− − "I am worthless and the government is not responsive (so I won't participate)."

describe remaining combinations of negative and positive self-images and negative and positive feelings toward government. In the diagram above, the likely behavioral consequence of each combination is given in parentheses.

If the two types of attitude are in fact correlated, we would expect not only that most of the cases would fall in the —— cell, but that more would fall in the + + than in the remaining — + and + — cells. Yet this may very well not be the case. The cell — +, "The government is responsive, but I am worthless . . .," is where we would anticipate finding Negroes subject to paternalistic modes of white-dominated government. And because southern government is in fact extraordinarily unresponsive to Negroes, a substantial number of southern Negroes presumably fall into the + — category as well as the —— category.

Whether there is or is not a greater incidence of lower political self-image among southern Negroes cannot simply be extrapolated from northern versus southern figures for Negro *nonparticipation* in politics. Because actual barriers to participation are encountered less often in the North, it is in the North that low self-image politically is most likely to have a strong association with nonparticipation. Are northern Negro feelings of political inefficaciousness substantially greater than among whites, once standard explanatory social and economic variables have been accounted for? If so, what if anything is there in the political system itself that can explain this? Is the system actually less responsive to Negroes, although not as severely so as in the South? Or is political cynicism somewhat independent of the way the political system actually works? Is it simply a minor segment of an overall pessimism and low self-image engendered by an informal social order which is not so strikingly variant from North to South as the political system is? These are critical questions that need investigation if any meaningful attack on the way Negroes learn to view and use politics—on their *political socialization*—is to be undertaken.

Agents of Political Socialization: the Family

Earlier the observation was made that much of the process of political socialization occurs "during the school years." One could as well say, "during the family years," because the two periods occur at roughly the same stage of life. If we who are concerned with the nature of the political education Negroes are receiving, formally or informally, expect to alter the course of things, we must face the grim prospect of ascertaining what the parameters are within which we can operate. Realistically, this means determining what contribution the school experience makes to political socialization, as against the contribution of the family or other aspects of the environment. Unfortunately, the school contribution is rather small, judging from what evidence is currently available. While there are certainly "school effects" — an increased amount of political information that can be traced to school experience, an increased movement away from the political attitudes of one's family, etc. — these effects are still only marginal.

By contrast, the "family effect" is striking. The extraordinary perseverance of loyalty to a given political party within families is well documented. Hyman reports a correlation of 0.9 between party preference of parents and children.[14] Party loyalty persists in great strength even in the face of conflict with, for example, social class. Martin Levin demonstrates that when family political-party preference is in conflict with the social or occupational status of the family, it is the family tradition rather than the occupational class which overwhelmingly carries the day. He reports that of high school students whose parents were both Republicans and whose fathers were of blue-collar occupational stratum, 91 percent considered themselves Republican. And again where occupational stratum and parents' political preference were in conflict—that is, where the parents were white collar but also Democrats—the children were overwhelmingly Democratic. In this case, 75 percent were Democratic.[15]

It is not only party preference which carries over from parents to children. There is also a strong correlation between the ideological positions of children and their parents. In this case, correlation is of the order of 0.5 rather than 0.9, according to Hyman. But still a rather substantial amount of rates of participation in politics remains roughly the same from parents to children.[16] Given evidence of this strength, it should not come as any surprise that the amount of political participation also tends to be similar within families.

In talking about parent-child political consistency, it is somewhat hazardous to lump both parents together. Of course there is a great deal of consistency there as well. In the case of conflict between the parents regarding issues, the parent more likely to be followed depends in part on the specific issue area. But on the whole, the tradition of "politics is a man's game" has its effect, both by making the father the primary guidepost for the child's development of issue positions and for bringing the wife into line, should she deviate.[17]

These are figures for whites. One must consider whether family life in Negro America is significantly different from that in white America and whether any such differences that do exist have political relevance. The observation that Negro family life is more matriarchal than that of white comes to mind immediately. (No claim is made that Negro families are predominantly matriarchal, but only that more of them are than among white families.) If the matriarchy proposition is valid, we would expect greater influence of the mother of the household on political attitudes, feelings about political activity, learning of political facts, and development of political skills. We should not immediately jump to the supposition that this would entail lower levels of information, activity, and interest just because American women as a whole tend to be lower in all of these than men.[18] If, indeed, the Negro woman is more likely to assume male roles in the family in general, there is no *a priori* reason to believe that she does not also assume the typical male political role in the family.

This author, however, has presented elsewhere some indirect evidence that in fact the Negro female does not pick up the role of political propagator within the family. In a study of Negro political participation in Durham and Winston-Salem, N.C., he observed a smaller difference in participation between Negro males and females than among white males and females, but he concluded that this was because of a drop in male participation rather than an increase in female participation.[19] If Negro women play a greater part in political socialization of their children than white women do for theirs, then the effect on the children would be lower levels of information, interest, participation, and skill.

There are several bases for the matriarchy theory. Some make reference to experience as slaves and even earlier as African tribal members.[20] Others convincingly point to the influence of the mother because of her earning power relative to the father in many Negro families. Perhaps most important is the larger incidence among Negro families of "broken homes"—broken through divorce, separation, lack of husband, and the husband's having moved North to earn more income. It is interesting to speculate what effect absence of a father has on the early political socialization of Negro children. Thinking again of the findings of Greenstein and Easton and Hess, does this absence make it more difficult to develop images of what political figures are like? Does a hypothesized greater difficulty in developing a strong, favorable image of prominent officeholders lead to greater cynicism in later life toward politicians? This line of thinking assumes that the early correspondence between an image of one's father and of the President or other officeholder, noted earlier, is not simply two instances of a generalized reaction to prominent males but is rather a specific projection of feelings about one type of male, the father, toward another who seems to the small child in some ways to be similar.

Agents of Political Socialization: the School

Most studies of the relationship between amount of education and levels of political activity or interests have been cross-sectional; that is, at a given instant in time they have compared people who in the past accumulated a lot of education against those who in the past accumulated very little. It is precarious to attribute the greater amounts of interest and participation on the part of highly educated people to whatever it is that happened to them during the additional years of schooling they had. Additional schooling and political interest may, in fact, simply both be dependently related to a common antecedent independent variable; namely, social status of the family.

Nevertheless, it is worth reviewing these cross-sectional findings, since some material on Negroes exists in this form. In this author's study of adult Negro political participation in Durham and Winston-Salem, he hypothesized the following: that while the general phenomenon of increasing participation with more education completed would hold for both races, the rate of increase for whites would be greater than it would be for Negroes. While those with high school educations in both races would generally participate at a greater rate than those with only grade school educations, the increase in participation from grade school to high school would be markedly greater for whites than for Negroes.

This hypothesis was only imperfectly demonstrated by the actual data. Excluding for the moment those whites and Negroes who had attended college, Negro and white adults with up to a ninth-grade education kept pace with one another pretty well; that is, participation by those who attended junior high school exceeded the levels of participation of those who only reached grade school at best by roughly the same amount for each race. Negro adults participated at a lower level than whites, to be sure, but the race differential remained essentially constant with the increase of education through junior high school. The hypothesis was borne out for those who attended junior and senior high school, however, with whites showing a greater gain in amount of political participation from junior to senior high school than Negroes, even though all, of course, increased in participation to some extent.

The most striking data were for the college educated. In Durham, Negro adults with college educations participated at a greater rate than whites of college education. In Winston-Salem, the gap in participation levels seen at the high school level was essentially closed at the college level; that is, college-educated whites and Negroes participated at essentially the same level. (These findings are presented in the diagram on the following page.)[21]

Now let us assume for a moment that these cross-sectional data also hold true in the longitudinal sense, that an individual Negro proceeding through school "loses ground" to his white counterpart through high school, but then, after having gone to college, he gains sufficient ground to draw even or to go ahead in amount of participation in politics.[22] Since the family environment presumably has not changed during all

HYPOTHESIS: As years of schooling completed increases, accumulation of political facts leads to increasing participation; but Negroes gain fewer facts, grade for grade, than whites do.

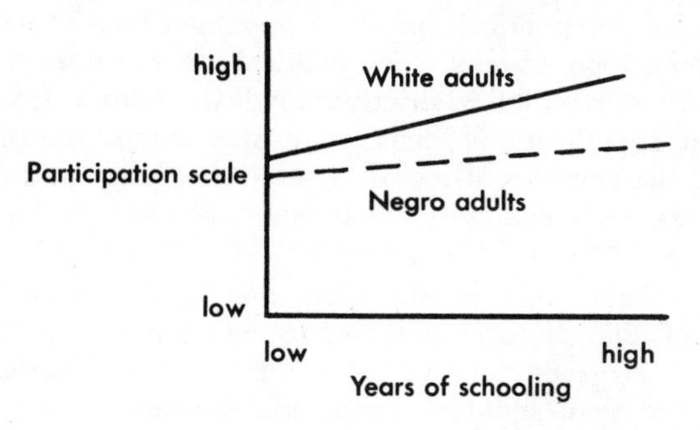

Durham: The more schooling completed, the more respondents participate in politics; the effect is strongest for college-educated Negroes.

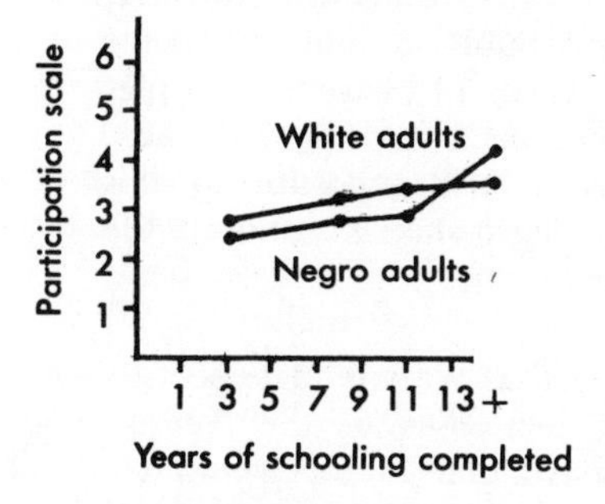

Winston-Salem: The more schooling completed, the more respondents participate in politics; the effect is strongest for college-educated Negroes.

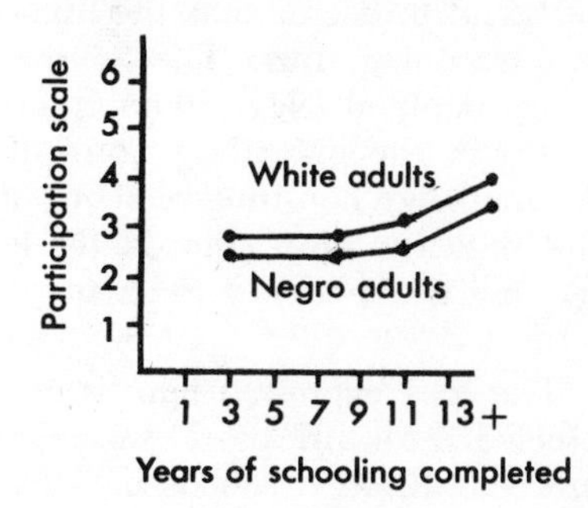

these school years and since there has been no change of social status, no change in parental levels of participation and interest, etc., it would be fair to attribute the increases noticed over the span of school years to the school experience itself.

Giving the schools their due (or more than their due), then, what kind of explanations can we suggest for the greater proclivity for participation among whites than among Negroes? One possibility is that, on the whole, Negro school children simply learn fewer political facts per year than whites and so are less capable, less willing, and less interested in participation by the time they come of age. A second possible explanation contemplates the school experience as a broader contributor to socialization:

> In this sense, schooling is seen as a means of inculcating persons growing into adulthood with patterns of expected behavior. Thus school becomes along with other major institutions of society, a teacher of norms, a preparation ground for "real life." In the political sphere, schooling usually involves "learning to be good citizens." The political ideas current in the world are rarely presented in strictly analytical contexts. Instead, the inherent superiority of democracy over totalitarianism is alleged, and the consequent moral imperatives are derived from the comparison—for example, "Everyone ought to vote." . . .[23]

Taking the school experience in this spirit, one would normally expect the inculcation of the democratic creed to increase proclivity toward participation. For Negroes, however, the total school experience may involve much more than simply learning the democratic creed. There are indeed other norms that Negroes may perhaps learn in school, especially in those schools which are all or almost entirely Negro.

> If schooling is primarily a matter of socialization, it might be hypothesized that Negro political participation rates would tend to decrease as the number of years of education increases, reasoning thus: The Southern Negro public school system [or possibly all-Negro schools anywhere] tends to inculcate Negroes with the prevailing norm of political behavior for that race; namely, non-involvement. The greater the exposure to this indoctrination (that is, the longer a Negro stays in school), the less the tendency to participate in politics.[24]

The idea expressed here is not literally that we would expect to find proclivity toward participation actually decreasing as the Negro child proceeds through school but that this particular factor would tend to dampen the rate of increase that might otherwise apply (as with white children).

This second line of speculation makes some rather gross assumptions about what Negro children actually experience in school. Do all-Negro schools consciously or unconsciously inculcate resignation, apathy, or cynicism about politics? If so, is this more true in southern Negro schools than in all-Negro schools in the North? Are reservations about the democratic creed which could lead to eventual apathy or cynicism actively stated by teachers, or are they simply observed by students who see teachers shy away from controversial issues and from active participation in sit-ins and other such demonstrations? Does even the Negro child in the predominantly white school in the North learn by indirection that his participation in politics is not especially treasured? Answers are lacking and needed.

Prospects

Leaving aside for the moment the possibility of major intervention into the school experience of young Negroes, the prospects for Negro political socialization in the coming decades hinge mainly on the tremendous inertia described in conjunction with the "family effect," modified by increases in the basic well-being of Negroes.

The obvious implication of the studies about the persistence of family political behavior and attitude patterns is that current political preferences of Negroes and current tendencies to participate or not are likely to continue for a great many years hence—in other words, low levels of political activity and extremely high levels of Democratic party loyalty. A *Newsweek* poll in 1963 indicated something like a 30-to-1 preference among Negro adults for the late President Kennedy over possible Republican opponents in 1964.[25] The nomination of Senator Goldwater may have pushed a Democratic preference even higher. A great chunk of this Democratic sympathy will never be expressed in ballots. Impregnable party preference plus low political activity are two behaviors well designed to foster political impotence. Harry Lee Moon has sanguinely described Negroes as a political balance of power.[26] And yet it is quite clear that no balance of power is operative when lack of participation is widespread and party preference is overwhelmingly predictable and immovable. In short, Negroes seem to be operating at far less than their potential; their strategy is bad.

Happily, grounds for optimism, for pushing beyond hidebound limits of traditional patterns, can also be found, again without resort to school intervention. From at least three standpoints, prospects seem bright, if greater participation by Negroes in American politics is in and of itself a desired goal. The first basis for optimism is the increasing economic and educational attainment, on the average, of American Negroes. Both of these characteristics are, of course, related to the amount of political participation.[27]

The second basis for optimism stems from environmental stimuli. Outside factors—wars, depression, floods—can create new levels of political interest and participation, at least for the short run. As for the long run, there is a little evidence and a great deal of theoretical speculation that major inputs of increased activity in politics continue to have their effect on the lives of those who have been touched by an important outside event. Thus it is argued that those who experienced the hard times of the Depression, and particularly those who were just coming of political age during the Depression, are more likely to be politically interested and active (to say nothing of being more Democratically oriented) for the remainder of their lives than people who had no such important experience. A generation of political activists is thereby alleged to have emerged from turbulent times. If the "generational effect" hypothesis is valid, then the turmoil of recent years that has caught the imagination of substantial numbers of young Negroes, dipping well down into the early teens, should by all odds show up in a "quantum jump" in average levels of Negro political participation in the years to come (as the present generation of young Negroes goes into adulthood.).[28]

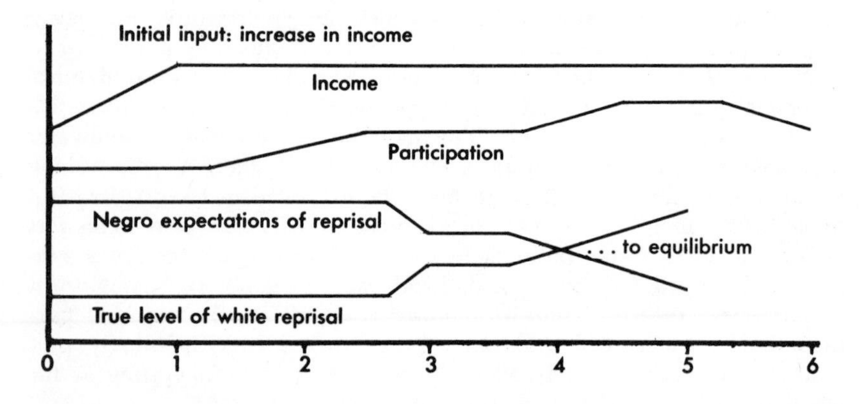

The third basis of optimism stems in great part from the previous two. It rests on some suppositions which are that and nothing more at this point. These are that there may be a "multiplier" that any initial increase in Negro political activity entails. (The dynamics of this multiplier are shown in the diagram.[29]) The essence of the idea is that an increase in participation leads to downward revisions in a Negro's estimate of how dangerous participation is and that this new estimate itself generates additional participation.[30]

We must remember that Negro nonparticipants still on the whole differ notably from white nonparticipants in that their unwillingness to take part in politics much more frequently can be traced to real or imagined fears of reprisal of one sort or another, ranging from physical violence to economic reprisal or even just personal insult, which after all is not often sought out.

Political participation and fears for what might follow from some such participation form an intriguing circle. If a change in the value of either the fears or the participation should occur, the "multiplier" presumably could take effect. Should the fears diminish, then presumably participation should increase; and if for some reason the participation should increase, the fears should also diminish. With serious exceptions, of course, southern Negroes' estimates of the amount of risk of violence or other reprisal are probably greater than the facts justify. The extra boost in participation arising from Negro discovery that their expectations of reprisal exceed the realities of reprisal is presumed to be primarily a southern phenomenon, of course, and then perhaps only an urban phenomenon in the mid-South. Among northern Negroes, nonparticipation is much less likely to be related to any fears of reprisal, and the underlying reasons for not participating are presumed to be quite similar to those for any nonparticipant, namely, a sense that "my vote doesn't count" or similar sentiments. Accordingly, one would not expect any "multiplier" to follow upon an initial increase in participation that occurred because of an increase in the level of Negro income or education.

I have held intervention in the school process in abeyance long enough. While there is much other than what happens to Negroes in school that puts them at a political disadvantage, this fact should not deter us from trying to maximize the impact the school experience can have on their later political effectiveness. I have called Negro political immobility "bad strategy." Perhaps the greatest contribution we as educators could make to the school-age Negroes who will be tomorrow's adult citizens is to reorient their thinking (and, incidentally, our own) about the development and use of political strategy. This means spelling out with approval the various techniques of bargaining, forced demands, concession, and occasional retreat that are used by politically successful subgroups in our society. It certainly means a reappraisal of the utility of strong party preference, moving from a position of blind preference to one of intelligent partisanship—not, I quickly add, to a position of political "independence." It means being candid on two scores when dealing with heterogeneous groups of students in the classroom—candid about the probable maximum of political potential that a given subgroup could have (just how successful Negroes can expect to be, given their total resources of numbers, money, effort, education, and so forth) and candid about the kinds of political techniques that are in fact being used currently or may be used in the reasonably near future.

Political activity in this day and age, after all, involves not only voting, contributing money, and writing letters to congressmen. It sometimes involves street demonstrations and civil disobedience. These need talking out in the classroom, too, not in normative terms but in terms of strategies which sometimes succeed or fail because they tread so close to the border of normatively acceptable political action. Our success in drawing Negro youth into active and thoughtful citizenship may ultimately rest on candid and imaginative teaching of a new politics that they and their parents are already creating.

References

1. The limitation to whites of research designs concerned with political socialization seems to be a consequence of a desire to simplify research strategy rather than to overlook an important variable.
2. Herbert H. Hyman, *Political Socialization,* New York, The Free Press of Glencoe, 1959.
3. Frederick W. Frey of M.I.T. observes increasing cynicism among senior high school students in a Boston suburb as compared with junior high school students. These findings are not yet available in monograph form.
4. Hyman, *op. cit.,* pp. 33–35. The literature is barren of research on how political *skills* are developed in the population at large.
5. David Easton and Robert D. Hess, "The Child's Changing Image of the President," *Public Opinion Quarterly,* vol. 24, 1960, pp. 632–644.
6. Fred I. Greenstein, "More on Children's Images of the President," *Public Opinion Quarterly,* vol. 25, 1961, pp. 648–654.
7. At least two of the items in the Survey Research Center's Political Efficacy Scale are ambiguous between these two attitudes. For a discussion of the relationships between a sense of political efficacy and political behavior, see especially Angus Campbell et al., *The American Voter,* New York, John Wiley & Sons, Inc., 1960.
8. Donald R. Matthews and James W. Prothro ingeniously demonstrate the substantial contribution of such political factors (as against social and economic) as formal voter requirements, state factional systems, existence of racial political organizations, party competition, and racial violence to one form of political activity, registering. "Political Factors and Negro Voter Registration in the South," *American Political Science Review,* vol. 57, June, 1963, pp. 355–367.
9. Levin encounters a parallel difficulty with the concept of "political alienation." Alienation is postulated as inducing four distinctly different behaviors: rational activism, withdrawal, projection, and charismatic identification. Murray B. Levin, *The Alienated Voter: Politics in Boston,* New York, Holt, Rinehart and Winston, Inc., 1960.
10. For a discussion of behavior and fate control, see John W. Thibaut and Harold H. Kelley, *The Social Psychology of Groups,* New York, John Wiley & Sons, Inc., 1959, pp. 101–104.
11. John Dollard, et al., *Frustration and Aggression,* New Haven, Conn., Yale University Press, 1939.
12. "My own case studies have led me to believe that persons who have a capacity for externalized aggression are more likely to become politically oriented than those for whom such external expression is inhibited . . ." Robert E. Lane, *Political Life,* New York, The Free Press of Glencoe, 1959, p. 119.
13. Child describes circumstances under which such controlled frustration leads to strong achievement drives among children. In one study, for example, children who were refused help in taking their coats off and putting them on—a frustration—but were encouraged in their own efforts to succeed in the task were observed to increase their desire to achieve. Irvin

L. Child, "Socialization," Gardner Lindzey (ed.), *Handbook of Social Psychology,* Reading, Mass., Addison-Wesley Publishing Company, Inc., 1954, sec. II.

14. Hyman, *op. cit.,* p. 74. A high correlation is helped, of course, by having only two parties to choose from.
15. Martin L. Levin, "Social Climates and Political Socialization," *Public Opinion Quarterly,* vol. 25, 1961, pp. 596–606.
16. Hyman, *op. cit.,* p. 72.
17. Fred I. Greenstein, "Sex-related Political Differences in Childhood," *Journal of Politics,* vol. 23, 1962, pp. 353–357. See also Hyman, *op. cit.,* pp. 83–84.
18. Lane, *op. cit.,* pp. 209–215.
19. Bradbury Seasholes, "Negro Political Participation in Two North Carolina Cities," unpublished doctoral dissertation, Department of Political Science, University of North Carolina, Chapel Hill, 1961, pp. 128-147.
20. See especially Melville J. Herskovits, *The Myth of the Negro Past,* New York, Harper & Row, Publishers, 1941, and E. Franklin Frazier, *The Negro Family,* New York, The Macmillan Company, 1939. Herskovits was particularly sanguine about American Negroes' ties with Africa. See also Harold R. Isaacs, *The New World of Negro Americans,* New York, The John Day Company, Inc., 1963, pp. 109-110.
21. Seasholes, *op. cit.,* pp. 86, 94.
22. There is obviously a problem here in that we can't reasonably talk about persons' level of *political participation* during their actual years of schooling, when at that age many forms of political participation are legally not open to them. It would be better to think of increasing the students' sense of favorable attitudes toward participation, of "If I could participate, I certainly would."
23. *Ibid.,* p. 84.
24. *Ibid.,* pp. 86–87.
25. *Newsweek,* vol. 62, July 29, 1963, p. 29.
26. Harry L. Moon, *Balance of Power: The Negro Vote.* Garden City, N.Y., Doubleday & Company, Inc., 1948.
27. The relationship has been demonstrated as holding for absolute gains in both variables. The fact that Negroes are not increasing income in amounts comparable to whites may dampen, but does not negate, the prospective gain in amount of participation. Matthews and Prothro, however, found the relationship between SES [socioeconomic status] and participation for southern Negroes less pronounced than one would anticipate, leading them to their analysis of political climate as a crucial consideration. Donald R. Matthews and James W. Prothro, "Social and Economic Factors and Negro Voter Registration in the South," *American Political Science Review,* vol. 57, 1963, pp. 24-44.
28. The "generational effect" is very difficult to distinguish in cross-sectional research from what we already know about the relationship of how old a person is to how much he is likely to take part in politics. Sustained longitudinal research, preferably using specific respondents over and over, is needed.
29. Seasholes, *op. cit.,* p. 262.
30. To make the figure apply more to the North, one could substitute "nonresults" for "reprisal" and make "true level of nonresults" (né "white reprisal") stay level or perhaps even decline.

The fundamental issues and questions raised by the consideration of Negroes' political socialization are the following:

1. Of what relevance are politics and political socialization to a discussion of Negro self-images?
2. To what extent is the "Negro revolution" accounted for and taken into account in the generalized analysis and projection of past patterns of Negro political thought and action?
3. What part can and should the schools play in providing a more adequate education for participation in government and politics?

Although none of these questions were answered with finality in the conference, the flow of discussion, sometimes heated, uncovered a variety of answers. In the pages that follow we shall attempt to recreate the essence of those discussions by letting the participants speak for themselves as much as possible.

Relevance of Politics

That politics and political socialization have bearing on the development and nature of Negroes' self-images was not immediately evident to some conference participants. In a discussion of the extent to which the Negro problem is more than just a problem of lower-classness, the following exchange took place:

> "I thought that the theme of this specific conference would take for granted that we're concerned with all children, but that we're going to look here at a problem that is very peculiar because it hasn't been looked at anywhere else. . . . This morning [when the working paper on Negro political socialization was discussed] I was thoroughly frustrated because I just didn't know where we were headed. I didn't understand why this whole thing about voting in the first place came into the picture at all, and that it was somehow tied in with what we're looking at. Other people asked this question last night, why this paper was even being presented, and there wasn't any good answer. Except that, well, they thought there were some ideas here, but I think it got us off on a wrong track."

> "Well, I don't think it has to. Somebody said that if you consider as political action what's happening now—the sit-ins, the demonstrations—that this is central, this is what we're talking about. And if we look at it with that point of view, it seems to me that this could be the very thing around which we build almost our whole conference."

"A real balance of power, not just who votes and who doesn't."

"Yes, and the whole problem of why is it necessary to have this kind of almost way-out political action. Why do you have to resort to sit-ins and boycotts and demonstrations?"

The central concern of the conference was actually low self-esteem of Negroes. The working paper on political socialization took the position that the demonstrations indicate an important shift among some segments of the Negro population toward positive self-image. One Negro participant viewed the demonstrations less sanguinely, as an emotional reaction more than a form of political strategy.

"As an educator, how do you relate sit-ins and demonstrations to the schools?"

"To where the school has failed, so that you can't go through your so-called regular democratic processes. And then the whole thing ties back to what is the problem. Why are Negroes revolting in Birmingham? How many people are dead down there now? I think it's seven, isn't it? I think one died last night. . . . I think that as individuals here we ought to be concerned with what the schools are going to do, if anything, about this situation."

The relevance of politics to objective Negro effectiveness in society and hence to the cultivation of higher self-esteem is perhaps best recognized and appreciated by those Negroes who have been able to practice politics with skill and success. In the 1950's and 1960's this has tended to be in those locations where urbanism, voting freedom, and a high proportion of Negroes converge. Because a large proportion of Negroes is part of the equation, this convergence has occurred more frequently in the mid-South than elsewhere in the United States. Negroes in the Deep South and in most northern cities (particularly those of populations under 500,000) have been relatively impotent because of lack of numbers and/or voting freedom. The two comments that follow illustrate both the efficacy of learning and employing realistic strategies of politics, such as "bloc voting," and the curious lingering guilt about doing so.

"The individual person in a democracy is so essential that there's no way you can get around it [political education], because without it you don't have a democracy. We believe in a reasonably educated person in a democracy, and this education takes place in the schools; and unless it is in some way political, you get people who vote as a defensive measure. We spoke this morning of voting in a bloc. Well, doggone it, I hate to vote as a bloc. I may *have* to, to protect a basic interest. . . ."

"My city may be a good example of what you call voting in a bloc, because the Negroes there really vote, and the present mayor owes his position to the Negro vote. And they don't let him forget it one minute, you may be sure of that. And when we talk about bloc voting, as far as the Negro is concerned, it seems to me that what we are doing is simply [counteracting] bloc voting on the part of the white. . . . When a man comes out and says, 'If you elect me, I will keep Negroes out of this—I will see that there's no integration. . . .' If that isn't the *white* bloc, what is? Whatever the Negro does is in opposition to this. . . ."

The guilt expressed by the first individual is a common by-product of the typical political socialization of Americans, which stresses the atomistic emphasis of the democratic ideology and underplays the essential role of group action in actual operating democracies. As with whites, the politics that young Negroes learn suffers primarily from being unrealistic in this and many other regards. Bringing reality into the study of government can potentially affect Negro self-images both positively and negatively. Learning the truth about current and past Negro acceptance in, and impact on, the political system is unlikely to improve Negroes' images of the system itself; and, as pointed out in the background paper, negative feelings about the system too often induce negative feelings about the self. But on balance, the case for teaching realistic politics is strong.

First, realism brings expectations and actuality closer together. Negative feelings about politics (sometimes referred to as "political alienation") flourish where the gap between expectations and actuality grows too large. It follows that the antidote may be to improve actuality, to adjust expectations downward, or both. Reform movements have seldom taken both elements into consideration at once; yet *effective* reform—reform that changes attitudes toward government and the individual's contribution to it—cannot afford to ignore the ultimate effect of unreasonable expectations.

Second, political realism can help to sort out two separate concepts that too often are used synonymously, political effectiveness and political success.

"We agreed that there is a distinction between being politically effective in the sense of knowing and doing what the circumstances permit, and necessarily being *successful*. . . . I think there is a real distinction between making an individual happy and skillful, and still not necessarily ensuring success."

"There is something I still don't know. Would you like for the Negroes in Boston to have equal political effectiveness with those of Irish descent? Is that the aim?"

The aim is not so simple to state as it might at first seem. In general, clearly the aim is not to assure to Negroes political success, but rather to assure them political effectiveness commensurate with their numbers. But the basic political drive of Negroes today is toward the guaranteeing of fundamental procedural rights, such as the right to vote—rights provided to all individuals and minority groups in a democracy. This drive requires *success,* not simply proportional effectiveness. A realistic approach to the study of politics could demonstrate how the principle of minority rights is upheld, or is won, by the construction of majorities in society whose interests in the principle can never be identical with that of any specific minority. But beyond basic rights, it is commensurate effectiveness, not necessarily success, which is the ultimate societal objective. Shifting the individual's question from, "Am I successful?" to "Am I effective?" increases the possibility of a positive answer and of a more favorable self-image. Realism effects this shift by stressing that politics is not a win-or-lose proposition but instead is characteristically a process of bargaining and compromise whose end result more or less reflects the various political interests, resources, and skills of the groups with stakes in the outcome.

Third, political realism can uncover areas of governmental activity in which lower-class individuals operate with greater skills and effectiveness than they realize.

"You know, it has occurred to me that this notion about the alienation of the lower class from political involvement is nonsense, because at the same time I read about how the lower class is involved with the police, with the courts, with all kinds of governmental bureaucracies—with the welfare system, and so on and so forth. They have an awful lot more to do with government than I do. And it's a different kind of involvement with government, not the kind we usually count as political participation or political involvement. . . . It seems to me that we have kind of overlooked a rather natural and obvious fact that while these people may not score high on an index of participation when you count voting, they may be highly involved in politics and government if you define the terms quite differently."

Although the above statement is perhaps overly optimistic, it does underline the fact that traditionally the study of government deals with other than this rich level of political activity. A considerable portion of policy formation and administration is colored by administrators' psychological identification with the goals of their clients. For example, the influence of welfare recipients on welfare policies and administration is probably greater through their direct contact with agency workers than through less focused political action such as voting and writing letters to officials.

Finally, a realistic approach in no sense excludes discussion of "what can be." It does require that "what can be" is properly extrapolated from "what is and has been." To the extent that this requirement is respected, the prospects of accomplishing the possible—in our case, substantially improving the life chances of Negroes—are considerably enhanced.

Impact of the Negro Revolution

The "Negro revolution," a term which may or may not be appropriate, refers essentially to the marked increase in dramatic forms of political expression—freedom rides, sit-ins, picketing, marches, and boycotts—that segments of the Negro population (with some white involvement) have engaged in. Although sit-ins protesting discrimination against Negroes had been used occasionally by the Congress of Racial Equality during the preceding fifteen years, the lunch-counter sit-in by students at North Carolina Agricultural and Technical College at a number of Greensboro variety stores in 1960 probably marks as good a starting date for the revolution as any.

By concentrating on low self-image among Negroes and its consequences—political apathy, passivity, mental illness, and so forth—the working papers missed the substance and significance of the revolution, according to some conference participants. A white social scientist put it in these words:

> "The one thing that appalls me over all three papers of the Conference is that every one of them totally underestimated the importance and the magnitude of the revolution we're in—the very thing that led, I think, to this meeting . . . and absolutely right, and yet it was underevaluated. And what bothers me—no matter what the polling agency, drawing different kinds of samples—we get the same results; that is, white America still does not understand what the revolution is all about. Sixty percent of white America or better thinks that the Negro is happy and has, as the question goes, 'a fair share of America.' And therefore doesn't understand why he's in the streets, and thinks that he's disorderly, causing trouble, that

this is a threat to the society. And our mass media reinforce this idea endlessly with the idea of violence.

"So far the only violence has been white violence against Negroes. That Negroes in Birmingham right now are screaming for Federal intervention is because the Birmingham police and the state police of Alabama are there to protect the whites from Negroes. But they know that these people are not protecting *them* from whites, as clearly the death toll continues. But instead of looking at it this way, and our working papers have either done this or ignored the revolution, we have to look upon the revolution—and I don't think it's hard—as a great boon to the United States. It has come not a minute too soon, and I think it's just in time to save us, not just saving Negroes, but saving the United States. . . ."

Two Negro conference participants were not unaware of the impact of the revolution on whites with whom they must deal.

"In conservative communities like in my state, I mean, this little 'image-building process' has the whole community shook up, our newspapers and our leaders; and a lot of my time is spent trying to. . . ."

[interrupting] "Somebody told me the N.A.A.C.P. stood for the 'Negroes Ain't Actin' Like Colored People!' "

"No, but if you read the northern press, and I don't know how it is in the South, but in our northern communities this new push is creating fear and apprehension. Our board of directors, which represents a good cross section of influence in labor, education, religion, and so forth—many times my own board members come to me . . . and they express to me these apprehensions and fears, so that I don't think we ought to underrate it at all, because it's a very serious problem in all of our communities."

Part of the difficulty in assessing the parameters of the revolution is that we fail to distinguish the revolution in attitude from that in behavior. A number of statements by Negro participants revealed the depth of feeling, of anger, that characterizes the attitudinal revolution. One of these, although long and somewhat rambling in content, is especially worth quoting:

"I'm rather disturbed, I'm afraid, about what I've heard . . . because somewhere in our comments about the culturally deprived we are forgetting the very peculiar feeling it is to be a Negro in this country, regardless of how much education and understanding you have of the country, of the other American people in it. When you go into a store, you're a Negro; when you go into a bank, you're a Negro first, before you're American and before you are a human being; and I think until we face this—and I feel very emotional about this—that this Conference has failed. I've heard all kinds of working around this and not facing up to it and what it means, because what it means is what you and the people in every part of the country think about me and my children, my people, whatever you want to call them, and I don't think we're facing it.

[crying] "Please forgive my emotion . . . but it's something that if America, white America, black America, whatever you want to call it, does not face, I have a feeling that regardless of whether we're 10 percent, as an example of a democratic process, we're going to be a failure to the world, because the world isn't white.

"Maybe I'm thinking a long way ahead, but whatever it is in our school system, in our political system, in our economic system, that has to make people defend, accept, what is obvious in our system, however disguised—the white supremacy—we're in trouble. Just as Germany was in trouble, South Africa's in trouble. I know we can use all kinds of words, but when you boil it down, it's a feeling. It affects me, and it will affect you, it will affect our country. We don't have to face it right now, but we will later, and it may be harder. When I go back home from here, it's not very nice where I live . . . the people that I see there who have been Negroes in this country for centuries and having all these [attributes] labeled 'culturally deprived.' Many of them are not culturally deprived, whatever that means. They are facing a very evil thing and a very real thing. . . . And whether it affects 1 percent of Americans or 10 percent, it really affects 100 percent of us. Because there, but for the grace of God, go you or me, and many other Negro Americans are not as nice as I am, or adaptable.

"I don't think I can make this very clear; sometime when the Conference is over, bring one or two men in off the street and hear what they have to say and feel, about their children and their positions in the community and jobs. Whether their idea of what is real is not what we think is true, it is there. Whether labeled or not, they are there. Whether they live in the country or the city, they are still a part of this American system, and this problem of mobility is going to make it a very real one for people who never thought that a Negro was anything but a word or a feeling. They're going to move next to them, work next to them; and how are we going to face this, unless we can face it now here as people who have far more behind us in terms of education and understanding than many people in the street? How can we dodge it? I think we have an obligation to really face it. It frightens me. . . ."

In a very real sense, the attitudinal revolution is the more important one, when Negro self-image is the focus of concern. And there is unimpeachable evidence that the attitudinal revolution has spread far and deep within Negro America, creating political awareness and feeling among persons who otherwise would be almost totally apolitical. This revolution can only be viewed as a contribution to improved self-image, because it refuses to accept the white world's estimate of Negro worth.

But if the benefit is to be long-lasting, the attitudinal revolution must be transformed into a behavioral revolution, into political action which can establish the conditions of social, economic, and political equality under which individual Negroes can demonstrate their inherent capabilities.

It is this transformation, from thought into action, which, some thought, has not gone as far as others claim. General Negro participation in the demonstrations of the summer of 1963 was not uniformly great, and in some instances was embarrassingly modest. The sit-in movement, for the most part, involves both at the leadership and follower levels Negroes of middle-class income and/or education. To the suggestion that the present Negro movement parallels the growth and power of the labor movement in the 1930's came this response:

"I hope your analogy of the rise of the labor movement and the great changes that came into American life in the 30's are comparable to this, but I don't personally see the organized program available to be enacted. I don't at the present moment see the effective political leadership to carry this into effect, the way it happened in the 1930's. In the 1930's, there was a backlog of demand that the Socialists and the Progressives in this country had been building up for years and years and years. These things had been waiting and waiting and waiting to be enacted, and all of a sudden these things broke through with effective leadership. I don't see that stuff in this country today. . . ."

Yet the fact that a combination of attitude and action in the current movement may involve substantial numbers of Negroes is indicated in the following:

"Who are the people who are actually participating in the present protest movement? What are the effects of this participation on their lives and their personalities and their self-conception, if you will? What is the effect of their participation on their children? On those surrounding them? On their co-workers?

"I did a little figuring. Dr. Seasholes said somewhere along the line that 'even today the drama of freedom demonstrations and the radical nature of the Muslim movement are, I am convinced, instances of political aggressiveness not typical of Negroes in general.' I really put a big 'no' onto that. I did a little calculation, very rough, no basis in evidence or anything like that. But I estimated that half of the participants in the March on Washington were Negro, let's say. This would be about 100,000 people. Let's say that on the average, each one of these has a circle of ten people—family, friends, what have you—ten people that support them, that listen to them, that they told their story to when they came back, anticipated going to this thing before going, got some food, got some money, et cetera. I think that ten is a relatively small number. Now this would be a million, which would be 5 percent of the total Negro adult population. But certainly 5 percent of any population in a political situation is a gigantic figure. To travel distances and to be involved in this sort of way, I think it's far from minor.

"A way of proving to myself that this was indeed not minor was to ask what would happen if 5 percent of the total American population, Negro and white, were involved in some kind of movement. This would be 20 million people. That's a lot of people. So I find it hard to go along with, and accept, this pessimistic estimate. I think you are making your estimate on the basis of information from the distant past—that is, last year. Things have changed. And the key to the whole change has been the rise of the Negro protest movement and all that surrounds it. . . ."

"All I can say about your comments on revolution and the extent of it is that I hope you're right, and I'm wrong [in underestimating its strength].

"I suppose it's partly a definition of where involvement that we would call 'aggression' begins and where it ends. I mean, where you make the cut-off point. . . . I'm quite aware of the fact that feelings about what is going on run very, very deep, that people are politicized to an extent—white and Negro, particularly in the South—way down in the SES [socioeconomic status] scale, where they normally wouldn't be. . . ."

"The key thing is not how many people participate in the sit-ins, but how many people are supporting it. Every revolution has had as active participants a very small segment of the population, and they've succeeded when they've had support and failed when they didn't have the support."

Aside from how far it has progressed, the transformation from attitude to action has not gone particularly smoothly, in the sense of being translated into rational, efficient political activity. Two political comments illustrate the matter. One called for a third political party as a vehicle of Negro protest. The other stated as the overriding "political" goal of Negroes forcing whites to face up to the fundamental moral issue at stake in the race question. While both comments were valuable as further evidence of the depth of Negro feeling, they betray a potentially disastrous flirtation with unsound, unrealistic political strategy:

"It is proper to say that youth, Negro youth in particular, has given up, is frustrated, is . . . impatient with adult leadership. . . . The answer to all this is a new party, a new political party. It is not going to get into all this red tape. . . ."

". . . If this were part of Africa, that would mean something, but you are only 10 to 15 percent of the nation. You have to learn patience, accommodation, the give-and-take that has got to take place. You can push, all right, but you can't expect much support. . . ."

Sound strategy, it would appear, would call for Negroes to act within the existing two major parties as a true balance of power. Sound strategy would also suggest *not* making the basic choices in the race question stand out boldly—not forcing whites to choose between personal self-interest and democratic principle—but rather attempt to play to both, or obscure the relevance of the former.

The nature of political units in this country, especially their geographical basis, makes bloc behavior by ethnic minorities feasible, appropriate, and effective for certain purposes. Election of municipal and party officials by wards facilitates the inclusion of Negroes in city and party government. The potentiality for minorities of using their *majority* position in small political geographical units, such as wards and Congressional districts, was well put in the conference:

"I think something that we talked about yesterday needs mentioning, and that is the fact of the geographical situation.

Where Negroes are pouring into the central city, you have, because of the exigencies of city municipal boundaries, a real potential for increased optimism on the part of Negroes. Because Negroes are forced into ghettos, they see themselves becoming a majority rather quickly within certain boundaries, and this can lead to optimism. I think we sometimes lose track in the abstract of the specifics of where Negroes are moving to, and whether politics is affected thereby."

"What we've got to do now is use this ghetto creatively. They put us in the ghetto, and, boy, there's a new day a-comin' when you can realize the very reason Adam Powell has been in the Congress as long as he has . . . and all the others—because they come from ghettos. We can use this ghetto in a creative sense. I'll bet you this will make a change in the nature of things. I think this will have some effect on the realtors on the way they'll sell us a house. This is a reality of the caste system that we see very clearly in the political world. . . . Look what has happened in New York and the power that is expressed by the way and place Negroes live."

The limitation of this reality and prospect is that, nationally, geographical units with large Negro populations (proportionately) are few in number, and most are in the dangerously hostile areas of the South. Consequently, Negro strategy for national policy still must face up to numbers.

"If you're going to play just plain out-and-out group politics—coalition forming and so forth—you've got to remember what size of coalition is going to have to be built, and on what basis it's going to be built on. If it's going to be built on an appeal to morality, to democratic ideology, it has got to be built within a framework of the existing status quo in terms of governmental process. To get back to what kind of revolution this is, it's a revolution that's going to need an awful lot of white sympathy."

On balance, the risk in being deceived by relatively small numbers must finally be recognized. Effective politics is more than numbers. It involves skills, internal group consensus, intensity of feeling, initiative, preparedness, and many other such factors. In the description by one Negro community worker of the dimensions of the revolution, many of these factors come to light:

"What I think is important to bring to this group, because it's of significance to those of us who are in political and social-action activity in various communities, is to point out the shift in the leadership patterns that is taking place in many of our communities where we have an appreciable number of Negroes. The shift is from the former paternalistic guidance and assistance which was given by white political leaders. This has been a shifting over now to Negro political leaders. And there's something so very significant in most of our communities. In the South, the Negro clergy is in the forefront. That pattern has not been followed so much in the North. Negro clergy are forced to share this responsibility with other community leaders, and that is the reason we are seeing differences in activity between North and South in political activity.

"My second point has to do with how do you count the significance, or weigh the significance, of Negro political activity. It's not a 1-to-1 ratio any more. I mean, you don't say one Negro vote or one Negro group, because in many areas of this country there's increased support being given to Negro leaders and to Negro organizations by white leaders and white organizations—and because it's becoming popular now to be, as we say, 'visibly connected' with the movement. And this was dramatized in the March on Washington. I've seen it in many communities. . . . Frankly, in my city, we couldn't find space the last two days for all the white groups and individuals who wanted to go because they said it was the thing to do when they were supporting action. Now, this is going to set a new pattern, and I think Negro leaders and community leaders are wise to this situation.

"Thirdly, I think this is something new on the national scene, and it may not be as significant to as many white leaders as it is to Negro leaders; but there's a new unity and cooperation among leaders. And that was dramatized in the March on Washington. You may not know it, but this was the first time to my knowledge—and I've been working in this field for about twenty-five years—that we got every single major Negro organization coming together, coordinating efforts, fund raising, and cooperating. And this has already been reflected down in the local community."

What Role for the Schools?

The importance of having children and adolescents learn realistic politics is well demonstrated in the context of the Negro revolution. A realistic approach holds the promise to Negroes of being able to maximize their possible gains through governmental action. And for the society as a whole, this approach holds the promise of reinforcing restraint against irrational, harmful radicalism on the part of both whites and Negroes.

But this promise asks a great deal from the process of political socialization. It asks a great deal from our educational system, where, after all, only a modest portion of learning about politics takes place. And within the educational system a series of substantial hurdles lies in the way of any major attempt to attack the problems of Negro political attitudes and information. Proposals to increase formal teaching about Negro political involvement, in order to paint a more realistic and in many respects optimistic picture for Negro students, run into the same difficulties expressed in the following comments of conference participants:

> "This notion of the contribution of the minorities must not be overdone, but the question is also asked of how can history be taught so that the meaning of the Negro in America can be known? It was suggested that every school in North and South should be required to have a course on Negro life and that such a course should be complete and cover all phases of Negro life. An additional comment was that too much power was being attributed to the school and that situations vary. . . .
>
> "It was pointed out that public education is just one institution. . . . The schools and the teachers can stress and press to the limits along with other institutions such as religion, labor, and so forth, in the education of Negro youth. Public schools need to face out and face up to the movement which is taking place in the country, and the schools would make a major contribution in providing information and background materials—history and preparation of students to meet and find answers to this vicious problem.
>
> "Another pertinent question is, 'Are the schools to "aid and abet" the Negro revolution, which seeks drastic changes in the status of the group? And is there danger that the schools may become a "tool" of the revolution?' The alternative suggested was, 'Can the revolution become a tool of the public schools?' "

Some disagreement existed in the conference over whether the objective of helping Negroes improve their self-images necessitates teaching emphasis on Negro contributions above and beyond an emphasis justified by the overall parameters of the social or political system. Should, for example, political education of Negroes go beyond a balanced, realistic appraisal of that race's accomplishments and failures in politics, to concentrate on political "heroes" who are Negro?

> "One suggestion was that the use of new materials in the classroom be put under 'Materials, Negro, or [inaudible]'—let's use that expression unless you want to change it. There's a

certain type of material, and how would you describe the kind of material which you use?"

"I would like to say 'materials which more nearly represented the contribution of various, or all, groups to American development,' or something like that. I mean, I don't think you want history books written from a Negro point of view or an Indian point of view or a labor point of view. . . ."

One commentator suggested that the message of political and social efficacy does not need to be spelled out in specifically ethnic terms, if the past history of education's contribution to the Americanization of ethnic groups other than Negroes can be taken as a valid precedent; nevertheless, frank *confrontation* of the Negro's *condition* in American life cannot be left ignored.

"Now, there are a number of peoples that have been isolated and set apart from the mainstream of American life. These include Negroes, they include Mexican-Americans, they include the homeless men, the skid-row people, they include some of the hill people in the country—all these are people who have been isolated, who have been isolated from the mainstream of American life. And we ask ourselves, as decent, thoughtful, liberal, nice people of America, we ask ourselves, 'How do we correct this, how do we bring them back into the mainstream of American life?'

"One of the solutions . . . is that education is the means. This has applied to the mass horde of immigrants that came to this country; they were dirty and stinking, it was felt that somehow we've got to make them clean and nice, and make them Americans. How did we attack this? We attacked this through the vehicle of our educational system, and this was successfully done. We were talking at lunch today about many of the immigrant groups; most of them have been successfully integrated into the mainstreams of American life. Now, I think when we talk about the culturally deprived, regardless of which particular group we're talking about, we're trying to rely on education as a means of bringing them in. Now, it's not guaranteed that this is going to work, because there are many forces that operate against this, but I think that we have a greater likelihood of convincing those people who are outside of the American mainstream that they should be a part of it, and convincing those who have kicked them out of the mainstream that they should allow them back in. . . .

"That is the first question that I raise—if we seriously

> tackle the question of bringing to the American people the nature of the American Negro situation. If we fail to do that, then all the efforts that we make with the culturally deprived of one sort or another will be to no avail, because they will know, they will know from their own internal situation, that we're liars. Because they will say, 'You're paying attention to me, you're doing a lot of nice things for me, but why are you kicking me in the pants?'
>
> "So these two separate issues, I think, need to be distinguished: (1) How do we bring to the American people, including *all* its children, the nature of the American Negro situation? and (2) a separate question, How do we improve the capacities, the capabilities, of those who for one reason or another have been isolated and shoved aside?"

Among the possibilities for school innovation, then, are the following: introduction into curricula of political "heroes" that are Negroes; greater time and stress placed on the Negro *issue* (slavery, segregation, lower-class status, and so forth) in American history and politics; and more emphasis on a more realistic, process-oriented teaching of politics, with no particular racial flavoring. (These possibilities, of course, are not mutually exclusive.) Any and all of these face problems of acceptance.

> "Since I'm supposed to be a realist, I keep asking myself, 'Well, for heaven's sake, what kinds of local school boards are going to buy any really major emphasis on Negroes?' They may buy something under the name of citizenship, or of a new approach towards trying to stimulate the lower segments of the social scale, and in so doing will hit on a lot of Negroes."

A number of school administrators seemed convinced that the uniquely Negro character of the overall problem is not, and cannot be, clearly identified, for political reasons.

> "In our state programs, we do not think of the culturally deprived child as any one particular race. Period. We have enrolled many, many people who can be very well classified as deprived in any way you want to use it, who are all white people. And we number them—they are equal in number to the Negro youths who live in the city. So for us in our state, we won't want to make this distinction, that it is just a problem concerned with a race. And when we approach a school board or a school district to help with a program, we talk about education of children—of the child who needs additional help,

a new kind of program, a different kind of a program. So, for us, I don't want this synonymous idea that the culturally deprived and the Negro are one and the same."

"What I tried to imply is that as a school administrator I wasn't going to take a stand because I was primarily interested in one group of children or another. I was going to take the stand that I was interested in *children*. Now, then, there is one aspect of my interest in Negro children. I find that they have certain factors, certain conditions, which pertain to them by the mere fact that they are Negroes; and this I have to take into consideration in trying to arrange an educational program for this in the school. . . . What I am trying to do here is I'm trying to point out that you take your stand, that you are in favor of all children, which you have to take as a public school administrator, but this does not exclude you from being aware of, and doing something about, the basic problem that this conference is, I think, concerned with."

"It's not just a question of making a class for Negro children or specializing in Negro children; this is a question of, that the Negroes are not the only ones affected by it. It isn't really a Negro problem at all, because the Negroes are not the only ones affected. It affects the whole school, but it's a ques- of where you put your emphasis, isn't it, and what you teach in your school."

While comments like the above reflect a laudably inclusive concern for the welfare of all culturally deprived children, some participants felt that they also are indicative of evasiveness, of an unwillingness to face up to the fundamental nature of our racial problem.

"When you talk about the culturally deprived, I think you're talking about the question of whom you teach. When you talk about the Negro in America, you're talking about *what* you teach. And I think the concept, the self-concept, the image that people have of themselves depends in part on what you teach and how you teach. If the content of what you teach about the Negro in American life is accurate and true, true to the facts and to the deep significance, then you will have an improvement in all children's conception of themselves, including Negro children. I think that if the way in which you teach them is faithful to individual dignity, then their own conceptions, everybody's conception of themselves will be improved. In order to do this, you have to face up to the hard facts of life without discrimination and segregation in the school situation as well as in other situations. . . . And by facing the Negro situation straightforwardly, clearly, and directly, we're in the end helping the white population . . . to face a central issue in American life, which means that we're helping them to face all of American life."

If evasiveness was to be found among the participants themselves, it was argued, the prospects for winning acceptance of major innovation in school systems at large must not be great. If it is hard to get school personnel to talk about Negroes, the prospect of gaining acceptance for substantial discussion of Negro *politics* is doubly discouraging. This is because, in the eyes of some observers, politics itself is a subject handled gingerly in American schools.

"How on earth can we expect the schools to teach anything about politics, when the schools have nothing to do with politics? That is, the school system in American society prides itself on being apolitical. The teachers, for the most part, don't admit to knowing what the inside of a voter's booth looks like. But how are they going to teach the kids anything about political life in American society? Well, I don't know what all the social science texts look like. I've seen some that deal with something called 'civics.' But I would suggest to you that it doesn't really matter what the textbooks look like or the reading materials look like, if all this takes place in an atmosphere in which politics is dirty, politics is evil, and education is something which must have nothing to do with politics. How on earth do you expect children to come out of such a school system with anything but a negative attitude toward real life politics, I just don't know. I would suggest that another element in cynicism and apathy is the education that children get in the school system about the nature of politics. . . . As things stand now, our schools are not producing a population which is, by virtue of its education, in a position to do anything about most of the things we don't like about the way the political system works."

"I think it's interesting that you brought up the point of the apolitical nature of our system. I said before that Negro teachers in southern school situations are 'chicken' on politics. I should quickly add that maybe teachers generally are kind of 'chicken' in this respect. I've known of a few instances of a fellow who tried to send out his senior class to examine the local power structure. That was disastrous, believe me."

Others are more charitable:

"Well, I'm much more optimistic with reference to the realities of the school situation . . . although I agree that we have a long, long way to go. Not only are there increasing numbers of social studies teachers in particular encouraging classroom discussion of strong issues, but also, the related political implications."

And there may be a simpler answer to whatever lack of political realism there actually is in typical high school social studies:

"Why aren't teachers talking about the reality of politics? Why do they keep talking about the Bill of Rights? There's a real time lag here in just what they learned in school. This approach to learning politics is a fairly recent one, and we've still got entrenched in the school systems a lot of people who simply learned this subject matter the old way and aren't particularly inclined to shift for *any* reason, let alone because they're afraid to."

In brief, no clear picture of what constitutes reasonable expectations for changing the education of Negroes for political participation emerges from the observations of the Conference participants. Partly because it was difficult to specify the specific innovations that might be recommended for introduction into school curricula and programs, it was difficult to anticipate what acceptance by school administrators, the community at large, and the students themselves might follow.

Summary

Politics, of course, is the process from which law emerges. Not only the enforcement of law but the *aura* of law can have substantial consequences on Negro self-images. The enforcement of law, in improving economic and social position and in removing racial segregation, has obvious bearing on self-images. But even without enforcement, there can be positive consequences. If segregation and discrimination persist after laws supporting them are rescinded, a certain psychological advantage accrues to Negroes. And even if positive new civil rights legislation goes unenforced or weakly enforced, Negroes have the psychological advantage of knowing that "The Law" is on their side, that they are "in the right." The fundamental sustaining force for Negro Americans throughout their struggle for equality has been their unwavering sense that law and justice are on their side, that theirs is not simply one more set of self-interested claims by one of many pressure groups. For these reasons, securing "idealistic" legislation, which often has at best only modest chance of real enforcement, makes more sense than might be apparent at first.

In the working paper on political socialization, this author said, "For Negroes eager to improve their images in others' eyes (and their own), political activity is not a clear-cut means to the end. For educators, the rugged job is to demonstrate more clearly the relevance of politics as a means to reach Negro ends." Part of that job is to make evident the benefits that flow from political activity, benefits that we have just been discussing. The other part of that job is to reduce the "costs" that go along with political participation.[1] Costs are those not only of money but more importantly of time and effort. Just the act of voting requires the time, money, and effort to gather information about the issues involved, to analyze the consequences of the various alternatives to be taken (voting for and/or electing one person as against another), and actually to go to the polls to cast a ballot. The job of the individual is to make sure that these costs do not exceed the expected benefits. For this reason, most of us take advantage of efforts by others to do these tasks for us. For example, we let newspapers do a great deal of the sort of information gathering that none of us would individually undertake.

The public education system is a major device by which political information is or can be obtained by persons at relatively little cost in money, time, or effort. To the student, there appears to be no money cost involved. At least until he is eligible legally to drop out of school, there is no time cost, because he has to be physically present in school buildings during certain hours of the day in any case. The only additional effort cost is that increment that may be added if political education of the sort proposed in this paper is "harder" than subjects that would otherwise be thrust upon the student.

Finally, the cost to the individual student of becoming politically informed and skilled is minimized in the school setting because he is still at an age when learning in any sphere is easier, when mental rigidities are not so severe as in later years. This is why the school years are, and the school experience can be, crucial in the process of political socialization.

> Plato and Aristotle were the first but by no means the only great philosophers to point out that the formation of citizens for any type of commonwealth is a task which begins in the cradle and extends to adulthood. . . . There is much we do not yet know about the details of political socialization, but we do know that patterns of political behavior, like other aspects of acculturation, are acquired subtly, almost imperceptibly, from the total environment of the child. Attitudes toward authority, and specifically toward political authority;

> identification with groups and symbols; expectations concerning adult political roles, including paying taxes, serving in military forces, voting, participating in politics—these are a few of the determinants of the quality of citizenship. . . .[2]

This is why it appears that our hope for developing more stable and effective *Negro* adult citizens lies in what can be done now and in the future with and for Negro *youth,* before set patterns of thought and action have become too well entrenched. Substantial, positive intervention in the early life of Negroes through the schools and other agencies needs to be made if we are to improve the life chances of our most disadvantaged minority.

Regrettably, the factual and theoretical foundation upon which successful intervention can be based is difficult to find. What little foundation there is we have tried to review in these pages. But fundamentally, the following observation of David Easton and Robert Hess summarizes the current situation:

> . . . Although in practice we may recognize that the political evolution of the child is critical for the maintenance of a system, there has been little actual research to indicate just what happens in the process of political maturation and how critical this process is. We do not have reliable knowledge about how a child acquires the political outlook that fails or succeeds in integrating him into a given political system and what alternative processes are more or less likely to do so.[3]

The urgency of proceeding with sound research into the way American Negroes in particular learn to relate to government must not be underestimated as an undertaking prior to or concomitant with actual intervention programs. This is not because we cannot afford to lunge ahead on a trial-and-error basis, in the monetary sense of "afford." We cannot afford to, in two other major senses:

1. We cannot afford to, because trial and error is time consuming, and time is short in America's racial future.
2. We cannot afford to suffer certain of the consequences of the "error" component of the "trial-and-error" process. With deliberate speed, however, the gains made by Negroes in the past in objective betterment and in self-dignity can be projected on an accelerated scale into the coming years. As one Negro conference participant put it:

> "There are real grounds for hope in this situation. During my lifetime, I've seen more changes take place in the status of the Negro than I ever expected to see in my lifetime. I re-

member well when I was sixteen years old, I remember in high school and college, if some of us just didn't have the strength, we wouldn't be where we are today. Now we're in a period when there's great acceleration. No one needs to be hopeless today—those of us who work every day organizing Negro groups, white groups, everybody, to speed this movement.

"But I share your feeling that there needs to be more done, and more done quickly, if we are going to save ourselves."

References

1. Anthony Downs, *An Economic Theory of Democracy,* New York, Harper & Row, Publishers, 1957, Part III.
2. Evron M. Kirkpatrick and Jeane J. Kirkpatrick, "Political Science," in *High School Social Studies Perspectives,* Boston, Houghton Mifflin Company, 1962, pp. 100–101.
3. David Easton and Robert D. Hess, "Problems in the Study of Political Socialization," in S. M. Lipset and L. Lowenthal (eds.), *Culture and Social Character,* New York, The Free Press of Glencoe, 1961, p. 4.

section three NEGRO YOUTH AND SOCIAL ADAPTATION: THE ROLE OF THE SCHOOL AS AN AGENT OF CHANGE

by William C. Kvaraceus . . . Director of Youth Studies, The Lincoln Filene Center for Citizenship and Public Affairs, and Professor of Education, Tufts University

The Position Paper

Commenting on his own school experiences, James Baldwin brings our topic into sharp focus. He writes: "School began to reveal itself, therefore, as a child's game that one could not win, and boys dropped out and went to work. My father wanted me to do the same. I refused, even though I no longer had any illusions about what an education could do for me."[1] Today Negro youth continues to fall out only to face the additional problem: there is less work opportunity.

Digging even deeper to the taproots of the major problems facing Negro youth, Baldwin insightfully admonishes us: "But the dispute has actually nothing to do with education, as some among the eminently uneducated know. It has to do with political power and it has to do with sex. And this is a nation which, most unluckily, knows very little about either."[2] Since Dr. Grambs's paper is more closely related to sex and Dr. Seasholes's is directly concerned with political participation, a discussion of the role of the school agency may appear to be less relevant, but hardly superfluous. Obviously, politics and sex represent a very heady mixture to be swallowed by American schools. But both are issues that must be faced.

Nevertheless, the compulsory classroom represents the universal vehicle—often the only vehicle—to self-realization, to achievement, to jobs, and to status for Negro youth. In mobilizing community forces to assist the culturally disadvantaged, social planners intuitively look to the school as a major—if not a central—resource. For the schools have all the children of all the people; they receive the child early and maintain close and intimate relationships with him for a long period of time; they have trained personnel (who are further trainable) to deal with children and youth; they aim to develop integrated and socially effective citizens; and they are found in every community. The school, then, as one of the community institutions that comes in close and prolonged contact with children and youth, enjoys a unique and strategic responsibility and opportunity for assisting culturally disadvantaged youth.

But the school's direct contribution in a community-wide program aimed to identify and assist the culturally disadvantaged will be realized only as "good schools" become "better schools." In this sense, the school's responsibility to the Negro student is no different from its responsibility to any other learner in the classroom, advantaged or disadvantaged, white or nonwhite—albeit his learning problems remain more concentrated and more complex.

The exact nature of the school's role (there are many role patterns) in assisting the culturally deprived Negro students will depend upon a clear differentiation of individual needs, interests, and capacities, as must be done with white students. In program planning at every grade level, we will need to consider the special problems of: (1) the Negro students who are already "well on their way" and who may try to out-middle-class their middle-class academic comrades; (2) those students who are in ferment—who are making the upward effort, but who are blocked and for whom there appears no legitimate means to chosen goals; and (3) those Negroes who are stable and are staying in the submilieu representing often the hard core of the defeated, the paralyzed, and the unmotivated.

Studies of the Negro pupil as a learner in the big-city school systems have frequently revealed him to be standing in a poor school posture if not in educational bankruptcy. His readiness for learning seldom reaches as high as the school anticipates. His nonverbal and nonacademic sets create a difficult motivational problem and perhaps call for a different teaching-learning style than is found in the conventional classroom. His reading and language skills fall far below the level of his grade placement. He is more often truant and more frequently counted among the delinquent. Thus, suffering the accumulated frustration due to failure, boredom, and constant pressure of the preposterous academic task, school becomes a place of confinement and the age of leaving looms like a welcomed escape hatch and a solution to his troubles. Although the Negro student is often viewed as a severe headache or burden to the school, the school represents an even greater headache and a heavier burden to him. And too often it is with a sigh of relief that the school may see him off to the street.

There are limitations on what the school apparatus can accomplish with and for disadvantaged youth. In the life space of the culturally disadvantaged, the school inserts itself only after much learning has already taken place. And always there are other powerful forces—family, housing, neighborhood, peer groups, labor organizations, mass media, the social and economic order—that impinge, in addition to the school experiences, on the growth and development of the young. Just what can the school agency do to maximize its positive influence with the young Negro?

The school agency will achieve its maximum effectiveness with the disadvantaged Negro to the degree to which it satisfies four major contingencies: first, if the teachers themselves provide good role models with whom many youngsters readily identify; second, if the curriculum of the school includes aims, methods, materials, and climate conducive to learning; third, if ancillary services, including testing, counseling, job placement, case work, and health services, are available and accessible to the youngster at the time of need; and fourth, if the school becomes a member of the community team and meshes its services with other public and private agencies that work closely with Negro youth and their families.

School as an Ego-supporting Institution

Children in the big city who enter the public schools in heavily populated neighborhoods are immediately absorbed in a massive educational system. Although the big-city school system accepts all children, it does so on its own terms. These terms frequently demand some renunciation of differences—personal, social, and cultural—and a constant submission to the processes of conformity and standardization. Most schools achieve their goals at the price of some loss of privacy, personal identity, and individuality. They require submission to external controls and to the pressures of the group; they invoke the severe competitive processes of selection and survival of the academically fit; and all too frequently they produce an artificial separation between the classroom and the life stream of everyday problems and activities.

These demands of the large-city school system are most destructive to the egos of the culturally deprived. Children and youth who are unable or unwilling to submit frequently join the ranks of the school failures, the troubled and troublesome, the truants, and the early school dropouts. They may even set up their own ego-supporting institutions in the form of juvenile gangs. It is imperative that the school, in working to achieve its goals, operate always as an ego-supporting institution. The destructive nature of the school experiences of many unadapted youngsters, Negro and white, shows up vividly in studies of school failure, dropouts, youth unemployment, and delinquency. How can the total school effort, via the curriculum, the relationship with the teacher, and the special services, combine to reinforce and strengthen the self-concept of Negro youth and aid in their social adaptation?

The Curriculum of the School

There are two curricula that will be found in every school. First, there is the overt curriculum which is made up of all the teacher-planned (in some cases, teacher-pupil planned) activities in which the young learners are engaged and which lead, hopefully, to some agreed-upon goals. But as Alice Miel noted at the 1960 White House Conference, the school curriculum represents "a changing assemblage of opportunities for educational experience." In a fast-changing world, the American schools have not changed fast enough. This educational lag between the outside world and the classroom has been handicapping to all categories of learners, both advantaged and disadvantaged. Second, there is the covert, or subliminal, curriculum to be found in the culture and subcultures of the school which sets up normative ways to behave and how not to behave. We shall consider special aspects of both curricula as they pertain to the school life of the Negro.

The Formal and Visible Curriculum

For many Negro youngsters, the curriculum experiences appear irrelevant and pointless. There is very little apparent connection between what goes on in school and the present or future life of the learner. In addition to the traditional function of transmitting the culture, school activities must connect with the child's present and his future. To ensure relevancy, school goals must be specified in terms of expected changes or modifications in behavior or in terms of the acquisition of new and desirable modes of behavior. As the behavior of masses of children undergoes modification, it may thus be possible to change the way of life and to improve the less effective cultural practices of the disadvantaged. School attendance and involvement in learning activities should make a discernible difference. This difference, broadly speaking, should be observable in the acquisition of new behavior or the changes in behavior of the learner. Such changes might be seen in the pupil's leisure-time activities, in his job competencies, in the management of his day-to-day home economics activities, in his decision-making and problem-solving behavior, in his maintenance of health and physical well-being, in the reading he does for information or pleasure, and in his capacity for further learning. Unless the pupil's behavior has been modified and improved and unless new and desirable behavior has been established, learning cannot be said to have taken place.

To illustrate this principle, consider, first, the traditional learning experience in English literature in the high school. A youngster is required to read carefully (if not with pleasure) a number of books from the "recommended reading list." A detailed appraisal of his reading reveals his recall of plot, character, setting, and theme. Having answered all or a sufficient number of questions to the satisfaction of the teacher, the young learner seldom or never reads another book. Yet he may receive a "passing mark" in literature, although his nonreading behavior has not changed. Or consider, second, the pupil in social studies who has learned to recite the Bill of Rights, chapter and verse, but whose behavior and conduct as a youth now or as an adult later reflect no understanding of the meaning or implications of these articles in his personal, political, social, or business life. The expected and desired change in behavior has not taken place. The youngster has not learned.

To reiterate, in planning a variegated curriculum to meet the different needs of all pupils, the course objectives, insofar as possible, should be stated as concrete and visible modes of new behavior or as improvements or changes in established and less effective ways of behaving. As this is done, curriculum planners will need to consider three related problems.

First, there is the current danger, already cited, of mass education that will lead to a standardization of the Negro learner in the stereotype of the "middle-class citizen and parent" or into a regimented array of "correct" opinions, purchases, leisure-time pursuits, and occupations. Stated conversely, the maverick, the independent thinker or performer, or the divergent creator should be carefully sought out among children and youth who are born and who live within the estate of lower-classness. How to educate—literally, to lead out or draw out—the Negro child from his subculture into middle-class milieus, if the school's objectives so demand, and yet preserve and develop elements of individuality, divergency, and independence represents a major problem facing the curriculum planners. Unfortunately the curriculum planners seldom consult with youth—white or nonwhite—or with their parents either in curriculum development or in curriculum implementation.

On this point, Anna Freud has made an astute observation:

> Educators, that is to say those adults who form the environment of the child, always want to make him what suits them, which consequently differs according to the century, position, rank, class, etc., of the adults. But all these varying aims have one feature in common. The universal aim of education is always to make out of the child a grown-up person who shall not be very different from the grown-up world around him.[3]

What the dominant society demands for and of the Negro often makes little sense either to him or to his parents. This is especially true of the nonmobile Negro who is stable and is staying in the subculture. Inarticulate and nonverbal as the youngster may appear (yet note the richness and creativity of his own hipster tongue), the dialogue concerning the aims and objectives of the school and the aims and objectives of the youngster and his family must be started even before he comes to school.

Anna Freud also indicated that an educator—unlike the child-caring mother—always wants something from the child. Many Negro children perceive this, and they appear afraid, unwilling, or unable to give back to the demanding authority. We need to inquire in schools why this is so.

Second, there is the constant threat of confining the Negro student and the potential or actual dropout to those educational experiences aimed exclusively in the direction of objectives that are immediate, extrinsic, utilitarian, and practical. Preoccupation with these goals runs the risk of placing a low ceiling on courses offered or chosen. The danger to the upwardly mobile Negro youth, whether on-their-way or in-ferment, is great. This is not to overlook what Riessman[4] has on several occasions pointed out: the need for concreteness and "down-to-earth learning by doing," especially in the initial stages and with the culturally less mobile Negro. Although accent on self and creativity may be alien to the culture of many deprived children, ideational goals should be held aloft and clearly visible, especially for the upwardly mobile and ultimately, through progression, for the less mobile. To diminish in any way the ideational goals in the education of Negro youth is to derogate. The current emphases on expansion of occupational training programs and on the development of marketable skills in many schools, as valuable as they may be, can in the long run further disadvantage the disadvantaged, whose educational sights may be lowered or whose stay in school may be shortened through the pursuit of terminal courses. Equal emphasis must be given to the development of school programs that place the accent on cultural enrichment, general education, and instructional improvement. Implicit in the differential student-course matching is the need for pupil personnel services, including counseling, testing, and job placement. To these we shall return later; but we have recognized at this point of goal determination that very careful consideration should be given to course selections as an aspect of career planning.

Third, to ensure desirable modifications in behavior or the development of new and improved modes of behavior, the school must provide richer opportunities to practice such behavior as a part of the learning experience and as an expression of the product of learning. This calls for the development of practice opportunities and laboratory experiences in school and community. Too much of school experience is theoretical, abstract, or, at best, vicarious. What is sorely needed in the curriculum of the secondary school is a graduated series of real-life experiences in problem solving and decision making, in participation within the social, political, and economic life of the in-school and out-of-school society. Most youth are cut out of the mainstream of community activities. They have minimal function. The exile, the disenfranchisement, the rejection are most severe and complete with Negro youth. At least, white youth have some cosmetic value in the dominant adult community. In contrast, few adults swell with pride at the sight of norm-conforming Negro youth. To be a nothing, to have no function, is hard for all youth; but it is doubly hard for Negro youth.

Courses of study in problems of democracy, for example, should be centered on the study of local community problems, as well as planning for their solution and actually solving them. It is true that only youth can solve the youth problem. The energies of American youth, white and nonwhite, have seldom been tapped for social and civic benefit. That Negro youth have the initiative, the inspiration, and the commitment to high social purpose cannot be questioned as one views their strong role now in the steady drive to freedom and job opportunity. Energies expended in demonstrations, sit-ins, and freedom marches can also be directed to goals of self-realization and social betterment. The question to be explored here is: "What kinds of laboratory experiences and practices can the local schools establish as an integral part of the regular curriculum to lend reality and significance to the focus of learning and to fix habits of behavior as explicated in the educational goals of the school?"

Now to point up our discussion of educational goals stated in terms of behavioral outcomes. The objectives of the school should be established and revised through continuous discussion with parents and with Negro youth themselves. These dialogues between school and home must be carried on a bivariate screen. On the following diagram we can scale the objectives of the school and of Negro youth on two dimensions. The horizontal axis represents a bipolar dimension of objectives on a scale ranging from conformity to divergency; the vertical axis represents a scale ranging from material-utilitarian to ideational. The bivariate chart invites consideration of current emphasis in programs now being offered to culturally deprived youth; it also offers material for reflection to curriculum planners as well as for those who run the courses. It is suggested that the participants in this Conference plot the objectives of current school programs that have been implemented, using the suggested schemata or some adaptation of the two dimensions.

But the goals of the school curricula are more than ordinary goals. They are projections of the future self-concept; they can promise a better future and a better self-concept, and they can beckon the learner to run the hard course of change.

A few selected comments are in order concerning the "materials and methods" of curricula with reference to the Negro student.

Motivation is one of the major problems that every teacher faces

Goals of education as projections of self-image.

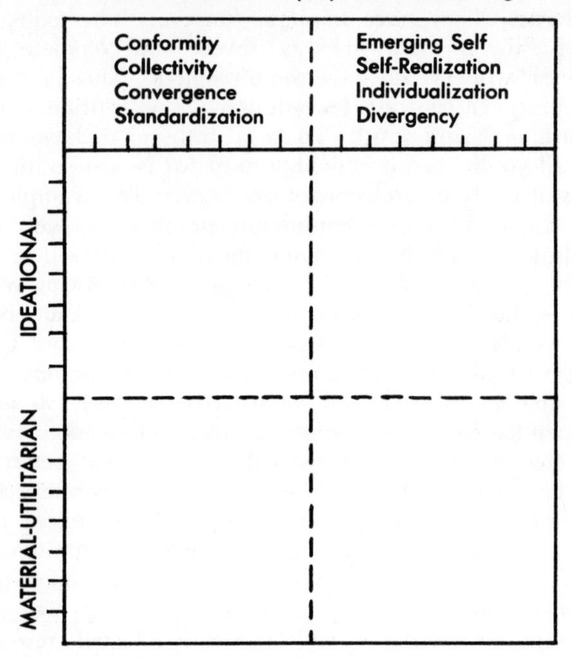

with the culturally disadvantaged. The pragmatic attitude and the anti-intellectualism typical of lower-class living lead to objectives that are predominantly utilitarian, with special emphasis on job procurement, as we have noted earlier. Ausubel,[5] however, makes a strong case for intrinsic motivation (the acquisition of knowledge for its own sake) as "the most promising motivational strategy" which can be adopted in teaching the culturally deprived learner or nonlearner. He points out that "meaningful school learning is more potent, relevant, durable and easier to arouse than its extrinsic counterpart." When successful, it furnishes its own reward. Also, since much of school learning cannot be easily rationalized as necessary for the everyday demands of living, only cognitive drive becomes the one immediately relevant motivation. He points out in addition that intrinsic motivation, unlike extrinsic motif, is not so likely to lose its potency or relevance in later life when utilitarian and career advancements are less and less a dominant life consideration. Ausubel suggests that

> . . . it is not necessary to postpone learning activities until appropriate interests and motivations have been developed. Frequently the best way of motivating an unmotivated pupil is

to ignore his motivational state for the time being and to concentrate on teaching him as effectively as possible. Much to his surprise and to his teacher's, he will learn despite his lack of motivation; and from the satisfaction of learning he will characteristically develop the motivation to learn more.

Paradoxically, therefore, we may discover that the most effective method of developing intrinsic motivation to learn is to focus on the cognitive rather than on the motivational aspects of learning, and to rely on the motivation that is developed retro-actively from successful educational achievement. This is particularly true when a teacher is able to generate contagious excitement and enthusiasm about the subject he teaches, and when he is the kind of person with whom culturally deprived children can identify. Masculinizing the school and dramatizing the lives and exploits of cultural, intellectual, and scientific heroes can also enhance the process of identification. At the same time, of course, we can attempt to combat the anti-intellectualism and lack of cultural tradition in the home through programs of adult education and cultural enrichment.[6]

In forthcoming discussions we shall follow up the emphasis on teacher identification and role models and the need for adult education and cultural enrichment.

In the research and the speculations of Clark, Deutsch, Riessman, Sexton, Wolfe, and others,[7] many inferences have been made concerning the low-level verbal and academic stance and performance of the culturally disadvantaged Negro and white learners. Deprived of a variety of stimuli in their early childhood, Negro pupils often appear seriously deficient in their equipment for learning. To facilitate learning, Deutsch has suggested that "the school must expect frequently to do a portion of the job traditionally assigned to the home, and curriculum must be reorganized to provide for establishing a good base."[8] For many of these youngsters, this will mean a downward extension of the elementary school to develop readiness for school tasks. Current studies now under way at Boston University[9] suggest that "intelligence," or the capacity to learn, can be significantly improved by means of exposure to enriched preschool experiences in the tradition of the good nursery school.

In coming to grips with the verbal and academic disabilities, little more than lip service has been given to the powerful medium of the picture. The language of pictures as a supportive medium of instruction—though never a substitute for the printed word—warrants far greater attention and study as an instructional tool, especially with the youngster who comes from a nonacademic and less verbal culture and who will in all likelihood inhabit the picture world of *Life, Look, Ebony,* the cinema, and the TV room. As Dorothy B. Jones has pointed out, pictures more than words can develop a new respect for actualities themselves. This is important for both Negro and white, lest either or both groups become too willing to substitute the words (*integration, freedom, equal rights,* and the rest) for the actualities themselves. She states:

> As the semanticists have pointed out, most of us tend to think in terms of good or bad, black or white, plus or minus. What we need to do, they tell us, is look about with greater objectivity, accept and think of things as they *are* rather than label them with words that inherently express inferences and judgments. If we can stick to *actualities*—to facts—then we can approach the "multi-valued orientation" that will facilitate social understanding and social change.[10]

If pictures rather than words remain for the vast majority of children and adults the usual or even preferred form of thought and fantasy, we should go to this more direct medium of communication in the classroom.

It is well to remember that instead of eliminating the desire for reading, studies have shown that viewing still and motion pictures may actually stimulate the child and adult to pick up a book. Since the advent of TV, the public libraries have reported steady increases rather than decreases in book circulation per capita. In a visual age, the classroom should reflect greater emphasis on visualization as a means of learning and thinking. This can be a crucial stimulant and tool for our target groups.

An example of the effective use of the language of pictures can be found in the recent publication, *A Pictorial History of the Negro in America,* by Hughes and Melzer.[11] Based on detailed research, the volume is written in a straightforward and easy narrative style filled with dramatic impact without sentimental or overemotional appeals. More of this type of instructional material is needed in all areas of the curriculum and at all grade levels.

Several years ago, Tilroe[12] studied school programs and adaptations in twenty secondary schools having high dropout rates (averaging 47.4 percent) with the educational practices found in twenty low-dropout high schools (averaging 8.8 percent). Highly significant and associated with low-dropout schools were the following: programs of family education, integrated activity programs, differentiated courses of study, wide selection of electives, more frequent group conferences for teachers, exit interviews, frequent parent-student conferences, and a remedial reading program. These give us some clues to reducing the inclination to drop out which has been so characteristic of Negro youth.

Perhaps of greater import than any practice or even the sum of these innovations is the implicit message that is beamed to both pupil and parent: "We want to hold on to you; we want to help you; we are not trying to get rid of you." High retention rates reflect more than school adaptations; they are also reflective of attitudes of school personnel. We shall need to consider the potential of the teacher in affecting self-concepts and social adaptations of Negro youth; but now let us look into the "hidden curriculum" of the school.

The Subliminal Curriculum

The school is more than an agent of organized society; the school represents a small and, for many culturally disadvantaged youngsters, a strange and separate society.

I have already pointed out, and perhaps overstated, that the formal curriculum of the school provides planned and systematic experiences through which new behaviors and/or modifications of behavior are developed. This curriculum operates in most schools in a monotonous routine and ritual of lesson assigning, lesson hearing, and lesson marking. In an earlier study,[13] from which I shall borrow freely, I have pointed out that there is also a second and perhaps more powerful curriculum which is to be found in the culture of the school. This is the way of life of the school, providing a normative structure of how to act and how not to act. This subliminal curriculum, like the hidden but major portion of an iceberg, is in a sense a natural extension of the visible and formal curriculum of the school. Though hidden, it may represent for behavior and misbehavior the more formidable and sometimes the more effective—if not hazardous—aspect of the school's program in developing real and significant changes in the behavior of high school youth.

The importance of this less visible aspect of the curriculum can be ascertained from the current protests centered on segregation in the New Rochelles, Englewoods, Bostons, and Birminghams. Intuitively, the lay public, including whites and nonwhites, appreciate the fact that the ethos of a high school with 90 percent Negro enrollment and the ethos of a high school in the same city with 90 percent white enrollment do represent a wide range of differences in the styles of school living and learning. The climate of the "students" of one school may award status and prestige to the truant, the nonachiever, the recalcitrant learner, and the early dropout. The climate of student opinion of another school may award status and prestige to the high achiever, the college-bound, and the activities leader. Those who seek to ensure a preferred value system through the mathematical criterion involving "better balance" of white and Negro students will be disappointed. For the answer lies in the focal concerns or points of reference representing values and norms of the effective reference group, and more particularly within the leadership of the effective group.

There is no such thing as "the culture" of the American public secondary school. A wide variety of cultures and subcultures exist and can be found in different high schools and in different communities. The ways of life in the large inner-city high school will differ substantially from the way of living in the more homogeneous upper-middle-class models found in the clean and neat suburban school; and these, in turn, will differ from the patterns visible in the small high schools that are now fast disappearing from the rural scene. Margaret Mead has explored some of these significant variants in her Inglis Lecture, *The School in American Culture*.[14] At the same time, it must be recognized that the structure of school society, not unlike the structure of the society outside of school, consists of a number of subgroups, each with its own somewhat distinct cultural characteristics. In the high school, these may cluster around class status of the family, college-going intentions, course elections, ethnic aspects of the neighboring community, etc.

Behavior and, of course, misbehavior frequently are only manifestations or reflections of the cultural imperatives of the school. The cultural imperatives of the secondary school are powerful and pervasive. They may and frequently do neutralize and even supersede the forces operating in the formal and planned experiences of the visible curriculum.

My purpose here is to analyze some common imperatives culled from the cultural milieus of the secondary school that frequently tend to shape or determine personality (modes of adjustment). We must recognize, of course, that behavior and misbehavior represent always an interaction of the organism and the external environment referred to here in a cultural sense. Since the factors within the culture are more often overlooked than the factors under the skin in studying behavior and misbehavior, this discussion focuses exclusively on the more common cultural imperatives which have been distilled from many different secondary schools. All of these cultural imperatives can serve to predispose the high school student to misbehavior and social inadaptation, since they expose him to frustration, ego distintegration, stress, anxiety, weak imitative example, and lowered self-estimate.

The American high school is unique in many ways when compared with many of its European counterparts. A point of greatest difference can frequently be found in the free-and-easy boy-girl relationships best symbolized by the insurance policy carried in the form of the steady date or the isolated couple at the school dance united in romantic embrace.

The sexiest spot in any American town today can be found in its high school. This is especially true in smaller communities and most visible in suburbia, perhaps more so than in the inner city. This theme has been caught in the melodrama of *Peyton Place,* where even the high school principal is hardly immune to the sexually oriented climate of his own institution and eventually capitulates. The identical theme is burlesqued in the Grade B Hollywood celluloid, "High School Confidential," which recently played the wide screens of the local movie houses. In this caricature of the high school, seniors (maybe they were only sophomores) speak frequently and glibly of the stag and stud roles of the male "students."

In a sense, the sex-crossed activities of the high school provide an important part of the practicum for the future husband-wife companion role but without verbalization and without theoretical orientation to the phenomenon and meaning of sex. Hence the young adult may somehow master the developmental task and mature into an expert craftsman by the time the male or female family role is undertaken. But until the transition is from the *how* to the *why,* youth will seldom attain a professional level of their husband-wife roles. What is sorely needed in the American secondary school is the opportunity to talk it out rather than just act it out, even though the acting may be done without injury and on the symbolic level. The heavy curtain of official silence that hangs around sex in an institution replete with sex-crossed activities presents the modern educational paradox. It is hoped that talking it out will develop restraint, good sense, and moral principle rather than further accentuating an overaccentuated subject.

How much of this sex orientation is attributable to the unrealistic adult romanticism of youth and love and adult fantasies and fears in regard to Negroes and adolescents could be explored profitably by research teams from sociology, anthropology, psychology, and education. For it is the high schools that house the teen-agers who are regarded by adults, as Edgar Friedenberg has pointed out, as a "hot-blooded minority." They are, he says, "in the process of being denatured; of becoming under social stress, something more acceptable to dominant society, but essentially different from what its own growth and experience would lead to."[15] Friedenberg continues:

> In the most formal sense, then, the adolescent is one of our second class citizens. But the informal aspects of minority status are also imputed to him. "The teen-ager," like the Latin or Negro, is seen as joyous, playful, lazy, and irresponsible,

with brutality lurking just below the surface and ready to break into violence. All these groups are seen as childish and excitable, imprudent and improvident, sexually aggressive, and dangerous, but possessed of superb and sustained power to satisfy sexual demands.[16]

The functional aspects of this teen-age stereotype for adults and teachers also need to be investigated, and the implications for teacher recruitment, training, and placement need to be drawn out. In this search we may find some answers to *de facto* (and other types of) segregation and to why a special effort must be made to recruit teachers for the inner-city schools, and also why high school dances are so closely and anxiously supervised. "The Black Board Jungle" made capital of adult fears, fantasies, and titillations by equating adolescence, delinquency, and aggressive sexuality in a high school setting for adult viewing. Front-page stories such as that of the marriage of Charlayne Hunter, the Negro co-ed who broke the color barrier at the University of Georgia, to Walter Stovall, a white Georgian, will always make exciting reading for some adults.

The fact that most private or independent secondary schools hold to their monolithic sex structure testifies that they continue to meet the needs of apprehensive parents who consciously or unconsciously seek out those school organizations which "protect" their young adolescents from the sex-crossed activities of the public high school. The presence of Negro students often underscores their apprehension. This is not to deny that there are other reasons, good and bad, that motivate anxious parents to send their maturing youngsters to private all-male or all-female schools. Integration has made a profitable business out of many bad private schools that were hardly solvent a few years ago.

Contrary to the practicum in relating to the opposite sex with its lack of information and discussion, the rest of the school's program at the high school level can best be described as information without application or implementation. For the period of his high school career, the learner is cut off from the stream of real-life problems. He finds himself in a deep freeze. The activities in which he must engage appear irrelevant to the Negro student's past, present, or future—especially the present. Since the high school is careful to skirt and detour around real-life problems and controversial issues involving race relations, alcoholism, materialism, religion, politics, collectivism, consumer competencies, marriage, and family life, it involves the learner in a type of artificially contrived busywork and shadowboxing that either lulls the adolescent into a stupor or drives him in his resentment out of school to overt aggression. In protecting youth from real-life problems, the school enters into a tragic conspiracy of irresponsible retreat from reality. The perversion of the high school curriculum to neutral and petty purposes emasculates the school program and distintegrates the ego. The complaints[17] of youth today are that the school experiences are stale and flat. Boredom in school is what drives many youths, Negro and white, to retaliatory and noncomforming behavior, to chronic truancy, and eventually to withdrawal. The best therapeutic device available for the noisy and retreating part of our adolescent society is an interesting, meaningful, and vital high school curriculum.

Nowhere is the listless play-acting more visible than in the so-called student governments in the high school. Seldom are youth trusted to make their own decisions and to experience the learning that can come from making moral choices or socioeconomic-political decisions on their own. The direction and supervision exercised in student government make a mockery of the democratic processes. Neither does the high school appear effective in finding any honest or real work with which to preoccupy the fast-maturing adolescent. The result today can be seen in the young adult who is convinced of his low status. He is a nobody, a nothing. He suffers from the lack of any utility function (except that of serving in the role of a perpetual scapegoat for the adult members of society who heap upon him all the debris of their own inadequacies). There is no more unimportant member of society than the adolescent. He is the outraged personality of the twentieth century, as indicated by the eloquent testimony in the mounting rebellion visible in the delinquency trends of any large city. Herein is frequently reflected the aggressive inferiority of modern youth. The nonfunctioning curriculum of the secondary school, coupled with compulsory school attendance, is rapidly turning the American public high school into an adolescent ghetto. Let us inspect the compulsory nature of this relationship between school and adolescent.

There are many captive students in American high schools. What proportion of its Negro pupils would the secondary schools lose if the compulsory school-attendance laws were revoked and if the attendance officers were taken off the job? In the educational mythology of compulsory secondary schooling, the public institutions have promised to educate every child of every parent in the strong middle-class tradition. For most pupils, as with Penrod, school has become "a place of confinement envenomed by mathematics," which we have recently replaced with a "new mathematics" curriculum and to which we have added a revised science program. Unfortunately these programs are not geared to all the individual differences that are visible through compulsory school attendance. The efforts made in improving and upgrading the math-science courses of study for the academically endowed and college-going student should be matched by equal effort and expenditure for the terminal high school student as well as for the potential dropout.

Unfortunately Dr. Conant's comprehensive high school is not comprehensive enough.

The tempo and rhythm of learning in the high schools is fast, brief, and staccato. The student studies by clock and calendar. Time concepts of Negro youngsters are not built on these two measures. Learning stops for frequent holiday and vacation periods. Entrance to school and withdrawal from school are based on birth certificates rather than on any criteria of ability, achievement, and readiness. Learning is always short timed and truncated. It operates in fifty-minute periods in which teacher and pupil study to beat the clock. All of this is alien to a studentship and a scholarship which is continuous and permeating and which must race in the long, arduous marathon rather than the fifty-minute dash in a five-period day. Much of the pseudointellectualism of our day can be traced to the "quickie" nature of the school's learning-teaching process.

Organizationally the high school program sorts out classes (not individuals) among teachers about every fifty minutes. The frequently shifted youngster belongs to no one. Even with a "home-room period," he suffers a feeling of rootlessness and impersonality. As a member of a class, he may achieve the status of a pupil, but he seldom calls attention to himself as a person except through misbehavior. Help may be extended to him, but it must be routed through the impersonal bureaucracy of the guidance department.

Secondary schools have shown a complete lack of imagination, of ingenuity, in developing programs that would ensure the establishment of strong and extended teacher-pupil and pupil-teacher relationships on which instruction and learning can be anchored. Attention should be given to the possibilities inherent in arranging programs in much longer time patterns by spending a half day or full day within each area of instruction, or even a week with the science teacher, followed by a full week each in the round of other teachers in other areas. High school programming will make learning and scholarship pervasive only when schooling itself is pervasive.

High school classes are very tightly grouped on the age-grade principle, with subdivisions according to interests in different curricula which reflect, in turn, educational and occupational levels of aspiration, resulting in strong social-class differentiation. Grouping tightly on the age-grade basis can affect behavior and misbehavior in several ways.

First, the grouping affects behavior by implying to both teachers and pupils an equality and homogeneity that actually does not exist and in consequence of which instruction is undifferentiated through the slavish use of the single text and the identical lesson assignment. This invites the problem of the bored learner at the upper levels and the frustrated learner within the lower ranges of ability and achievement.

Only by individualizing instruction within the classroom can the great educational superstition be broken that all children of the same age who come to school can learn the same things at the same time at the same place and to the same degree. High school students taught under the American superstition of readiness and equality are bound to suffer the trauma of a bad hangover once they leave school and walk into the competitive climate in the world of work.

Second, grouping in tight age brackets tends to reinforce the already overly strong youth subcultures. The teen-ager notoriously would rather be wrong with his peers than right with his family or other adult authority. When this happens, as Margaret Mead has pointed out, American youth tend to surrender some moral autonomy for the comforts of the irresponsible crowd. This is the inherent nature of the delinquent act, particularly of the "group-intoxicated" and "socialized" types.

How much leeway is possible in grouping more broadly, but within the chronological age span of the secondary school, presents a real problem. Surely more could be done in the six-year secondary school by overlapping membership in some classes, such as music and art, and by adhering more closely to ability-achievement criteria in others, thereby breaking the solid age-grade-status grouping that now prevails. At the same time, the pressure to differentiate instruction for extremes will be lessened.

Contrary to some fears and even some evidence that preadolescents, adolescents, and postadolescents cannot be effectively grouped for instruction, careful observations of the social and emotional situations on the ski slope or in the swimming pool or on the stage (where instruction frequently is imparted to groups having very wide age ranges, but in accordance with a continuous-growth principle) will reveal many positive outcomes, particularly in terms of a reciprocal respect and a camaraderie rare even in closely knit pressure groups.

In connection with problems of homogeneity and grouping, two principles culled from the investigations of Riecken on the efficacy of work camps in changing attitudes are noteworthy. He reported that "attitudes could be more easily and successfully changed if a group rather than an isolated individual is the object of attempts to produce change."[18] He also has found that personality traits underwent the most positive changes when his subjects were introduced into totally different situations and when they were faced by radically different sets of relations from those to which they were habituated. Dr. Coles's intensive study of Negro and white youngsters in integrated schools in the South generally reaffirms similar positive changes, though not in every case.[19] There is powerful persuasion in the peer group, as many investigators have found. To shift one's values and to find oneself alienated or deviating from one's reference group can be hard; however, when a shift in values establishes a group standard, every pupil's new behavior will be reinforced by the class members. To organize classes in homogenized—if not homogeneous—units may lessen the opportunity for eliciting change. Implications can be drawn from these studies to strengthen open-enrollment programs and to answer questions concerning racial imbalance in predominantly Negro schools.

One implication, in view of the very strong hold that neighborhood segregation has on composition of enrollment in city schools, may be the necessity of forced mixing of children with varied backgrounds to provide positive racial encounters at an early age. In the event that this adaptation is made, it will be necessary to take into consideration other important variables, such as class status, which may prove to be more crucial than skin color. This may be one way, perhaps the only way, to raise the inferior status of schools that are found in low-income areas, as documented by Sexton in her big-city study.[20]

Merely shifting youngsters from one school to another or redistricting in and of themselves may create problems, as well as providing the students with a rich opportunity to learn and value other students of dissimilar backgrounds. Social integration and lessons in democratic living will not accrue automatically and certainly not without careful prior planning. Much more can be done at the elementary school levels before racial and class-status ideologies have taken root, as Dr. Coles's study of younger Southern children in segregated schools bears out. But much more effort and skill will be required to work with older youth at the high school level. As Hollingshead reported of Elmtown, most interactions among students in school follow along social-class lines.

> By the time he reaches adolescence his personality is formed. Also, he has developed conceptions of (1) himself; (2) the social structure; (3) his place in it along with appropriate roles and statuses; (4) forms of behavior approved and disapproved; and (5) means of doing what he desires even though it involves the violation of laws and mores.[21]

At the secondary school level, a direct approach to the problem should be tried out in which the students themselves carry out self-studies of the impact of social-class differences on students (and perhaps on teachers). This could also be enlarged into a neighborhood study via such courses as problems of democracy, introduction to sociology, or psychology. High school pupils would thereby be encouraged to isolate and define problems, gather data, consider alternatives for action, and help to implement change.

Status in school is always linked to successful achievement in the classroom. For the adolescent, one source (often the only source) of teacher approval can be found in academic achievement via the report-card route. Unless the student shows a satisfactory level of attainment, he is not likely to find himself surrounded by smiling and approving adult faces.

School failure is frequently a concomitant and forerunner of deviant behavior. Studies of delinquents and nondelinquents[22] indicate a wide split between the educationally bankrupt and the educationally affluent. Delinquents frequently make a success of failure by using this means to thumb their noses at the school.

It is easy to understand how failure can be used to strike back at the teaching authority, or to demolish the school, by students whose neighborhood or peer-group value system is contrary to that of the school or of the dominant society. It may not be so easy to understand how the upper-middle-class child can use failure as a powerful weapon to cut down his parents. When school success becomes a paramount issue to the parent who draws selfishly his own brand of personal satisfaction from the achievement of his youngsters, academic failure can prove a subtle and satisfactory boomerang for any youngster. In fact, this is one of the few ways that many middle-class high school adolescents have of getting back at their predatory parents.

How to ensure success for the less academic or "nonacademic" pupil in the high school presents a difficult curriculum problem. Until this issue is met, students who must enter high school will run the risk of breaking their backs as they reach for unattainable goals. When satisfactions that can come only through achievement, success, and approval are not attainable, the youngsters may well resort to other means to achieve some measure of success. These means may frequently be the antisocial route of misbehavior.

The American school, if it is to diminish deviate behavior, must aim to develop inner behavioral controls that will make its graduates less dependent on the supervising, monitoring, and policing authority. Self-discipline as contrasted with external-control dependency has been the aim of the secondary school, but this aim can hardly be attained so long as the school culture continues to dominate with adult controls and to tell the student what to do, when to do it, how to do it, and whether it is right when it is done. Such heavy dependence upon forces of external and formal discipline tends to deepen the misunderstanding and resentment that exist between youth and adult and to intensify the hate and hostility now manifest in much of the deviate behavior in youth culture. Both the sociologist and the psychiatrist have independently come to the conclusion that the culture of formal and external controls, when it succeeds, frequently creates a reluctant and recalcitrant conformist living close to the letter of the law. When it fails, it creates "the outlaw," best exemplified by the overt, aggressive delinquent who is a member of an "outlaw gang" in the depths of the big city.

These and other cultural determinants found operating in most public secondary schools will continuously precipitate crises, tensions, and frustrations for the high school student. David Segel[23] has pointed out three kinds of behavior solutions that can follow on frustration in the high school: (1) regression, as exemplified by school leaving; (2) aggression, as seen in disorderly conduct, overt attack, and vandalism; (3) fixation, as found in the sitting out of the school activities, or "going through the motions."

Of all these behavior solutions to inimical school situations, perhaps the most wholesome or promising will be found in the overt-aggression pattern in which the youngster is doing something about it. He is putting up a fight. He is adjusting the best and usually the only way he knows how. He is calling our attention to himself and to his problem situation. He is not retreating, nor is he giving up, nor is he resorting to fantasy in solving his terrible problem. There is much that is positive—even wholesome—in the delinquency phenomenon. Needless to say, this is not well understood generally and can be readily misunderstood.

Knowledge of these cultural imperatives of behavior and misbehavior in school and classroom will enable the professional youth worker in school and community, together with the parent and the pupil, to plan cultural change. By changing the behavior of large masses of young people, the great American public school of the future may even be able to change and influence the culture of the community.

Role of the Teacher as a Person and as a Professional Worker

The most direct and effective way to strengthen the school as an ego-supporting institution is to improve the interpersonal relationships between teacher and students. It is the individual teacher who generally enjoys the most intimate and continuing relationship with the child outside the home and the family circle. Through the powerful instrument of this relationship, the teacher can do much to promote, via the normal educational processes, better mental health and educational growth. To achieve this, he must be a mature adult, committed to his responsibility of helping children and youth and presenting a positive image with which to identify. He must be aware of conscious and unconscious motivations (his own as well as those of the pupils) and be able to communicate with others. This is where those responsible for teacher preparation and in-service training of staff can make their most telling contribution: by seeking to improve and help teaching personalities as well as teacher competencies.

Every teacher faces the same basic problem. He must define and maintain his role as a mature professional adult. Teachers in the big-city school system usually operate in a cumbersome bureaucracy. Surrounded by administrators, supervisors, and specialists, they often become uncertain of their own functions and the extent and direction of their own responsibility. Of particular significance is the study of the National Education Association[24] indicating that a substantially larger proportion of teachers in large school districts than teachers in small school districts felt that they lacked the rights and authority needed to maintain "effective control" over their pupils. This same study found that those teachers who felt that they had the necessary authority did have better-behaved pupils and fewer troublemakers in their classes.

It may well be that teachers in larger school districts, as compared with those in smaller districts, are less likely to have an important voice in determining the educational and disciplinary policies of their schools. Consideration should be given to including teachers of larger school units in any discussions related to policies and practices dealing with youngsters who offer learning problems and who are prone or vulnerable to social inadaptation.

At the same time, teachers constantly face the problem of resolving conflicts arising between their school-organization role and their teacher-helper role. The organization commitment pulls in the direction of the enforcement and maintenance of standards of middle-class achievement, speech, dress, and behavior; but the teacher-helper commitment demands the assistance of the young learner in terms of his basic needs against the reality setting of his effective reference group.

For example, in assisting the nonachiever or near-failure, the teacher-helper provides the pupil with individual instruction and emotional support, but at the end of the marking period the organization role may force the teacher to fail the pupil in spite of the learning effort expended or the extenuating circumstances of the pupil's learning difficulties. Such a situation may lead to hostility directed at the very pupil the teacher has been trying to help, but who also precipitated the role conflict. In working with Negro youth in particular, the teacher must be conscious of the problem he faces with this type of conflict.

Many teachers in big-city systems today indicate strong job dissatisfaction and low self-concept, which often tend to reduce their frustration tolerance. Watson has pointed up the lack of hero images in the education field. Answering the question, "Why do we not have heroes in education?" he states:

> Somehow the idea is current that all educators and teachers are equal in competence. Therefore, none of them should be honored as exemplars, for this necessitates making choices among equals. Since some worthy person may not be honored, none should be. Or, when everyone is honored, none are distinguished. As a result, we have no figures which we hold before the youth or our graduate students saying, if you wish to succeed in education, be like these heroes.

He concludes:

> So to outsiders, educators appear as a spineless amorphous group lacking a clear image of its heroes.[25]

One almost hesitates to raise the question as to what youth from the other subcultures really think of their teachers!

It is difficult to tell whether the figures on pupil misbehavior in big schools and big districts reflect, in fact, a true difference in the incidence of social inadaptation between big-city pupils and suburban pupils or whether they merely reflect significant differences between irritability levels of city teachers who work with great numbers of culturally deprived, including Negro, youngsters and teachers employed in smaller schools and smaller communities who are more frequently in contact with middle-class students. The fact is that many teachers today seem to be fearful, anxious, or angry. This is especially manifest in the teacher's relationship with the reluctant and recalcitrant learners in the big cities. The frequent cry heard for sterner and harsher measures in dealing with these pupils and for their removal from the regular classroom or exclusion from school would indicate that too many educators are now more concerned with the academic reputation of their school than with the welfare and well-being of the nonachieving and nonconforming students.

Some teachers unconsciously fear their disturbed or disturbing pupils and resent their presence in the classroom. In relating to these children, the teacher may find forgotten fears of the past suddenly unlatched by a chance remark or episode. These unresolved threats and hidden anxieties can blind and deafen the teacher to classroom realities or can paralyze him temporarily. Sensing the precipitant of this recall process, the teacher may strike back at the pupil, using him as a symbol of the earlier offender. At times, the teacher may even try to work out or resolve his old problems through the problem behavior of his students. In a searching study of desegregation and its effects on Negro and white students, Dr. Coles has recently recommended greater emphasis on the teaching personality: "In desegregated schools teachers will be dealing with not only the problems of their children, but those of their own lives, their habits, and expectations. These teachers should not spare themselves careful self-examination."[26]

Nevertheless, there is also great strength to build on within the classroom teacher's commitment. Dr. Coles reports that he found in his interviews with teachers in Atlanta and New Orleans "a deep sense of professional integrity, of identity as teachers which transcended their private feelings about race."[27] None of this was lost on the students, white and Negro. This may constitute the pivotal resource around which the school agency can begin to build and improve in its service to Negro youngsters.

Teachers who work with many nonachieving and inadapted pupils are apt themselves to experience strong emotional difficulty. Someone must help them resolve the personal difficulties arising from work with these children. In the big school systems, aid can be provided through therapeutic counseling by psychiatrists, psychologists, and psychiatric social workers operating as mental health consultants. Help can come from a positive and understanding school administrator or supervisor who lends his ear to the troubled teacher. The principal of the school may even use his office as a way station in which the teacher can freely express his innermost anxieties and fears. To this end, consideration must be given to a much-needed shift in focus on the part of school-centered child-guidance clinics, whose effectiveness may be strengthened and broadened by their becoming more and more teacher-guidance clinics. The classroom is seldom without mental health hazards for the teacher. Unfortunately, most teachers have little direct or easy access to mental health aids.

In most classrooms, the cognitive aspect of life experience and the learning process are played up and the emotional aspects are played down. We understress the emotional life of the Negro pupil until his difficulties are so pronounced that this dimension can no longer be denied. The teacher generally does not trust emotions—his own or those of his pupils. Too often he only seeks to repress or deny them.

Teachers act in many classrooms today as though their Negro pupils were "clothes without bodies." In fact, the classroom is often used as a pacifier to calm down creative feelings, as though the school's aim were to produce dispassionate young adults. The result is often a boring ritual of learning and teaching.

The bigness of today's city schools and classrooms can breed anonymity, impersonality, and apathy. There is a growing threat of mechanization and isolation in many crowded classrooms today. In solving the problems of overcrowded classrooms and teacher shortages, innovations involving the more frequent use of self-teaching machines and devices have been widely recommended. There is the danger that this automated learning will reduce teacher-pupil interactions. Increased dependency on the TV screen, language tapes, teaching machines, movie and film projectors, and recordings should be justified not only in terms of learning increment but also in terms of the time saved for an increase rather than decrease of opportunities for more and deeper human relationships in the classroom. Otherwise teaching machines, robotlike human teaching as well as automation, can become a major threat to the adjustments of pupils who need the security and respect of a warm and reassuring human relationship in the big and impersonal world.

Teaching as a process involves planned interpersonal intervention aimed at changing ways in which other persons behave. The success of this process hangs in large measure on the extent to which pupils can establish a positive relationship and perhaps even identify with the teacher. "Who wants to be like you?" is a hard pay-off question that every teacher should pose for himself. A more uncomfortable question is, "Do I really want to stay with you?"

An effective relationship involving mutual trust and respect, with the acceptance of the reciprocal obligation reflected in the give-and-take of the learning-teaching process, will call for delicate classroom diplomacy between teachers and their Negro pupils. Differences in status, age, class, and skin color may interfere with the easy establishment of a good working relationship. We need to know more about the process of identification of Negro boys and girls. Teachers who are respected, accepted, and admired can become powerful objects of emulation. They can fill the need that exists in the paucity of good role models for both Negro boys and girls, but especially for boys. We do know that all youth are more impressed by what the teacher is and what he does than by what he says.

Baldwin testifies to the strong influence of a Negro principal in New York City. One can only speculate what the effect on Baldwin's own work might have been if the model had been a male Negro principal and if he had had more male Negro teachers.

> At the time I was going to school in Harlem the only Negro school principal as far as I know in the entire history of New York was a Mrs. Ayer, and she liked me. In a way I guess she proved to me that I didn't have to be entirely defined by my circumstances, because you know that every Negro child knows what his circumstances are but he cannot articulate them, because he is born into a republic which assures him in as many ways as it knows how, and with great force, that he has a certain place and he can never rise above it. Mrs. Ayer was a living proof that I was not necessarily what the country said I was.[28]

The difficulties in identification—even the advisability of close identification of Negro youngsters with their teachers—represents a complex and only slightly researched classroom phenomenon. The early Greeks described adolescence as a period of trying on and taking off of different masks to find the mask of best fit. Switching masks frequently can annoy—even scare—parents and teachers. But the youngster must find his own identity, and it is true that keeping on the mentor's mask too long can inhibit or distort the best development of the growing child's personality. Adelson points out:

> In adolescence especially they [identifications] sometimes seem to provide the means through which needed restructurings or

> crystallizations of personality take place. In some cases, the student can become himself only by first becoming someone else. He may find it difficult to acquire new and complex skills unless he protects himself psychically by borrowing, through identification, the teacher's power. Or he may use the identification as a mask, as a form of camouflage; while he pretends, to himself and to others, that he is being a certain someone, achieving this or that identity, he is actually accomplishing the inner changes that will allow him to achieve an identity closer to his own talents and dispositions. In all of these uses the identification is shallow and temporary; it is used as a prop, a crutch, a smoke screen or a shield; once it has served its purpose it is dissolved. The identification serves as the means of achieving a new and necessary identity.[29]

Perhaps this is where the teacher-pupil relationship can be most supportive via the temporary role modeling to enable easier transition from one value system to another or from one subculture to another. Since the identity needs of Negro students vary from those of white students, as well as from other colored students within the Negro spectrum, it is not possible that any one teacher can hope to serve as an appropriate and attractive model for all the students in his class. It is important to have many teachers available in the parade of role models; it may even be necessary to import successful hero models from the Negro community in the form of resource personnel who may contribute to learning experiences of the pupils by discussing and describing their vocational and avocational skills, interests, and achievements, thus making learning smart, respectable, and obtainable. It is also necessary to recognize, as Adelson points out, the pluralism in teaching: "the many styles of influence, the many modes of connection that bind student and teacher to each other."[30] There is need to explore the typologies of relationships to Negro pupils in which various forms of interaction can be studied in terms of personality development and achievement in school.

Insights concerning the adult leader's role in catalyzing desired adaptations within the subculture of adolescents which have direct implications for the teacher's role in developing self-direction and participation in community betterment come to us from studies carried out by the Center for Community and Field Service of New York University. Lukoff, Patterson, and Winick have reported:

> That emergence of an adolescent sub-culture characterized by self-directing community participation is not likely to occur without specific adult leadership which
> a. Gives supportive guidance; *i.e.,* is responsive to adoles-

cent problems, needs, and interests, both in terms of individuals and the group.

b. Is positive and symbolic; *i.e.,* in its behavior encourages identification with relevant values.

c. Practices appropriate process manipulations; *i.e.,* is sensitive and effective in both intervention and withdrawal tactics designed to maximize self-direction and community participation.[31]

The staff found that "where such an adult role was played subculture innovation developed; where it was not played . . . innovation either failed to occur or . . . [did not] last."[32]

Judging from the litany of repulsion as reflected in the school failure, disinterest, dislike, school vandalism, truancy, and dropout of Negro pupils, it may be even more urgent to study the strong powers of revulsion that are found in certain types of teachers. Perhaps as important as the "hero models" are the "antimodels" among the teachers who spawn discipline problems, distrust, and eventually defeat among the Negro students. The high incidence of the "transfer teacher," who flees from the classroom in the depressed areas of the inner city, provides grim evidence that many teachers would rather not be with the Negro student—to answer the question raised earlier.

Since there is no surplus of exemplary role models in home, neighborhood, and school for Negro youngsters, there is an urgent need to provide materials—including books, films, recordings, slides, etc.—that offer rich examples of Negro achievements and contributions in the United States and in other part of the world. These should do more than reflect the Bunches, the Andersons, the Robinsons; they should tell the dramatic and heroic story of the middle-class and lower-middle-class Negroes whose station in life is nearer that of the majority of pupils, but who have made the upward move against familiar and difficult obstacles.

In a poignant biographical statement, Lena Horne comments on her own search for identity and cites the problem of the remoteness of the George Washington Carvers and the absence of any female images between the silent kitchen slavey and the streetwalker:

> I certainly never learned anything about my identity in school, because the only Negro mentioned in history books was George Washington Carver, and he was too pure and good to believe, though I did learn that other races had backgrounds they looked upon with pride. I kept trying to find some reason to feel the same way. Eventually, when "interested" people began to try and give me different "images" of myself, I came to the realization that nobody (and certainly not yet myself) seemed to understand the Negro woman who stood between the

two conventionally accepted extremes: the "good," *quiet* colored woman who scrubbed and cooked and maybe made a respectable servant, and the whore. . . .

So, by the time I was 16 and had returned to Brooklyn after spending seven years in the South, I may not have known who *I* was, but I had a pretty good idea of what white people were, and what *they* thought *we* were.[33]

Langston Hughes and Milton Melzer have given us a promising publication in *A Pictorial History of the Negro in America* that makes many little-known facts of the Negro contribution to medicine, science, industry, arts, and political science available to schools. The contributions of Negroes in the fight for freedom from the Revolutionary War to the present are featured. But this is only one example of a much-needed classroom aid; we need a library of such readers for every grade level.

What the teacher expects and does not expect of his Negro students and how he perceives them can serve to stimulate or to stunt the aspiration level and the development of Negro students. In recognition of the stereotypes of the Negro and the white-black (good-bad) thinking and projections that victimize these students, as elaborated by Dr. Grambs, safeguards must be set up to prevent premature foreclosure—conscious or unconscious—of what the culturally disadvantaged Negro can do or how far he can reach. Progress of the Negro student will be limited until all teachers free themselves in the classroom from the judgments, the assumptions, and the prejudices with which adults—even professionals—have for a long time approached the matter of estimating the nature of the individual Negro pupil.

Attention has been focused in recent years on the education of teachers who work with culturally deprived youngsters. Riessman has indicated the following traits and skills essential to the effective instructor:

> The best type of teacher to win these children over to learning is a person of action who communicates in many ways and is not too dependent on words alone as a means of teaching. The leaders in the class and the rest of the children are likely to accept this type of person readily because he is close to the model after which they would like to pattern themselves. . . .
>
> The most successful teachers in terms of the culturally deprived children seem to combine the traditional concepts of structure, order, discipline, and strong external demands for achievement with the newer methods of down-to-earth learning by doing.[34]

Some consensus is visible within the Great Cities Projects suggesting that teachers in the deprived areas do need special understandings, skills, and insights concerning the social matrix in which the Negro and white youngsters live and the kinds of special learning problems they present. There is also agreement that this preparation cannot be carried on by the teacher-education institutions working in isolation; rather, it calls for joint effort in recruiting, planning, training, placement, and in-service support and supervision between the city school systems and the colleges preparing classroom personnel.

Improvement in instruction will call for a reevaluation of the teacher-education curricula cutting across three major areas: (1) the substantive area—teachers must be well grounded in their major areas of instruction; (2) special methods—teachers must acquire special skills via a practicum tied to a methods-theory course or courses to bring the prospective teacher into close classroom contact with the culturally deprived youngster, his family, and his neighborhood; and (3) self—an awareness of himself as a person with reference to the dynamics of the teacher's own behavior, including his needs, job satisfactions, reactions to others, and their reactions to him. It is this last area that is most neglected in the preparation or improvement of teaching personalities and of teaching competencies. Experiences in the study of self can come through individual counseling in the advisory or supervisory situations, through group counseling sessions, through human relations training, and through psychiatric consultations. As implied in the foregoing section, this third area is most in need of further discussion and exploration.

Special Services for Pupils and Teachers

The big-city school, with its large enrollment and broad base of financial support, can economically provide many special personnel services, including guidance, counseling, remediation, and health services. Teachers have real limits to their competencies in diagnosing and helping the socially inadapted pupils. There are also limits to the time that they can spend with the many individuals who need help. To this end, the big city must offer to the teacher the services of the school psychologist, psychiatrist, case worker, vocational counselor, school nurse or doctor, home visitors, etc. Too often such services tend to cluster at the secondary school level. They need to be equally available to the primary school staff, who are better able to put forth preventive effort with incipient problems.

The student personnel worker or counselor is a constant reminder of the inadequacies and malfunctioning of an overcrowded and perhaps overambitious school agency. He represents, in a sense, a community gesture to repair the wear and tear of an inadequate curriculum which does not accommodate to the wide span of needs, interests, and abilities represented in the big-city school; of the bigness and impersonality of the school; of inadequately trained and overworked teachers; and of sterile homes and strained family relationships. However, it is not enough to keep providing more and better personnel services in a valiant and expensive effort to prop up the classroom. It is imperative to shift the focus of the personnel services and attack the basic causes that result in a demand for these services in the first place. The long-term goal of school and student personnel services should not be more and better services; it should be the elimination or solution of the school-community problems that created the need for such services in the first place.[35]

As a relatively new innovation in the school, the counselor suffers from a strong urgency to succeed. Consequently, counselors are prone to accept any and every referral. They become omnibus functionaries who often promise more than they can deliver. They must be more selective and discriminating in the cases they undertake to serve and thus limit their mounting case loads. This will call for a clear understanding of their own competencies for dealing with certain types of cases and for a more realistic time concept in the rehabilitation process. Office-oriented sessions conducted two or three times a month will seldom effect any permanent change in school or out-of-school behavior.

Many of the problems of the nonlearner and norm violator take root in the curriculum. In trying to assist these youngsters, many counselors, case workers, and psychologists suffer severe job frustrations. Lacking a comprehensive and balanced curriculum, the best they can hope to accomplish is to persuade the disinterested and failing pupil to return and to adjust to what is basically an unsatisfactory and unpromising learning situation. Personnel workers can best serve their present and future clients by addressing themselves more and more to the improvement of the curriculum of the school. Otherwise the effectiveness of counseling, testing, social work, and attendance services will be severely circumscribed.

Counselors and psychologists frequently depend on tests to help adjust pupils to the tasks of the school. The indiscriminate and perfunctory use of standardized tests of ability, aptitude, and achievement with Negro students from culturally deprived neighborhoods has been the concern of many investigators. Use of a standardized measure with any subject must first satisfy the following three conditions: (1) the child must have had the same opportunity to learn as the normative group; (2) he must be equally motivated; and (3) he must have had equal practice in taking such tests. These conditions are imperfectly met by most Negro youngsters, which invalidates their test performances as bases from which to argue as to their abilities, achievements, etc. The problem of the hidden IQ and the undeveloped potential still awaits the development of culture-fair tools. Any permanent labeling of the Negro from his test performance on existing tools runs the risk of misclassification and of setting a low ceiling of expectation.

In counseling deviant pupils, personnel workers must be alert to exploit the unusual talent and the bizarre backgrounds of Negro youth rather than to prune them back to conform to classroom ritual and routine. Most guidance workers have fallen into the soft trap of uniformity and conformity as an ideal toward which all students should be trained. There is little space or sympathy for digression in the public schools today. Paradoxically, this cutting back to "normal pattern" (usually middle-class) via the routine guidance to conformity may actually defeat the counselor in his major aim, which is to develop each individual in accordance with his unique talents. Digression from the pedestrian pattern should be encouraged in the guidance process.

Guidance workers and other specialists must spread their influence to more pupils by working with and through the teaching staff. This can be accomplished if a mutual relationship of trust and respect exists between teachers and personnel workers. Many social workers, psychologists, and guidance workers could make their influence felt on a school-wide basis by conducting group counseling sessions for the staff and by creating opportunities for individual counseling of staff members.

Personnel workers cannot afford to "fly solo" or to act out their roles in discrete circles under the tent of the school. They need to fly in tight formation with other school workers and with professional personnel in the community who come in close contact with Negro youngsters and their families. This is in recognition of the teamwork principle, multiple causation, and the interdisciplinary approach to understanding, diagnosing, and adjusting the youngster in the need of help.

Finally, the personnel worker, if he is to be a practical and effective operative, must be research oriented—both as a consumer of research and as a director or participant in action research. Keeping up with the significant research and fact gathering is not an easy or simple task, especially for the busy practitioner who must do this on the run or on a marginal-time basis.

The School as a Cooperating Community Agency

There are multiple social-cultural-economic forces that have a strong impact on the Negro pupil, his family, and his school. Some of these include rapid immigration of lower-class socioeconomic groups into the inner city, who settle in the depressed and deteriorating areas; the steady influx of large numbers of rural families with little or no formal education or occupational skills; the exodus of white middle-class families to outlying areas and suburbs; the rapidly changing enrollments in neighborhood schools, creating conditions of *de facto* segregation; multiplication and concentration of families lacking a father and reflecting the pattern of a female-based household; high rates of unemployment among adults and especially among youth; limited employment opportunities, especially for Negro adults and Negro youth; and high rates of crime and juvenile delinquency.

These forces and movements involve problems of health, housing, employment, truancy, child welfare and protection, politics, leisure time, as well as schooling. Many of the educational problems of the young Negro stem from forces in the social matrix that are outside the control of the school agency. Again we must recognize the community nature of the problem and the limitations of the school agency, as it works alone or in isolation.

Implications for the school are twofold:

1. The school must reach out to the home and family of the Negro student and develop and maintain a close working relationship.
2. The school should serve as a central agency in a coordinated attack on the problems of the inner-city and culturally disadvantaged families via a multisided approach involving all community resources, including government agencies at all levels (local, state, national), housing, church, hospitals and clinics, police courts, mass media, labor, industry, etc.

We know that parents of Negro pupils living in culturally deprived areas do not evidence the close feeling for the schools that is so prominently visible in high socioeconomic neighborhoods in which the PTA flourishes. There are many reasons for this lack of communication. The schools are inferior, and the Negro knows it; so does the school staff. It is not easy to establish a relationship when one party is being shortchanged. Also, the Negro parent is helpless. His own education is lacking; his language and dress reflect his status in contrast to that of school personnel; he feels unacceptable; he lacks self-respect; there is no evidence in the home of intellectual interests; and he knows he will soon be moving, that his child will be in another school—no better and perhaps worse than this—so why bother.

School people know all this. They are very sensitive to the inadequacies of the school and to the lack of achievement; they feel guilty about it; and it is almost impossible to communicate across class barriers with inarticulate parents whose problems of living make school problems shrink to minor proportions. And most important, the school people rarely show any real knowledge of, or sensitivity to, the community in which they work. They commute to the day's task and return to their own suburban haven. There is no lingering in the neighborhood after the school day is over.

Sam M. Lambert, NEA Director of Research, in a review called the "Economic Status of Teachers" at the 101st NEA Convention in Detroit (1963), listed among the three major roadblocks to further progress "the widely held view that teaching is not a full-time job." Teaching Negro youngsters and working with their parents is a full-time job. It cannot be done by commuting teachers who leave the school in midafternoon. To get this job done, it may be necessary to subsidize teacher-family residences within the school neighborhood and to program detached-teacher workers on a full-working-day basis. Seeding the community with families of teachers can have other benefits and would easily justify the extra costs.

The school must reach out to the Negro home and family. It must begin the educational dialogue with them even before the child comes to school. A preparation for the school program should be set up, enlisting the cooperation of the parent. Materials need to be loaned to the home. It is important to note in the *Newsweek* survey (July 29, 1963) of the Negro in America, taken on a cross section of the Negro community across the nation, that 97 percent of the Negro parents stated that they wanted their children to complete high school, and a large proportion indicated that they thought their children were getting an inferior education. With this kind of mind set, the Negro parent may be much more ready to engage in educational dialogues with the school than the school is ready to admit or accept.

Let us return to the school's role as a cooperating agency working with other organizations in a coordinated program. Since no two neighborhoods or communities have the same problems or resources, local approaches to cooperative efforts will vary as to form and focus. In examination of community programs involving coordination and participation of all agencies, two principles manifest themselves: (1) there is need for full-time trained leadership to give direction to overall planning and action; and (2) although schools have been visible in cooperative community planning and action, few neighborhoods have yet felt the full force and power of their potential contribution to helping the Negro family and its school-going members.

Delmo Della-Dora, Deputy Superintendent of the Wayne County Board of Education, Detroit, Mich., has suggested an even more active role of leadership for school neighborhoods where little or nothing is being done to intervene:

> Schools should initiate action to see that the problems are attacked in a coordinated fashion if no other agency has already done so. In practice this means calling into being some kind of school-community planning group. Each high school could serve as the locus of activity. If not, whatever can be identified as natural communities within the city should form the basis for action groups. The questions to which a community planning group should address itself are:
>
> a. What is each of us doing to help raise the level of living in this community?
> b. Where do we see an inappropriate or unnecessary duplication of effort?
> c. In what areas can we, and should we, work together?
> d. What do we know about total community needs and problems? Which of these are not being met adequately? What

needs to be done? Who *should* do it now? Who *can* do it, in terms of financial and personal resources? What are the short term solutions and the longer term solutions to these unmet needs and unresolved problems?

A coordinated effort to solve total community problems spearheaded by school people does not imply that the schools should undertake to perform additional societal tasks, nor is it our intention to suggest that social agencies should take over functions of the individual or the family.[36]

Since coordination is such an acceptable principle, the question must be raised why we see so little of it. There is much in-fighting in school and community that reflects different philosophies, theories, practices, and emotional involvements and invested interests. These conflicts—sometimes covert, sometimes overt—can tend to drain off the administrators' and teachers' energies which should be better applied to helping the Negro youngsters. Many of these conflicts can be found along the following bipolar dimensions: action versus theory; rehabilitation versus restriction; centralization of services versus localization of services; subjectivity versus objectivity; student activity versus student passivity. Lack of any real coordination or teamwork can frequently be attributed to these conflict issues.

Summary

The school stance in working with the Negro pupil from the culturally disadvantaged home and neighborhood often reflects a variety of moods. The orientation can be repressive, or even retaliatory; it can reflect the helping hand of the humanist; it can breathe with messianic hope; it can counter with therapeutic aids, as found in the special services of the school and the child guidance clinics. In this paper, I have emphasized the cultural-reconstruction orientation as a working base line. This approach assumes that the basic problem in many—if not most—inner-city classrooms involves values and value systems. The cultural and subcultural determinants of behavior are studied, and the learner is viewed as reacting to the demands and the standards set up within his primary reference group as found in the family, gang, neighborhood, school, and community. Concern is expressed for the child's rule book as found in his milieu. Community forces—home, church, school, club—regard themselves as "change agents." This approach is only now making itself felt and promises a much-needed supplement to the more traditional school-community efforts.

Today many schools, caught in the press of the educational critics demanding more and better mathematicians, scientists, and linguists, appear more than willing to sell any misbehaving nonlearner down the river to preserve the academic reputation of the school. Little hope or help can be forthcoming from schools that are devoid of respect and redemptive love, that fail to provide a therapeutic climate, and that have little or no effect on the behavior or way of life of those they are committed to change through the educational growth process.

School personnel must work to develop greater differentiation of curriculum and instruction. In differentiating the curriculum, attention must be given to the current structure of the monolithic upper-middle-class curriculum that assumes that all high school pupils will become daily readers of the *New York Times* and will subscribe to the *Saturday Review* and will eventually turn out to be worthy alumni of some university or college—preferably of the Ivy League. Attention must be directed to the development of a meaningful curriculum for the nonmobile, or stable, lower-class youngster for whom middle-class goals do not represent reasonable or realistic goals. The core of this revised curriculum should center around the communications skills, leisure-time pursuits, husband-wife relationships, child-rearing skills, beginning job competencies, and social-civic responsibilities. Universal education will remain an American myth under present curriculum conditions. Indications are that the holding power of the public schools, presently graduating annually 60 out of 100 persons seventeen years of age, has probably reached its peak. Unless the curriculum is broadened, for many youngsters the American school will remain an ordeal to be sweated out.

In a rapidly changing socioeconomic-political scene, the schools must remain experimental, flexible, and fluid. Many critics of the American schools in the Rickover-Bestor tradition are urging "change and improvement" by regressing to the college-preparatory curriculum riveted to the "hard-core subjects" of mathematics, science, and languages. At most, only about 25 to 35 percent of the youth (a generous estimate) have the ability to profit from this traditional emphasis. This highly recommended and prestigious science-math-language diet will regurgitate defeat and frustration for most youngsters and will emit an early school dropout. Dropping out of school has been known to overlap with social inadaptation.

In addition to its time-honored function of transmitting the heritage and of developing the rational powers, the modern school must view itself an an agency for cultural renewal and change. The objectives of character development, worthy use of leisure, vocational training, worthy family membership, and civic and social competency must be placed in proper perspective as we raise the question, "What are we educating for?" and as we reexamine the objectives of the school against the needs of all pupils and the needs of our urbanized and technological society.

Furthermore, school objectives must be stated and evaluation of the school's program should be made in terms of development of new and desirable behaviors or the modification of old and undesirable behaviors.

If schools can modify the behaviors of large masses of children, thereby changing the culture (the way of life), they may ultimately live up to their potential as agents for cultural renewal and change. Otherwise the schools must face the imminent danger of becoming the most expensive irrelevancy in the American economy.

School staffs must direct their efforts to improve the subliminal, or covert, curriculum as found in the culture and subculture of the school. This is the way of life that sets up norms telling the youngster how to act and how not to act. The culture of the school society is frequently characterized by sex-crossed activities, delayed and postponed responsibility, learning by clock and by calendar, homogeneous age-grade-class-status groupings, undetermined or unspecified goals, external controls, and compulsory learning. All of these combine to make up a way of school life which varies from school to school and from community to community, but which is always effective in determining how a pupil will behave or misbehave.

The surrogate role of the teacher must be maximized. Who wants to be like the teacher? Many teachers do, and more could, serve as imitative examples in the old tradition of hero models by developing strong interpersonal relationships. With the threat of oversize classrooms, teaching machines, and listless mentors looming, anonymity, impersonality, and boredom can combine to emit a school dropout, if not a delinquent.

For those youngsters who manifest learning difficulties and symptoms of social-emotional maladjustment, the school must procure and maintain certain special and essential services. The teacher's time and competencies are limited. He needs the help of the school nurse, the school doctor, the counselor, the psychologist, and the case worker. To the usual array of services, we need to add those of a social analyst. Drawn from the disciplines of sociology and cultural anthropology, this functionary would aim to help school personnel to understand the society of the school and the cultural and subcultural currents within the school and the community. This social scientist would be concerned primarily with the dynamics of behavior as found in the individual's mileus and would serve as a strong complement to the psychologists or guidance workers who tend to concern themselves almost exclusively with psychic determinants of behavior.

The principal, school counselor, and school social worker must provide therapeutic counseling for the staff. Teachers are persons and, like their pupils, they also have problems. When a problem-laden teacher meets a problem-laden pupil, watch out for behavioral explosions. Teaching a large class of different and often difficult pupils day in and day out makes unusual demands on the teaching personality. When the going gets rough, teachers need ready access to an accepting and understanding administrator or counselor to whom they can gripe, beef, remonstrate, and unload. If relationships with staff are positive and of a nonjudgmental nature, these functionaries should be able to play the therapeutic-listening role of the good administrator or supervisor. In this way the principal's office can become a comfortable listening post or haven for the overworked, hard-pressed, harassed, and unhappy teacher. This is the easiest form of counseling and one that can do the least damage. If no one on the teaching staff ever comes by to discuss his problems with the administrator or supervisor on his own initiative, it is probably the administrator who needs help.

In summary, there is no one thing that the school, acting by itself, can do that will make any great difference in the self-concept of Negro youth and in their social adjustment. In a sense, the school's responsibility toward the Negro does not differ from its responsibility to every and any learner or nonlearner. He is not a code number on a computer card or a cumulative record. The Negro youngster is a growing and sensitive person. He has a face and a name—and feelings. He is surrounded like other children by parents, peers, teachers, and youth workers. All of these individuals are in a strategic position to help him or to hurt him. The Negro does not live in a vacuum. He learns, he plays, he works, or he finds refuge in a culture or subculture. The realities that he must face and the values that he inherits are seldom of his own making or shaping. Yet he must learn to face his reality, to adjust to it, and sometimes even to change it if he is to survive in the depths of the big decaying city or even in the highly waxed environment of a new suburbia. Not unlike the terrible plight of the "little boys for little chimneys" of Charles Dickens's day, the American Negro, caught in the impersonal and technological culture of today's industrial society, represents a big boy struggling in a big chimney. The opportunity and the responsibility to help the cultural disadvantaged rests not just with every youth and family worker but with every American citizen, and especially with every parent and every school worker.

References

1. James Baldwin, *The Fire Next Time,* New York, The Dial Press, Inc., 1963, pp. 32–33.
2. Baldwin, *Nobody Knows My Name,* New York, Dell Publishing Co., Inc., 1961, pp. 101–102.
3. Anna Freud, *Psychoanalysis for Teachers and Parents* (Barbara Low, Translator), Boston, The Beacon Press, 1960, p. 45.
4. Frank Riessman, "Teaching the Culturally Deprived," *NEA Journal,* April, 1963, p. 22.
5. David P. Ausubel, "How Reversible Are the Cognitive and Motivational Effects of Cultural Deprivation? Implications for Teaching the Culturally Deprived Child," Urbana, Ill., University of Illinois Bureau of Educational Research, p. 15. (Paper presented at the Conference on the Teaching of the Culturally Deprived Child, Buffalo, N.Y., March 28–30, 1963.)
6. *Ibid.,* pp. 15–16.

7. Kenneth B. Clark, "Educational Stimulation of Racially Disadvantaged Children," and Martin P. Deutsch, "The Disadvantaged Child and the Learning Process," in *Education in Depressed Areas,* A. Harry Passow (ed.), New York, Bureau of Publications, Teachers College, Columbia University, 1963; Frank Riessman, *The Culturally Deprived Child,* New York, Harper & Row, Publishers, 1962; Deborah Partridge Wolfe, "Curriculum Adaptations for the Culturally Deprived," *Journal of Negro Education,* Spring, 1962; Patricia Sexton, *Education and Income: Inequalities in Our Public Schools,* New York, The Viking Press, Inc., 1961; Albert Reiss and Albert Lewis Rhodes, "Are Educational Norms and Goals of Conforming, Truant and Delinquent Adolescents Influenced by Group Position in American Society?" *Journal of Negro Education,* Summer, 1959, pp. 252-267; Robert J. Havighurst and Lindley J. Stiles, "A Statement of National Policy for Alienated Youth," *Phi Delta Kappan,* April, 1961.

8. Deutsch, *ibid.,* p. 177.

9. Burton Blatt, *Educating Intelligence: A Study in the Prevention of Mental Retardation,* New York, John Wiley & Sons, Inc., 1965. A report of an experimental two-year study with retarded children from a culturally deprived area.

10. Dorothy B. Jones, "The Language of Our Time," *Quarterly of Film, Radio, and Television,* Winter, 1955, p. 176.

11. Langston Hughes and Milton Melzer, *A Pictorial History of the Negro in America,* New York, Crown Publishers, Inc., 1963, p. 340.

12. Dexter Tilroe, "Holding Power in the Six-Year Secondary School in New York," doctoral dissertation, New York, New York University, 1952.

13. William C. Kvaraceus, "The Behavioral Deviate in the Culture of the Secondary School," *Frontiers of Secondary Education* (III), Paul M. Halverson (ed.), Syracuse, N. Y., Syracuse University Press, 1958, pp. 18–27. ——— "Helping the Socially Inadapted Pupil in the Large City Schools," *Exceptional Children,* April, 1962, pp. 399–404.

14. Margaret Mead, *The School in American Culture,* Cambridge, Mass., Harvard University Press, 1951.

15. Edgar Z. Friedenberg, "The Image of the Adolescent Minority," *Dissent,* Spring, 1963, p. 148.

16. *Ibid.,* p. 150.

17. James S. Coleman, *The Adolescent Society,* New York, The Free Press of Glencoe, 1961. Note here the prestige values attached to sports and popularity over the academic, and Edgar Z. Friedenberg's interpretation in a recent issue of the *College Board Review* vindicating the adolescents' value systems against the reality of the academic requirement of high school.

18. Henry W. Riecken, *The Volunteer Work Camp: A Psychological Examination,* Reading, Mass., Addison-Wesley Publishing Company, Inc., 1952, pp. 30–31.

19. Robert Coles, *The Desegregation of Southern Schools: A Psychiatric Study,* New York, Anti-Defamation League of B'nai B'rith, and Atlanta, Ga., Southern Regional Council, July, 1963.

20. Sexton, *op. cit.*

21. A. B. Hollingshead, *Elmtown's Youth,* New York, John Wiley & Sons, Inc., 1949.

22. William C. Kvaraceus, *Juvenile Delinquency and the School,* New York, Harcourt, Brace & World, Inc., 1945. ——— *The Community and the Delinquent,* New York, Harcourt, Brace & World, Inc., 1954.
23. David Segel, *Frustration in Adolescent Youth,* U.S. Office of Education Bulletin 1951, no. 1, 1951, p. 65.
24. National Education Association, Research Division, "Teacher Opinion on Pupil Behavior 1955–56," *Research Bulletin,* April, 1956, pp. 51–107.
25. Fletcher G. Watson, "The Hero Image in Education," *Bulletin,* Harvard Graduate School of Education Association, Fall, 1962, p. 1. Reprinted from *Science Education,* December, 1961.
26. Coles, *op. cit.,* p. 24.
27. *Ibid.,* p. 17.
28. James Baldwin, "You've Done Everything You Can to Me . . . ," Conversation with Mr. Baldwin taped by WGBH-TV, Boston, Mass.
29. Joseph Adelson, "The Teacher as a Model," *The American Scholar,* Summer, 1961, p. 389.
30. *Ibid.,* p. 394.
31. Irving Lukoff, Franklin K. Patterson, and Charles Winick, "Is Society the Patient? Research and Action Implications," *The Journal of Educational Sociology,* October, 1956, pp. 106–107.
32. *Ibid.,* p. 107.
33. Lena Horne, "I Just Want to be Myself," *Show,* September, 1963, p. 62.
34. Riessman, *The Culturally Deprived Child, op. cit.,* pp. 21–22.
35. William C. Kvaraceus, "The Status and Function of Personnel Services," *Education,* vol. 81, December, 1960, pp. 202-209.
36. Delmo Della-Dora, "The Culturally Disadvantaged: Educational Implications of Certain Social-Cultural Phenomena," *Exceptional Children,* May, 1962, p. 470.

Discussion, Comments, and Issues

All discussants looked to the school agency as the central and strategic resource for upgrading the self-concept of Negro youth. The schools were viewed as the major—and in some cases the only—avenue through which the slum child, Negro or white, could work his way out and overcome his dual environmental handicaps found in the prejudices surrounding him and in the inadequacies of his cultural background. The conviction was expressed in all groups that somehow the American schools, if they were to justify their very existence, should greatly accelerate the processes of assimilation, self-realization, and adjustment.

Although all participants agreed that the educative process is greatly complicated for the Negro youngster from the big-city or rural slums whose homes and neighborhoods are characterized by poverty, instability, conflict, and exploitation, no universal agreements were forthcoming as to the crucial factors in the dynamics of the Negro youngsters' handicaps to learning nor of the exact role the school should or could play in overcoming the many obstacles. But one conviction was ever present: *the school had an important role, and it could do much more to help the Negro to realize himself.*

Most of the discussion that stemmed from a consideration of the third working paper on the role of the school has been organized around the following major issues:

1. Class status, values, and schools
2. The school as an agent of change
3. The curriculum and the teacher
4. Limitations on the role of the school

Early in the discussion, the group was warned about the vicious talking cycles and the need for the schools—and every other agency—to break through the circular argument that stalls action. The school agency can be a most strategic force. Every agency must make a start, and schools can start with textbooks or with token integration; but start they must, lest they get caught on dead center and be verbally immobilized.

> "Frequently we have talked about vicious cycles and we've used this kind of phraseology: 'You can't do this without doing that,' 'You can't do thus unless you do so'; and it seems to me in considering this whole theory I have come more and more strongly to feel that this is not helpful when you are formulating the problem, because it invariably leads us into inaction and letting the status quo prevail.
>
> "Here is the obvious argument which is made: the educational situation is attributable to the housing situation, but the housing situation in turn is attributable to the economic situation; and in turn the economic situation is attributable to the educational situation. There you have a nice circle, and you can't cut in. It seems to me that every institution, every institution of society, has to tackle the problem insofar as it concerns itself."

> "It seems to me that the school can start in one way with its textbooks. I am very conscious of this as a history teacher. The Negro is considered only as a slave before the Civil War and a problem since the Civil War. Now this is taught not only to Negroes but to everybody. Hence most students come up with this idea that if you could present a true picture about the Negro's place in history, it would change concepts on both sides. We've also found in Atlanta that concepts have been changed as a result of school integration. As you know, we don't achieve total integration, but even where you've had

three or four Negroes in an all-white school, you find evidence of change of concepts and attitudes. I think the schools can start doing something about this. They may not be able to solve the whole thing, but it's going to have to begin in the schools, because this is where we can reach people and change attitudes much more readily than you can in the communities at large."

Class Status, Values, and Schools

Some of the participants raised the questions: "Why the Negro revolution and ferment now?" and "Why are we having the consciousness of the revolution at this time? What does this imply for schools?" As one behavioral scientist put it:

"Despite the just complaint about a hundred years of gradualism, things have been happening for a hundred years—by no means rapidly enough—but what is it that is rubbing on what, just now, that creates such an extreme awareness of friction? I think we can answer that and direct the answer rather closely to what the school represents. I think the real reason that we are getting so much overt conflict—violence and everything else now—is that for the first time a relatively large proportion of Negro Americans are attempting to consolidate essentially lower-middle-class status. The previous status pyramid left most Negroes below this, and those who were not, if you look back at their patterns of achievement, I suspect almost tended to by-pass this particular status. They were very few in number. There was no confrontation at the lower-middle-class level. Even now, of course, I should think many people would verify this from their own experience. There is hardly any difficulty at relatively high status levels provided the Negro candidate has somehow managed to avoid being destroyed in the process of getting there. It's rather easy, comparatively at least, for upper-status academics or people rather well placed in the arts. At this point the conflicts don't arise.

"It's been corroborated a great deal that it *is* in lower middle class that you find the most repressive, most antiliberal—I can't call it conservative; it's nothing of the sort and never has been—the most punitive, hostile, and also passive ideology, not merely with reference to race but with reference to anything else. If you think back to what you know about the F scale and the authoritarian personality, you will remember that the great intellectual tour de force is that they were able to predict and identify these extremely authoritarian characters, in both senses of the word, from items that had to do with no ideology whatever, but only with diffuse interpersonal hostility. Your real anti-Negro individual, then, is a person who agrees with items like 'The sex life of the ancient Greeks and Romans is nothing to what goes on around here and sometimes where you would least expect it,' or 'Most of us will never know how many decisions about us are taken in smoke-filled rooms.' The whole constellation which is now being fought head on—there is at least some consolation that this bumpy bit of air is after all only a stratum, dangerous as it is. But it's not going to be like that when you get above it. On the other hand, it's an awfully pervasive stratum: these people are to be found in every Western developed country and, I suspect, in Eastern developed countries, too. For example, the Russian Decency Police do manifest themselves on beaches, in cafes where jazz might be played, and stuff like that. So that there is, in short, a crisis now partly because Negroes in large numbers are bucking the area where, in large numbers, the neo-Fascists are.

"Now the other aspect of this which seems to me to be so important—which may produce rather a mixed response among the group, depending on their primary group affiliations—I would say that the school has become, generally speaking, the instrument of this lower middle class—a highly constricted and rather passive group."

But if the social class representation here is so constricted, a question must be raised of what school people are really like and what are the characterological modes of the school. Granted that all school teachers are different, of course there are still central tendencies; and central tendencies become institutionalized—certain kinds of behavior become reinforced. Now answering the question:

"My own impression of most of the public educational institutions that I know of—this would be true to a certain extent at the college level where the place is run rather like a high school—is that the general pervasive atmosphere is of a kind of defensive, narcissistic, passive hostility which strikes you in the face as soon as you come in. The ways of being hostile are—well, they're rather like the ways of the jellyfish: you send out nematocysts that sting people, but at the same time you turn in on yourself.

"There is a paper-barrier set of procedures which are designed not only to keep people and pupils at bay but to keep the administrative staff from having to become really aware of the realities of life in school and out. There is little or no tendency for any real interaction to develop. People just withdraw, in effect, from each other more and more. But there are always small kinds of friction that cannot be resolved.

"One thing that I found out working with high school students disturbed me quite a bit. The kids, in talking to me about my interview materials and the study I was doing, would occasionally raise questions. One of their responses was, 'Well, I'm not sure if this is what they want. I'm not sure if this is what they're getting at.' It was very noticeable that they never said *you*. It was quite inconceivable to them that an actual agent—somebody who was really doing something—had appeared at this place to do it himself. They knew, of course, that this was a cooperative research division project, so I take it they felt that they were really too unimportant. I know that a good many people who get research grants do hire field workers rather than do the actual field work; but it was mostly, I think, that the artificiality of the situation—as they understood it—precluded their even assuming that anyone who was real in the external world could have found their way into the place at all. I had to be something like the unicorn, at best, and quite possibly not even that—maybe simply a myth, or somebody who had been sent in to do a job. I don't know; they didn't even raise that kind of question.

"As to the time schedule and the clock—I had terrible difficulty with that in every high school I've been at. You couldn't schedule in the ordinary way, because the kids didn't know what time it was or would be. They knew what period it was, but since the interviewing didn't follow periods exactly—I mean it just didn't work out that length of time—they were allowed as much time as they needed—I had to keep having people waiting all over the place. I couldn't ask them to come at particular clock hours as they just didn't know what they would have when, what they wanted to cut or when they had study halls. In the fantasy and ritual of school, there was little or no contact with the realties on many dimensions, including time."

Some concerns had been expressed concerning the conservatism—even anti-intellectualism—of many classroom teachers. Other participants wondered whether the complaints of Conant[1] and Koerner[2] concerning the education and miseducation of American teachers would have a traumatic effect on many teachers—particularly those who had received much of their preparation in normal schools, teachers colleges, schools of education, and/or on a part-time basis. It was pointed out by other members that, regardless of the effect on teachers, most of whom were already inured to the quips and complaints of their many critics, most of them did come from the lower classes and retained many of the lower-middle-class characteristics. What Conant and Koerner are really saying is that more teachers should be recruited from the upper-middle class to begin with, although they dare not say it directly.

> "When they [Conant and Koerner] complain, say, about the part-time teacher and leave her feeling like a second-class citizen, what they're really saying, of course, is that people who come up with the experiences of wanting to be upward-mobile into this system and this kind of a life from an even lower status—that they are, in fact, likely to have certain characteristics that go along with it that are partly the result of what their part-time education didn't do, but are more likely to be the result of what their upbringing did do—that will make them the kind of person among whom general propositions—liberal thought—not in the sense of an ideology, but a free play of ideas—who, in other words, are quite likely to act in the way that I have been talking about. But certainly this isn't a universal principle.
>
> "I fear that Conant and Koerner were as reluctant as we are, and unfortunately so, to talk openly and directly about social class and its implications for Negro education. You can talk about segregation, because it obviously exists and therefore it can be viewed as bad. It is bad, but it can be viewed. Whereas social class we can continue to pretend doesn't exist in our democracy."

> "The social-class characteristic of the teacher is, I fear, what they are really complaining about when they say, 'If you don't want teachers to be educated or "trained" in the way that they are, look for people, then, with higher social background,' i.e., those who didn't have to get their education piecemeal or on the side."

The Negro participants stressed over and over again that the problems of the Negro were more than a class problem. They were adamant in the thesis that the Negro's problem was anchored to the race problem and that his handicaps in school and community were bound by the chains of the caste system. Most of the white members of the Conference appeared to agree with their Negro counterparts, that is, those white members who were really listening and hearing. The Conference strongly rejected the Bettelheim[3] thesis that the confusion in American white-Negro relations stems from an unwillingness to separate a class problem from a race or caste problem. The theme that the Negro's problem was more than a problem of class, that it was compounded by caste and poverty, but differed essentially from the problems of the lower-class whites, was reiterated regularly. The following comments reflect this conviction:

"Social class is not unimportant. The question of poverty in this country is an urgent problem. What we are saying with respect to race is, and if we are going to look at the Negroes in this country, we can't be misled by the references and the commonality of this group to a lower class. We must also be very much aware of the caste status of this group, of what has happened to a people who for three or four hundred years have had a consistently negative treatment in a given society.

"But at the same time as we look at caste and class, we must recognize that most Negroes are poor; and we've also got to look at the fact that poverty in this country is a major problem."

"The people who object to our talking about poverty also object to our talking about race, because they are so closely tied together, and we don't solve one without the other."

Problems of the teacher's role and autonomy in the school system were discussed in relation to decisions and opportunities for upward mobility: freedom of movement and freedom of choice that can come only when caste restrictions have been withdrawn. There is an opportunity for fundamental change and improvement in the educational system within the present crises.

"But you only get change under a particular set of conditions, and that condition seems to be whether the power structure, particularly the superintendent in the individual school, is going to allow the teacher to have the same kind of active role that the teacher should be asking the child to have; and unless you go from one stage to the next stage, you can't have effective modification of the system taking place where the child's been capsulated or the teacher's been capsulated. You must have changes within the very structure of the power system. This goes back to the original remarks in terms of the nature of the crisis. There is an opportunity within this crisis for preparation of, for introduction of, fundamental changes in the system.

"Changes in the system will be demanded by the Negro community, because it's absolutely necessary if children are to be prepared in jumping social-class barriers and overcoming caste limitations; they have to be prepared for the automated kind of future that's taking place. They can only be prepared with the types of programs that will result in a metamorphosis in the system.

"There's just one other point on this that has come up again and again—that social class has to be understood, that when we deal with the Negro revolution, we're dealing with a caste and class problem; but we're dealing with a problem where many people, many lower-white-class people, have made a decision that they're going to stay lower class. Many Negroes might make the same kind of decision. Sometimes it would be voluntary, sometimes it would be built into the system; but the thing that we're striving for, the Negro community is striving for, is the freedom to move any place in the social status without there being any caste restriction.

"One other point: there were specific suggestions, and I just want to give one illustration of the kind of possibilities that exist. We had some discussion of the importance of the community, and I gave an example of an experience that we had last year on a pilot group of 150 parents in which we found out—it goes back to the whole question of self-image—that the parents had no pictures of their children. We found out that 80 percent of the children had never seen a picture of themselves. It's a kind of gimmick, but it's something that also works. We took pictures of every single child in some kind of intellectual activity—working an alphabet board, reading a book, with the tape recorder. We gave the pictures to the children and had amazing behavioral reactions. Children would say, 'That's me! That's me!' It was real excitement. But more important than that, we gave pictures to the parents, put the pictures on the wall and on the furniture. The attendance at our parents' meetings went up from 25 percent to about 75 percent, mostly mothers, of course, after this one instance of showing some kind of interest in the home.

"It's interesting the extent to which you can get parental cooperation. There has been some expression that Negro parents are often reluctant to cooperate. I think that the reluctance is initial reluctance until you have won a certain amount of trust and demonstrated that you have something to give which can be meaningful in terms of their high aspiration level, not for themselves, but for their child. Now when you've demonstrated that, the parent will come along and will be very helpful."

The School as an Agent of Change

Strong exception was taken in some quarters to the concept of the role and function of the school as an agent of change. The myth of a monolithic middle-class society and the predominant and exclusive commitment of the schools to preparing middle-class citizens had been questioned. "Should not the schools also prepare for a law-abiding and honorable estate of lower-classness," asked an educator, "without at the same time closing off or narrowing the avenue to a middle-class way of life?" Someone else asked the provocative question: "Is it possible that the Freedom Marchers will discover that they have really lost some freedoms once they have marched into the middle-class pit?" Strong convictions and stronger feelings are visible in the following comments stemming from these concerns:

> "And it bothers me when I hear that programs ought to be geared down to lower-class objectives, because many of these Negroes are in the lower class not because they want to be, but because they are forced to be, because of the caste system. We ought to be more careful lest we lower the ceiling as a result of our high school curriculum. I'm thinking of my own situation. I teach in a Negro college, a very poor college because it is a private, church-supported school. We get people from rural Georgia, and these are by no means middle-class people. They're likely to be upper-lower class. And they need encouragement rather than the kind of arrangement that would gear them only to lower-middle class."

A Negro parent stated rather bluntly:

> "If you're hungry most of the time, if you don't have the opportunities, if you lack the material things, the middle class is attractive to you. I don't care whether or not my kids wear the middle-class label, although they do show it. But I do want to make sure they have a choice. And unless, again, the school provides this, it's not going to come any other way."

The following lengthy comment pushes the question of middle-class values and sharply questions the school's ability to function as an agent of change and the desirability or the possibility of specifying educational goals and outcomes, particularly under the general headings of diversity and nonconformity. Implicitly the school agency is seen in its time-honored role of transmitter of the culture. The question remains: Can the school also play a second role, the role of a change agent?

> "I've been struck by how often this eminently middle-class group has been willing to insult the middle class. That is not surprising, because everyone knows about the middle class; one of the features of the middle class is its consummate art in insulting itself. In fact, the middle-class intellectual learns very quickly what's wrong with the middle class and utilizes it. It always seems to me that we avoid the use of the term *middle class*. I think we ought to broaden our sense of what the middle class has always been. And one of the truths, it seems to me, about the middle class is that it uses criticism of itself to main-

tain itself exactly as it was. It's a telling truth. One of the things the middle class learns very quickly is to assimilate its critics and utilize criticism of itself by way of maintaining itself."

"Now we talk about nonconformity. Can we really be very explicit about what goals we want by way of nonconformity? I would like to suggest that one thing you cannot do with the nonconformist is to indoctrinate him into the future. When you're really dealing with nonconformity, you haven't got the slightest idea what goals you are to expect of the nonconformist because, in fact, it is you and me and the school system which he is being nonconformist about. What I find is an obsessive, detailed categorization of goals, which seems to me the ultimate conformity. What you're asking children is that they approximate not a person, but a label. Whether that label is located in the past or the future, it is no less a conformity to a category. And I am frightened, frankly, by this appropriation of goals as if we really knew what tomorrow would be; not only appropriation of these goals, but a formulation presumably of an educational system which would approximate these goals. If we believed in freedom in this sense and nonconformity, we would not have the slightest notion of what to expect.

"A school system which is doing its duty should be one which is trying to discover and, in fact, value its own tradition. Call it middle class, that's an insult; call them the Judaeo-Christian heritage, that's modish; call them what you will. What good is a school system which is so rhetorically committed to the sickness of the system and to the ease with which it can be criticized? We speak about character in our teachers and heroes. It seems to me it's not a question of making a personality—this too is indoctrination into the future. It's giving people a commitment, a conscious understanding of what is valuable and then, in presenting what is valuable about it, if the student wishes to be nonconformist, let him be nonconformist over and against it and let him not be crushed by the show of aggressiveness."

"It's my hunch that you cannot begin to control culture at the level, subtle and deep, at which the Kvaraceus paper comprehends and probes it. It might be that a more frontal, more ignorant, more aggressive, and a more moral frontal attack upon this system would accomplish the very changes which are described so delicately, but which seem, to me, admit of no manipulation whatsoever. What I wish to know is not whether we are going to change the roles of the school or whether the school is going to face up to what has been in fact the complicity in injustice which has been the role of the American school. If there is going to be an awareness in the school, let it be an awareness of the values of justice and injustice. If there's going to be self-consciousness, let it be self-consciousness of its own complicity, not of its ability just for having a conference to institute changes. Schools ought to be discovering their heritage and tradition and they ought to be themselves in that sense, making people nonconformists over and against them if they wish, if they have the power and if they have the values of a human being."

An expert in comparative education responded that the basic question raised by the Kvaraceus paper was no longer a hypothetical or theoretical question; nor was it a matter of academic opinion or debate. Recent changes in industrial societies with mass education had demonstrated in the United States and other countries that the schools are already in fact helping to build a new social order.

"Counts[4] raised the question: Dare the schools, can the schools, build a new social order in the thirties? I'm not so sure that this is a hypothetical question any longer. In examination of political structures in Western European industrialized countries, one finds that the school geared to mass education has only been around for a few generations—it's a relatively new phenomenon. At the same time, there are some things we can say about the process of education that don't seem to be a matter of opinion as they perhaps were back in the thirties. We do know that as a country industrializes, there is mass education—I know of no exceptions. We do know that as the school age goes up, the curriculum becomes broader; we do know that groups previously excluded are included as the culture becomes increasingly interdependent, economically, socially, and politically, regardless of what the past relations are of people of different races, ethnic groups, or religions. Perhaps there is some kind of an emotion or direction in terms of an increased inclusiveness in this complex, interdependent culture. Perhaps the Negro revolution is, in part, a revolution that's been repeated several times as in England, Germany, USSR with other minority or divergent groups.

"I wonder if the question that was raised in the thirties is debatable today. In the industrialized society, inevitably we begin to raise questions in educational theory about who can learn. We find periodically that the nature-nurture controversy is resolved. Each time a group breaks loose, lurches again toward some kind of greater franchise politically, socially, and economically, the question of intelligence or the capacity to be creative has been revived, particularly in urban areas, now focusing upon the Negro as another group seeks greater involvement. I don't think the nature-nurture question is really a fruitful one to raise any longer. I think the school is involved, whether it likes it or not, in the process of constructing a new social order."

In addition to transmitting the heritage, the school agency has taken on an added responsibility which it could no longer avoid without becoming an anachronism or an expensive irrelevancy. A goalless school agency is difficult to conceive and would not be worth maintaining unless it made a difference in the present and future lives of Negroes and whites. One of the basic goals of the school is to make differing students even more different through the process of self-realization. For the Negro, this means that the schools should aim to ensure his self-realization and identification by becoming even more a Negro rather than a copy of a middle-class white.

Baldwin, in his "Talk to Teachers," pointed out that ". . . one of the paradoxes of education was that precisely at the point when you begin to develop conscience, you must find yourself at war with your society. It is your responsibility to change society if you think of yourself as an educated person," he told the New York City teachers.

In the same address, he comments on the purpose of education and stresses the need to examine and to change society—no matter what the risk:

> The purpose of education, finally, is to create in a person the ability to look at the world for himself, to make his own decisions, to say to himself this is black or this is white, to decide for himself whether there is a God in heaven or not. To ask questions of the universe, and then learn to live with those questions, is the way he achieves his own identity. But no society is really anxious to have that kind of person around. What societies really, ideally, want is a citizenry which will simply obey the rules of society. If a society succeeds in this, that society is about to perish. The obligation of anyone who thinks of himself as responsible is to examine society and try to change it and to fight it—at no matter what risk. This is the only hope society has. This is the only way societies change.[5]

Apprehensions were expressed lest the schools be used by special-interest groups to achieve certain objectives. The need for free and open discussions on all issues, including the Negro problems, is recommended, without propagandizing. It is suggested that the Negro movement can become an educational device to be used by the school in aiding and abetting the learning processes.

> "I was a little bit taken aback by some of these remarks, and a little frightened by them, because it seems that now we are frankly saying that public schools are to be utilized directly to aid and abet the Negro revolution, which I would personally wish and do; but there are hard questions which educators must face when they so frankly select and so consciously utilize their teaching material in order to effect change. Now to raise a concrete question. Suppose in the pursuit of infinitely greater frankness in the schools and freedom of discussion, certain materials are introduced. . . . Let's put it this way: the local NAACP is dissatisfied with the class discussion, which to them doesn't seem to be forwarding the movement. The point is that if you're going to be really frank and have teachers pursuing the problem, the way teachers ought to pursue problems, then you've got to take some lumps with some advantages in presenting all the facts. All the material isn't going to be pleasant, and all the material isn't going to forward the movement. In any case, are we going to now have watchdogs over the curriculum of the school from the civil rights groups and the NAACP, even as we deplore such watchdogs in other connections?
>
> "Well, I think there are two quite different aspects, one to say that any particular line will be pursued, and on the other hand to say that a particular issue—in this case, the Negro issue—will be pursued in all its ramifications. This means allowing in the classroom situation, or in any other situation, for the expression of negative attitudes. I think if we don't get the negative attitudes expressed in the classroom, it's a lousy job that's being done, because no one can tell me that the vast majority of the American population is in love with the Negro. No one can tell me that. It's not true. So the negative feelings have to come out, they have to be expressed—all the reservations, all the anger, all the hostility—all these feelings have to come out so that they can be dealt with. Without this, you're just not facing the problem. I would say it's not a question of standing guard and saying, 'This must be discussed in this way, or else,' but rather, 'This must be discussed.' "
>
> "But then you need skilled people to reflect this and to channel it."
>
> "Yes, otherwise it would be interpreted as aiding and abetting the revolution."

"No, it's going to be interpreted as aiding and abetting the counterrevolution, which is really the point I'm making. Yes, I think you have to have the faith that the truth will make you free with a vengeance, to take it. My own feeling about civil rights groups is that they wouldn't be a problem because, well, take your example of the NAACP. They'd be so delighted that there was a free discussion finally in the public school system that they'd be prepared to take the lumps once they were assured that the whole thing was in good faith. I didn't mean to imply that the educational system would then be essentially the tool of the revolution. I was saying it just as much or more so the other way. The revolution is a tool for the educational system, to teach many, many things which are now being taught, but not successfully, because they're not hooked into anything that's meaningful and relevant."

On this issue, Havighurst[6] has noted two major functions of schools in relation to society:

> First, it is a stabilizer or perpetuator of the society, and second, it is an agent for change. As a stabilizer, education mirrors what is already in the society and reflects it into the lives of the next generation. As an agent of change, education acts under the direction of technological or ideological forces to make each generation different from its parents.

Havighurst offers the opinion that the "kinds of social change most effectively promoted by education are those (1) which can be taught readily, and (2) which the society generally approves." In contrast, therefore, the areas of social change least open to educational influence are those in which "there is (1) a taboo, or (2) a controversy."[7]

Since there is so much taboo and controversy concerning the Negro in the educational, social, economic, and political spheres, it should not be surprising that questions which concern the school's opportunity —even responsibility—for advancing change and improvement for Negro youth and adults should impel violent and irrational reactions in many quarters. As Havighurst insightfully points out, school personnel generally tend either to ignore such issues or to play it safe, which usually means conservatively and in such a way as to avoid change. In this sense, resolution of the Negro controversy will not be aided by the school without reorientation to its potential role as an agent of change.

The Curriculum and the Teacher

The Educational Policies Commission in its recent report, *Education and the Disadvantaged American*,[8] indicated that the successful school program must attack the problems of the culturally handicapped on three fronts simultaneously: it must demonstrate to pupils a close relationship between school and life; it must include the remedial services that will ensure academic progress; and it must arouse aspirations which can alter constructively the courses of young lives. Throughout the Conference, many concerns and recommendations could be heard in these three areas, as the excerpts below will bear out.

Of major concern to the membership were such factors as the unreality and meaninglessness of a large part of the school curricula for many Negro youngsters, the pressing need to develop and improve reading competencies, the need for hero models among teaching staff and especially in the male category, the restrictive and disabling effects of low ceiling of opportunity on levels of aspiration of pupils.

A young Negro educator expressed some of these concerns in the following fashion:

> ". . . curriculum has an essential element of irreality for most kids; that is, it seems to lack a future. Much of the experiences through which we put kids in our schools are meaningless to them, immediately perhaps, and certainly in the long run."

> "But I wonder how much we are keeping in mind the limited and limiting framework within which the Negro youngster lives. There is a low ceiling under which the Negro operates. He is too adjusted—or too used—to this, so much so that it will affect what we will hear when we talk with him, when we get him to talk out, or when his parents try to talk out. Their vision has been limited, and this will limit seriously what he wants to get out of school, what kind of life, what kind of child we want. We tend to overlook this continuing effect of the low ceiling on the youngsters. Not enough consideration has been given to this factor. This is evidenced by the Kvaraceus paper when it talks about three different types of Negro: the one who is on the way to middle class through the one who is very firmly entrenched in a lower-class way of life. This is in itself, I think, an admission of the fact that you have left this ingredient out as one of your overriding concerns in the Negro culture and in terms of what you can do with many Negro youngsters. How do we expect, in view of the constancy of the low and repressed ceiling which the youngster is very aware of—how do we expect to bring the youngster out from under and into the full enjoyment and participating membership of an unburdened class citizenship?"

> "Generally speaking, however, the lower-class and upper-class youngsters have many values and aims in common, al-

> though the differences in their opportunities or resources for attaining them, of course, result in totally different styles of living. But in both cases, the orientation is likely to be more subjective; that is, you are less interested in getting a good credential out of the people who observe you and more interested in what you are told to do by your own inner life. Now if you're an upper-class pupil, you also get other kinds of nonschool experiences that lead you to defer impulse gratification longer because somehow you know this pays off better. Thus you can develop more easily those modes of behavior that are acceptable to the dominant middle-class school for quite different reasons until you can get past this school point. It's much harder if you are a lower-class youngster; in this case, you know the hard fact of life is that you probably will never get paid off, and you will never cash in."

The discussion that followed suggested that the aspiration level held up by the school was usually false and misleading. What invariably happens is that the Negro youngster is consigned to the slums and to unemployment, regardless of his performance in school. Unfortunately, the necessity for coming to terms with the school is in itself imposed upon the young learner. You must procure a high school diploma to escape the lower class and to move up, just as you need a passport to move from one country to another, because there has been a somewhat arbitrary agreement to demand this of every traveler. Suppose, however, that such an agreement could be abrogated with a slight shift in the total sociopolitical arrangements; and suppose you could get a reasonable number of major employing industries to select their young workers on the basis of aptitude for their particular kind of work and not to ask for academic credentials, just as some states forbid requesting photographs or statements of religious affiliation on the grounds that this kind of information permits discrimination based upon irrelevant and phony grounds. One result would be to superimpose a realistic demand upon the high school curriculum: the former pupil would now face the challenge of making it partly on his own terms, that is, by demonstrating what he could actually do on the job and for people. Instead of requiring the artificiality of a diploma of every youngster, with its built-in demands to please and get along with enough school people, a number of other alternatives to high school were offered. A Youth Conservation Corps, a Domestic Peace Corps, some adaptation of the NYA (National Youth Administration) of the late thirties, or an apprentice system might present reasonable alternatives to high schools. Several of the participants suggested that high school students be paid twenty-five dollars a week while in attendance provided they maintained a decent academic work productivity. The last alternative suggestion to bolster the high school curriculum performance invited a sharp questioning from several doubting Thomases in the Conference along the following lines:

"Would you really give that amount to all of them?"

"Of course; there shouldn't be a means test on the thing. That would be very insulting."

"What would your purpose be in giving them this money?"

"To make them more autonomous, to give them a tool, the only thing, in other words, that will be listened to in a person of their age in a culture like ours; to give them the means of expressing and giving physical embodiment to some of their own values, purposes, and implications. The money may probably be spent foolishly by a large number of them, though I wouldn't ever expect an ultimate disaster of the scope of, say, the Manhattan Project. It probably wouldn't cost quite as much to do it. But if you really want to see a discriminated minority in this country, look at adolescents themselves and quit asking what color they are. That really becomes secondary. These are the only people that don't have any kind of a franchise, that can be tried in different courts, for whom certain acts are offenses in law which are not offenses in law if committed by adults."

"Yes, but in the light of your statements on adolescence, what you're saying now, that they be paid twenty-five dollars a week, is amazing. Instead of giving them attention and love and interest, which they need, you just want to buy them off."

"Who said *instead?*"

"This is a form of respect. And coming back to the Negro problem, the Negro is seldom without some affection, as a number of researchers have pointed out."

"But he wants affection from the white man, doesn't he?"

"I think he wants respect. I'm now quoting from the same researchers. If you have twenty-five dollars in your high school pocket, I believe you would build respect."

The fanciful supplement of a weekly payment to reinforce the curriculum—meaningful or meaningless—of the high school student was not resolved by the Conference. What the discussion does point up is the fact that many participants felt that the curriculum situation is a desperate one and radical reforms and imaginative alternatives are very much in order, especially in this time of crisis.

The Conference group agreed with the importance of the concept of the subliminal curriculum as developed in the Kvaraceus paper and felt that this was an area to be examined carefully and with particular reference to bringing about changes in values and in behavior. Summing up this topic, one discussant stated:

> "Yes, I think that the subliminal curriculum is one which has been overlooked to a large extent in our thinking about what is going on in our schools. The questions that Dr. Kvaraceus has raised are, I think, very succinctly stated, but they need to be investigated further before they can be applied in school and classroom."

Help in Reading

There was no disagreement among the participants on the importance of reading and the fact that disability in this skill was closely tied to the lack of academic success and frequently resulted in early school dropout of Negro pupils. A superintendent of schools who had faced up to the problem of the "nonreader" in his community offered the following comments:

> "The fundamental purpose—at least, one of the basic purposes—of the schools is to teach children to read and to write, because these skills unlock the doors to the other types of knowledge in the world, and knowledge is necessary for many of the adjustments that have to take place. One of the most important and direct contributions that the schools can make is to do a much better job of teaching reading to Negro children. The answer to a great deal of this urgency rests in the primary grades or perhaps even earlier than the primary grades. There is a strong school of thought developing in this country which suggests that we may be starting children in school much too late. This is an area in which we need more research. . . . If we would take Negro children into our schools at an earlier age and find out where the blocks are that prevent their reading, and then pour into the school the resources that make it possible for us to overcome these blocks, a child would have a greater degree of success. With success comes self-esteem and confidence in the ability to go out and face all the other problems that you meet in the world. For instance, there has been some reference here to speech patterns. We in Buffalo have had a

little bit of experience in one of our experimental schools. We are convinced that one of the things that makes it difficult for many of the children of Negro background to learn to read is because of the speech patterns. The words as they appear in print and the words as they are spoken in the homes of these children are two completely different things."

"I believe you've hit on an important research need right there."

"To be sure, there is a growing body of knowledge in this area, but there certainly is nothing conclusive yet. Here's an area where we definitely need some help. I was told a few months ago at a reading conference that this was all settled—we knew all there was to know about reading. Maybe we do. Maybe the gentleman who was making the remarks knows all about it, but frankly the knowledge that he has hasn't filtered down to me nor has it filtered down to a lot of the teachers in our schools nor to our supervisors."

"You mentioned providing special reading helps; did you mention in what grade or grades?"

"I think you ought to start a special program the very moment the child comes to school. I'd say in the first school contact you should begin to work on speech. You can't do much before school entrance. I'm not going to go as far as some people do. Some say you should take the children away from the parents even earlier. This I'm not prepared to do. I am not sure what the optimum grade level or the age level is that the child ought to be taken away from the home and brought into the school. We have thought it was age 5 for a socializing experience, and then age 6 when you start teaching reading. A few years ago, this was absolutely fixed. There have been some studies in recent years to lead us to question this absolute notion. I'd like to see this varied and experimented with—not on a small sample of a handful of experimental children, but on a much wider scale. Maybe at 4, maybe 5, maybe 6—I don't know what the most propitious age level is for introduction of reading instruction for white or Negro."

"What about extending the school downward to a preprimary level for Negro youngsters?"

"A prekindergarten doesn't mean too much unless you know what you're going to do with these kids. Now we ran nursery schools, too, in Buffalo, and when World War II was over, we dropped them. Many of our school people felt this was a social welfare activity so the mothers could go to work. Well, if this is your concept of a nursery school, this isn't going to solve the problem that we're dealing with here today."

Improving the Self-concept and the Image of the Negro Through the Study of Negro History

"You must relate the child to something in his past that's positive, if you want him to respond in a positive way," spoke up a young Negro teacher as she described her experience in a Freedom School in the Boston area. Here is an example of how teachers, parents, and youngsters became students and stayed to learn of Negro American history and of the problems they faced in developing materials and methods. One problem that the teaching staff did not encounter was the problem of disinterest or the disturbing nonlearner.

"In the school in which I taught, the ages run from ten through adult. The biggest group was a sixteen-year-old group, and the fourteen-year-old group; we also had about twenty or thirty adults, mostly parents, who came on two other nights. A few college students, and many of the teachers became students. Some teachers felt they weren't qualified to teach any American Negro history, but they stayed and they contributed to discussions, and they learned; and they knew a lot of American history, anyway. They just didn't know where the pieces of Negro history fit in. And to me as a teacher, I was thrilled, because I know even where I teach we have a lot of discipline problems. I never had to say one thing once about behavior, about paying attention. They did any homework you might ask them."

"What did you use for material?"

"Anything I could get. I gave a few books myself, because my parents had books on Negro history. Naturally, many of these are above the students' heads, and you have to break it down for them. What we did was we made up lesson plans, because we knew we couldn't find teachers who were that well read up on Negro history. Many of them were one or two lessons ahead of the students. And we asked contributors. We had people who were doing African Studies at B.U. [Boston University] who gave lesson plans in modern and ancient history. I didn't get a single history teacher to give their time this summer, that is, from the Negro community; not that we had that many here, unfortunately, but this I felt was a lack perhaps for many reasons that I don't know. Not that they weren't interested, but it's a question of getting texts like the one that was mentioned in one of the papers, the *Pictorial History* [*A Pictorial History of the Negro in America*].

"They cut out newspaper articles, and they noticed of their own free will that there was a difference in the reporting between four and five different newspapers; and many of them became critical for the first time of newspaper reporting and read something past the first page and the funny papers. This carried right through the summer, and they would bring in newspaper articles from magazines, or we bring the magazines and give them to them, like the *New Yorker* and the *Saturday Review* and the *Nation*, etc., and let them take them home and compare them. I think some of them learned quite a bit about how to read a paper and read between the lines and really understand what was going on. And in two weeks they will start up again. And I think as a result the parents who came may have told their children that this was a good thing, and maybe the children who came told their parents. We didn't get quite as many men as we'd have liked to come, but I'm just saying that when you relate the child to something in his past that's positive, he's going to respond to it in a positive way."

"Some of the teachers cut out the last page of the Muslim paper where they have been carrying a series called 'Vignettes of Negro History,' which has been pretty well done, especially on the slave insurrections and the Underground Railroad. Some of the students of their own accord went back and reread *Ebony* magazines. Most of them hadn't even looked at this Negro history section before. You know, this is the 'square' part of the magazine. They cut these out and made notebooks out of them. Then another group deliberately went around to survey and study what was going on in the community. In other words, they felt that they were living and making history.

"Pictorial materials were difficult to find. Negro organizations and libraries can, of course, contribute and help. We used all the libraries. We have even placed *Ebony* and some of the other magazines in our public libraries so that others would have a chance to see them."

"And all of the students wanted to know, 'When are we going to have this again?' For the first time, they were proud of themselves. They heard things about Negro history, and more accurately American history, because you can't teach the contribution of the Negro to history unless you do go back into what really happened in America. Negro pupils—and white, for that matter—have many misconceptions of just really what happened here in the beginning of this country.

"Due to the requests of many parents and students, we intend to continue some type of schooling during the summer and through the year where Negro history would be taught, and particularly the contributions of the Negro in American history, as well as some understanding of ancient African history and what is happening in modern Africa today; and end up with a picture of the community these students now live in. Actually, their understanding of a community is very dim. They don't even know what's going on in the next block. They don't even know what facilities are available to them. They have very little pride in Boston as a city."

There was consensus among the participants that it was equally important that non-Negro students also should have some understanding and appreciation of the Negroes' contribution and place in the development of the country. Mixed sentiments were expressed on the advantages of having Negro teachers leading the discussion and guiding the learning in Negro American history. One of the Negro teachers expressed a majority opinion as follows:

"But colored students still don't live in an all-Negro world. They go home perhaps to a neighborhood that's predominately Negro, but when they go to work and when they travel, they must talk to and relate to white people. I hate to talk in terms of 'colored students,' because I'm speaking about human beings; I don't believe that in this city we have that many Negro teachers, anyway. Just because you're a Negro teacher doesn't mean you know anything about Negro history, either. I think every teacher should have an awareness of the Negro role and participation in American history."

At this point, we must ask the question, "What does the future hold for the Freedom School as a desperate and valiant attempt to help upgrade self-concept, to erase misconceptions, to overcome ignorance, and to improve attitudes of whites toward their Negro neighbors?" Also the question of the role of the public schools must be raised. Why is it not possible to carry on with the same enthusiasm and devotion in the publicly supported classrooms? One answer that was heard frequently indicated that the teachers in the public schools were fearful of, and unprepared for, the task before them, as will come out in a later discussion. The following comment provides a clue concerning the future of the Freedom School, at least in this one community:

> "I wouldn't like to think of it just in terms of a crash program. I would like to think such emphasis would become a regular part of the curriculum of all schools. But in the meanwhile, if we are going to continue with schools that are segregated, whether they are segregated *de facto* or *de jure,* we have the responsibility to make certain that Negro students know that their parents and forefathers have contributed something positive to American history. The teacher would have to know this first of all. And few do.
>
> "I don't know what the final outcome will be in the Freedom School program. There will be revisions. We felt that there were some things which can't go too fast. We sort of spotlighted high points in history. You would get comments from children, if you asked them what was the Underground Railroad—just to learn their awareness—indicating they thought it was a train like the subway. They had never heard of Harriet Tubman, and yet there is a Harriet Tubman House in Boston which is a Neighborhood House. When you'd mention Dr. DuBois, they didn't know who he is, and yet he should figure in American history as well as reflect the Negro's contribution. Frederick Douglass is another. Many Negro names are important in Boston's history alone; the social studies program for the schools could do a better job on spotting local Negro heroes, making children aware of what their own city has done in terms of Negro American history."

A professor of history who teaches courses in the history of the Negro and other courses in American history took issue with some of the assumptions implicit within the idea of stressing the contributions of the Negro through the simple or direct expedient of presenting more and more Negro heroes to the students. His argument follows:

> "I think an important distinction has to be made, and I don't think we have made it. We keep speaking of a *contribution,* and there's no question that every minority group in America has its sense of its own heroes. I have a book on my shelf at home called *Famous Musicians of Jewish Origin,* and you would be amazed at the people who have now been discovered who are of Jewish origin. In the Chicago schools, for a long time the hyphenated groups were very, very active in getting their particular heroes up front and center. I am afraid that we are now discussing the problem in terms of

a kind of quantitative coverage. Let's get a certain percentage of Negro names, Negro figures, Negro dates, Negro events on the record. . . .

"And frankly, I think the whole notion of contribution is a misleading one, and I would substitute the word, 'What has the Negro *meant* in American history?' not what has he contributed. And here I don't think it's a question of what's in the historian's mind. Now, I give a course in the Civil War, and I would say that my whole professional reputation is based on the notion that this country would not have had a civil war were it not for its bad conscience about slavery in the South. That is not a romantic, sentimental notion which television producers use on three-hour programs; that is, the innermost sense of American history, the meaning of our history, is right there. Now, there is simply no—there *is* American history without the Erie Canal, but there is no American history without the Civil War; and I think you're quite right to say that in a sense what's happening in America today is a culmination of what America meant, what themes it has returned to, what sores it has found underneath in its conscience; so that if we could get away from this word *contribution,* which is really false, getting heroes so maybe Jackie Robinson or Marian Anderson will have a picture on page 143 of the textbook, and really move to what is the central meaning of the American experience and failure, too, it seems to me that would be a very important distinction. It's not a question of coverage; it's a question of simply making sense of what's happening in this country."

"I would like to recommend that every school, north and south and across the country, in the cities and rural places—that they require a course for white and Negro students in the Negro in American life. This would include the historical aspects, and it would include the political aspects. It would include the economic questions, and it would include questions of society, questions of sex, and questions raised by simple speeches, as mine, and questions raised by all things that have been brought up. I'm going to say my piece as I think it. I struck upon this particular recommendation in spite of all the obvious difficulties—and there are many obvious difficulties—because to me this represents a recognition that the Negro question, if you will, in the United States goes to the very heart of American life. If we don't as a nation face this issue, then we don't face ourselves, the American past, present, future destiny, etc. It's not *an* issue, it's not

> one of many. It's one of *the* central issues of this era, and if you face this squarely in your efforts to teach youngsters about America, about themselves, about life—if you face this, then you're facing the *whole* question of American life. If you don't face this, then you're not facing America. You're facing an America that has involved a series of isolations; that is, a series of groups have been isolated away, segregated away, from the mainstream of American life. One of these, and today it's most striking, is the Negro. Another is the *whole* laboring classes of the United States. I think all that you've said about the history of the Negro can be said likewise about the history of the workingman in the United States. So this sort of restates in this course—the Negro in American life states for me what is necessary to be faced, and I think brings out my retort to what you are saying. What you are saying has its validity, but I think only if one recognizes that the Negro question is one of many questions can one take that point of view. The Negro question is *the* central question of American life today. If one says that, then you are sort of forced into another point of view about textbooks and about courses and preparation of teachers."

Finally, some discussions turned around content of the curriculum, particularly on the question of determining exactly what would be included in the teaching of the history of the Negro. Generally it was felt that there would be no way to distinguish between what was to be included and retained and what would be excluded unless the schools and the community first determined what is more important in the world of the student. This was recognized as a call for the establishment of priority of values.

One of the social scientists who had had considerable first-hand experience in working with white and Negro groups in the South spoke with feeling of the importance of certain content and learning experiences.

> "I think content does make a difference, and the gap in content which is seen in this area is a content about what it means to be a Negro. Opening up this question in integration groups in the South is a searing experience. It is particularly explosive to the Negro group who alone may explore its raw facets. I've heard them say, 'I don't want to talk about it, I don't want to talk about it. I *can't* talk about it.' I've had them leave in tears with Negro and white after a mutual exploration. It's too painful—the taboo area of self-examination, self-acceptance, self-understanding. If we're going to break

the vicious cycle, I would say, 'Here we can intervene. Here is missing content.' But there is such deep emotional involvement in it, both on the part of the guilty whites and the hostile Negro, and guilty Negro, that we face a traumatic impasse."

"There could be some value in history. If you do it by indirection. . . ."

"Whether it's history or what's your vehicle, this is the missing ingredient; and I think one of our problems is that we in professional circles meet what I call the 'white' Negro. I've been fortunate in meeting the 'Negro' Negro personally, not just professionally, in the South, and I've met their kids in particular situations; and it provides a new and more valid perspective and one which I think we are closed off from in our own professional environments too much, because we get the articulate, bourgeois, educated spokesman who has been able to work through, like many Negro representatives here who are able to cope with this situation. My experience has been that this is incredibly difficult and is *not* easy to cope with, and we need content, techniques, and strategy so that adults can be more competent in supporting youngsters."

The Fearful and Unprepared Educators

Even the most casual listener within the Conference group could not fail to catch the strong reluctance on the part of the white educators to face up to the issues. Several problems emerged:

1. Most school people had little or no awareness of the nature, the meaning, or the speed of the Negro revolution, although they were being swept along by the swift current of events.
2. They appeared timid about presenting historical data that were unfavorable or unpalatable to the dominant white, middle-class community almost as though the shame and guilt of the past had immobilized them or as though some fearful consequences might befall them.
3. School personnel seemed to ask for and await a set of blueprints for action from the behavioral scientists and the community-organization workers. Many appeared at first unwilling or unable to apply the information that was being presented.

Reluctance of the educators to look at historical facts squarely is visible in the following interchanges:

Historian: "The whole idea of not considering the Negro, always working him out, has been a real cultural conspiracy, not by individuals necessarily; but I think it has been taught as a part of our whole cultural background of 'inferior' and 'superior' race which is built up very early to justify certain kinds of attitudes in America. If pupils grow up with this attitude, history must therefore wipe it out. But I think as we become conscious of this and as we interpret what the Civil War really meant, we can break up what amounts to a conspiracy."

Educator: "Let me ask you a question. Would you wish that said in the classroom? Let's formulate it: 'One of the indications of the way America has avoided facing the problem of its own Negro peoples, its black peoples, is not to discuss them in schools; and therefore, boys and girls, the discussion which we are having in this history class of the Negro today is one of the first which has ever happened in American public schools.'

"You see, I understand and I agree with your notion that there has been a conspiracy—conscious or not, it doesn't matter—to keep the Negro out of the textbooks, and that this in some sense has been a tactic of domination. That's one of the ways domineering people keep people in their place. They keep them out of textbooks. That's always been true. Now, that's a fact about America you've just stated. Do you wish to state that fact in a classroom? I just raised the question."

Historian: "What would be your point? I don't see what you are getting at."

Educator: "Well, it seems to me that you've stated this as a fact of American history. This goes into meaning and interpretation when you say you would ask a class to comment on this. You would ask a teacher. What is the point of her saying this?"

Historian: "You want a teacher to say—let's get down to hard tacks—you wish a teacher to say, among the many things a teacher has occasion to say about American history, that one of the things which is true of our history—that those people who, for example, in the past have made textbooks have not given complete and fair representation to the Negro. Now, this is another sign of the domination by makers of opinion, makers of minds. . . .

"Again I say you cannot even begin to treat this problem until you ask 'why' as well as 'what,' without in some sense morally blaming, without taking some moral toll of America, blaming the past. I don't wish to compare America to Nazi Germany. That's an irreverent comparison, but you understand that the analogy breaks down at that point. Even if the Germans had, as we expected the Germans to admit in their history classes, 'Hitler was a bad guy,' similarly we cannot begin to make sense of the Negro in America without assessing some moral guilt. It's a parlor game today. Everyone calls themselves guilty. One can't talk about the American past with regard to the Negro without dealing in terms of guilt and shame and failure in some degree. Now, I raise the question, 'Do you wish these subjects'—and I just raise it; I'm not suggesting an answer—'do you wish these subjects to be dealt with in the public schools' treatment of the Negro? Do you wish teachers of high school students to say, "Well, what did we do wrong?" for example, as one question? Why has it not happened before? Or how can we account for the fact that one hundred years after the Emancipation Proclamation so little has been done toward the establishment of equality?' "

Educator: "I can't see any objection to your approach to this. I wouldn't hesitate personally to teach a history class this way at the high school level. On the other hand, I do think that there is a greater power being attributed to the public school around this table than what I, as a working school teacher and school administrator, think the public schools have. If you want to reform society, you do it very, very slowly through public schools."

Historian: "To answer in another way, let me give an example. In the Montclair schools, in the junior high schools—and the reason I know about this is because I participated in the planning—a group of colored youngsters found out that even in the history class and all the discussion there was no mention of the contribution of the Negro. They took it upon themselves, with the help of the YMCA and the Youth Council, a very strong group of about eighty-five youngsters in high school, to do something about it. Now at first—and this concept is self-image—at first the colored youngsters were too much afraid to talk about DuBois and all the rest out in the open, so they made a group project out of it. They agreed to assign at least two people in every class or wherever they found themselves where assignments were given who would ask for a special assignment with a Negro focus. Well, it worked. Surprisingly enough, it worked. Inside a semester, not only had the colored kids overcome their fear and apprehension of discussing the contributions of the Negro, but in the next semester they had white kids asking for assignments, because it caught hold. You see, it was done through indirection, and this whole group of colored youngsters had a new esteem for themselves. They took some delight in doing themes, and it caught hold. Now, if the teacher had tried to do it, she would have been a very creditable teacher to have achieved the same results."

Social Scientist: "I did a fifteen-program TV series called 'The Epitaph of Jim Crow.' There was a choice between my series on every educational television station in the country and a TV series on Retirement. Almost every city except for New York that I thought needed my series a little more than they needed Retirement chose the Retirement one, particularly when the educational station was in the hands of educators. If it was in the hands of the Board of Education of a city, they almost invariably chose Retirement rather than 'The Epitaph of Jim Crow.' I admit some personal involvement in this, but apart from that, as in the case of Chicago, they refused on the same grounds: they said my approach was too inflammatory. I made it clearly a matter of shame, something that had to be looked at. I think the difficulty in the matter of a shame approach is that most of white America is not prepared to accept this."

Educator: "But I am teaching people who are going on to teach American history, and I supplement the texts because these potential teachers do not find anything in American history about the Negro. We need to give them something to incorporate in their American history as they go along so that when they go out to teach youngsters, they can do the same. I tell them quite consciously, yes, just what you have said; and therefore we need to give them much more background; we need to supplement the textbooks, but I don't know whether I'd say this in a public school or not. I just never thought about it."

Historian: "What I'm suggesting is, very frankly, that you *do* think about it, because if you understand my distinction between what the Negro has *meant* in American history as apart from what he has contributed, there is simply no facing the question of what he has meant without at some time saying he has meant less than he has because there has been in some sense a conspiracy of silence. If the student has any feeling of the changes that are taking place now, I can't imagine how you can begin to discuss the Negro without being forced to face the student who says, 'Why? Why now, and not yesterday? Why has this not occurred before?' You cannot begin to answer the question 'Why?' without saying, 'I believe,' in our school classes. You must face the question, 'Why? Why is it? Why is it that suddenly on television I see all kinds of Negroes shaving? I didn't even know Negroes shaved before. Why?' "

But the problem of fear, intimidation, and uncertainty is not peculiar to the white educator; the same problem can frequently be noted with Negro educators, as one of the Negro participants reports out of his own experience:

Negro Publisher: "It bothered me this morning when someone mentioned the schools' golden opportunity to help the Negro youth take a new role. I live in a segregated county in Maryland. When I talk with the Negro principal of our high school, who is probably one of the best principals in the county, about the problem of integration and preparing the youngsters in his school to move into white schools, he tells me, first, 'I'll lose my job,' and second, 'I'm at a good school. Am I to help these youngsters not to want to come to my school?' You see, it's a real dilemma which the Negro leadership often faces.

"Someone here asked why, at the sit-ins, the Negro youngsters knew so little about their own situation. The Negro schools are as reluctant to open this area up for discussion, it seems, as many of the white schools; and also they get 'clipped' if they do, at least in our community.

"At this particular high school, I talked to the faculty. They were very much divided as to whether their major effort for these kids should be to upgrade their speech habits, change their grooming habits, or take them from where they were and not worry about these other problems, which would really shake them up, because they weren't quite ready to have their speech habits changed, they weren't quite ready to be made middle class; they wanted a skill they could use in the shop or some place. The faculty themselves were having quite a tussle over it. I am afraid that we don't begin to use education with the creativity or the impact that's available to us. We're just role playing and shadowboxing. Take the first-graders. You can do fantastic things with their ability to communicate and move out and be competent. Schools could do much more than they are doing."

Chairman: "I'd like to hear more from the educators to see what really are the limitations that they feel."

First Educator: "These protests—I'm not sure you can get away with it in my state."

Second Educator: "You can't get away with it in my city, either."

Third Educator: "And the Freedom Schools that the churches are running with the NAACP—we couldn't do it in our schools as public institutions, I'm sure."

Social Scientist: "With reference to the comment about the dust settling over our backs after this Conference is over and the question of the moral commitment, I'd like to make a comment. I believe that the multiplier effect Dr. Seasholes talks of is relevant here. He mentioned the multiplier effect when the Negroes showed some aspirations; these were soon followed by more and even greater aspirations. I believe there is a multiplier effect with regard to courage. Courage is most relevant here in our deliberations and at home on our jobs. If there is not going to be any dust resettling, there must be a chain reaction of people taking stands that are important now on these questions. I am speaking with reference to the moral question and the educator's responsibility as a person and as a professional."

Attention was frequently called to the silence of the teacher as a person and as a professional worker on the issues related to segregation and to the problems of the slum school. Silence on the part of the classroom teachers and other school personnel tends to reduce them to ineffective spokesmen and to weaken their influence in finding alternatives and solutions. If they do not feel free to speak out, since they are so close to the situation, much is lost, and the dust will surely continue to settle on the schools in the slum areas.

All the dialogue points up that educators need help and support and that they cannot be expected to do the job unaided. Attention must be given to the selection and preparation of teachers and to their counseling needs. In-service training should provide substantive help in areas of ignorance. But in addition to the didactic approaches, in-service training should also provide therapeutic opportunities for all those who find it difficult or who are unable to cope adequately with the daily pressures of the inner-city classrooms.

In the middle of the four-day Conference, one of the behavioral scientists attempted to evaluate the progress of the group discussions. He complained about the level of the discussions and the constant demand that the focus be on action and programming. He felt the need to broaden the discussion, to face the issues of the Negro demand as well as the citizen role of every individual, in addition to their institutional role.

> "I was hoping that we'd get to what I consider to be one of the most fundamental things that are facing us now in terms of the Negro revolution, the Negro demand, and I don't think we are. In fact, I think we've hardly touched the surface. In a sense, I'm still perfectly satisfied, if we are social scientists staying in our own private world, me included. I fear the teachers have been too concerned from the very beginning about being practical, constantly wanting every concept and finding translated immediately into practicality. I would hope we could be very practical in the things we come out with on Thursday, but I wonder if we haven't been too concerned with that on Monday and Tuesday, the first two days of a four-day conference. I think this tends to water down getting to the basic problems of the Negro. It seems to me we're always trying to translate this into institutional terms, and we might translate this into some other terms, too. We're all citizens as well as related to educational and social institutions. I was hoping to broaden the discussion to what most people who dedicate their lives full time to race relations consider to be most of the fundamental problems that we're still facing; and it doesn't look yet as though they can be identified or solved without some outside intervention and help."

In short, the educators do not sound heroic. Who wants to be like the timid teacher—uninformed and ambivalent? Such are hardly the hero models with whom youngsters—Negro or white—will hasten to identify. One of the behavioral scientists observed privately that he had found southern schoolmen frequently to be more informed and more insistent on change and improvement than many of the educators working in the schools of the northern cities.

The Teacher as a Model for Identification

A number of participants frequently referred to the crucial factor of the sex-role identity as the central developmental task for all adolescents—Negro and white—pointing out the singular difficulties presented in the development of Negro youngsters, and especially the males, who are so often brought up in female-based households. The background of this problem has been accurately described in the report already cited, *Education and the Disadvantaged American:*

> So long as the rural society was stable, a boy could learn his own life role by observing men at work in the fields, whether or not he recognized one of them as his father or as head of his family. Girls, too, could learn an adequate adult role by observation. But such learning is difficult in the cities. There

> the child cannot observe the occupational role of male members of the family group, who, when employed, work away from the home; and often no man lives regularly with the family. Nor does family tradition fill the gap as it does for many children, by providing the concept that the father is provider and head of the family. The mother is often incapable of providing for her daughters a model of homemaking appropriate to successful city living. And the playmates of the migrant child, who are likely to be as disadvantaged as he, are unable to compensate for the failure of his home.[9]

Evidence has been presented by a number of investigators indicating that the American male Negro has had a significant problem in maintaining his masculine status, not only because of the structure of his family but also because of the emasculating pressures of the white community, against which effective retaliation has been impossible up to the present. Much of this symbolic emasculation, it is pointed out, may begin with the little boy's sensitive awareness that his father or father-surrogates are very vulnerable in relation to white males. The psychiatrist Eugene B. Brody[10] has added that it is most unlikely that a relationship with a mother as the most important power, no matter how benign and secure, can serve as an adequate basis for the development of a stable social identity in a boy, whether in terms of sex, color, or other significant element.

The whole tenor of the Conference indicated that the school should be careful to play out an ego-supporting role as suggested in the Kvaraceus paper. It should not add to the emasculating forces in the outside community. School failure can be destructive. In addition, much comment was heard on the necessity of developing strong interpersonal relationships between teacher and student and student and teacher. The Conference agreed that there was a dire need for more Negro teachers in the classroom, especially males, although the complex dynamics of identification were recognized. One of the Negro teachers indicated that some of her pupils resented her, somehow sensing that their teacher had something that they and their parents lacked and might never attain. Reorganization of the school in scheduling classes was also suggested in an attempt to bring the pupils into closer and deeper contact with one or two teachers and with one another over a longer period of time than the usual one-year period. It was also proposed that more effective use could be made by the school of prestige Negro males in the neighborhood and community. Programs in which prominent Negro businessmen, politicians, municipal and government workers, Army and Navy personnel, ministers, scientists, and others could participate during school hours and in the evening with Negro parents and pupils were recommended. The caution that such a human resource listing should not draw exclusively from the highly visible and successful Negro in the Robinson-King-Anderson tradition was sounded. Rather, it was recommended that local heroes be used from within the local neighborhood and community, including any and all vertically mobile Negroes within reach. The following excerpts from the discussions will reflect some of the major concerns that have been summarized briefly in the preceding discussion:

> "I like, too, what was said about the importance of a teacher staying with a youngster or a group of youngsters long enough so there is the kind of interaction between them that can make a difference. The more I read about the development of the self-concept, this comes from other people's interaction with you and their perception of you. And one of the kinds of questions I was raising in my mind, as I read the Kvaraceus paper, was whether or not we shouldn't be giving a lot more consideration to the kind of organization of our school program that makes it possible for the same group of youngsters to stay together long enough to interact in meaningful ways and to develop some responsibility toward each other. I am raising the question of the importance of continuing the same group of students with the same teacher for a portion of the day together. In one college study involving university students, it was reported that students who did not feel themselves socially accepted in class spent 50 percent of their class time wondering about how they could become more socially accepted by their fellows. I think this has something to do with how we might go about improving academic achievement. It also seemed to me as I read the third paper, Kvaraceus was talking about helping people identify with an adult role in which Negroes were identifying as Negroes. I keep hearing this as I try to see what's happening on the social scene. One of my big problems up till now has been attempting to get whites and Negroes to identify with humans rather than with just whites or with just Negroes. I've been working for some time now helping pupils to see past color. I've worked with myself on this, too. Now, is this only the kind of thing which you work with with people who are in a favored position? Or is this equally important in working with identification within any segment of the population?"

The enormity and complexity of the teacher's task in motivating and guiding the Negro student to higher academic goals and achievement were never underestimated by the participants in the Conference. Whenever some educator appeared overly cautious—even timorous—the social scientists and community workers stepped in to reassure and to lend a helping hand. Need for further training and deeper insights was urged by one member as follows:

> "Problems of class, caste, and values are ones that we find very, very difficult for us to examine, because we lack the training for it. We ourselves as teachers are culture-bound, and we are so much a part of our middle-class culture that we can't even stand back and look at how we behave in it. We're just in this automatically, and we make the assumptions that everything that we have learned to do is good for all these for whom we are trying to help negotiate in the political-social structure which we call reality. The most difficult thing in American education will be to get the kind of cultural-anthropological and psychiatric insights which will help us to step out of our implicit framework and somehow get a different orientation so that we can provide a pluralistic set of experiences and pathways for children, so that those who do not wish to take on middle-class ways of behavior—sometimes we automatically assume it's the only good way to live—will have some reasonable alternative. Years ago when we set up that pyramid structure and assumed that everyone was going to want to move automatically up in it, and maybe it was because I came from a working-class orientation and knew working-class ways, I said that there would be many people who would not want to join the country-club crowd and serve with the Rotarians and do a number of other such things; that they would prefer to stay in a working-class pattern of life, but still be able to go to the theater or to listen to music or provide a vacation for their kids or to buy more food or do a number of things in a different dimension entirely. This is essentially one of the most difficult tasks we are going to face. We will have even more difficulty because we haven't understood the nature of the task—the problem of giving a realistic and useful educational opportunity to people many of whom don't want to live on our terms."

There was general agreement that teachers were ill prepared to cope with the learning-teaching problems in the inner-city slum schools. But the Conference was not willing to prescribe new or additional training programs without a closer look via the research route at the special needs presented by the pupils in these learning centers.

Coordinating and Supplementing the Curriculum

How to tie the school curriculum into community activities and how to coordinate volunteer youth activities to the mutual advantage of the school, community, and youth preoccupied the many participants. In the following comments, a Negro community worker relates the opportunity that is being fumbled by the schools in his district, and a word of caution is expressed by a social scientist concerning the volunteer youth activities instituted in a large metropolitan area and aimed to uplift the self-concept of youth.

> "What school people haven't done in the past is to make full use of all the resources that are available in the community—sometimes to help guide and educate, and sometimes to take the pressure off of themselves. Now the schools could readily take over some of this image building that's taking place. Negroes are building an image for *themselves* now. I enrolled about 400 people to go to Washington, including many high school youngsters. Right now they are well organized in my community. All last week in my office they have been working on Food for Peace. The kids are ready to go. Now, what's going to happen in the schools? The kids are ready for action. They take this movement right into the schools, and the poor teachers don't know what to do, so they put out an SOS. I have to leave my office and run over to the high school to do some trouble shooting because the teachers and the educators are not oriented to what we call the accelerated action movement now on foot in this country and which affects every community where there are Negroes, regardless of the size of the Negro community."

> "I'm sure that many of the teachers are frightened out of their skins. Yet it strikes me as a golden opportunity for public schools. Here is, at least for disadvantaged kids, something realistic outside of the school system to which they can now relate; and this is why I liked what someone said earlier about facing the problem out. It seems to me this is one thing public education can do for the protest movement which, in a sense, the protest movement cannot do for itself—that is provide wide-scale information; but I'm thinking about a much more feeling level than just information—a sort of gut-level perspective on the whole problem in which they're involved. Very frequently they get involved in protests, and they work very hard, and this has marvelous personality effects and so forth; but in talking to sit-in kids and Freedom Riders, I've often been taken aback by how little they really understand of the movement. Here is where the schools can come in to coordinate current events with the past and to tie in this movement with all other phases of the curriculum."

It was suggested that there are many ways to involve school youth—Negro and white—in community life and thus to build in a feeling of self-worth and function. Operation Kindness was described, but one member expressed serious reservations concerning certain assumptions underlying such volunteer activities of youth.

"In a nutshell, Operation Kindness enrolls youth in voluntary community service. There are thousands of high school, junior high school pupils all over Metropolitan Boston—from about 190 high schools—literally involved in thousands of activities, meaningful and important activities in mental hospitals, homes for the aged, settlement houses, museums, and other social-service agencies. The program represented one of the first breakthroughs for youth as far back as 1958. High school young people as far down chronologically as fourteen years of age are working in the community on many fronts."

"This plan of having youngsters work on community projects serves a twofold purpose if you are involved in a racial crisis. We frequently found that when you send them out in teams, Negro and white, or Jew and Negro, that they get to know one another much better working in the community situation than they ever do in schools. That may be an added dimension."

"At this point, I might introduce as a social scientist the issue I was raising earlier. Because this is the first I've heard of Operation Kindness, therefore nothing I say can or should be interpreted as pejorative to it specificially. I know nothing about it, but the underlying assumptions are an example of the kind of thing that I would guard against, although there would also be accruing the many values that you refer to. Take, for example, the specific instance that you've given of having youngsters participate on the wards in mental hospitals. This certainly reinforces—and this is all right, as far as it goes; it's fine—it does some things that the middle class generally thinks are good. It reinforces kindness. You call it *kindness,* which is an endorsement of this particular value, in contrast, say, to Operation Fortitude or Operation Dominance—a number of other values that certain other social classes have frequently found to yield gratification. If you think in terms of recent studies of mental institutions, the mental hospital itself represents a society with its own power structures. People who come in as nurses' aides or volunteers do a number of things that are awfully good for the lower-middle class and fairly good for the patient, sometimes bad for the patient, and sometimes pretty ambivalent for nearly everybody. They permit nurses to redefine their responsibilities as more administrative, and therefore to do less 'dirty work.' They add to the complexity of the procedure whereby you use a status system within a hospital to maintain your power over it. In other words, people who view the functioning of the mental hospital from the point of view of the patient find out that, wherever there are volunteers, they become used in effect as pawns in the power structure of the hospital itself, sometimes to the patient's advantage, sometimes to the patient's disadvantage. At any rate, you can't in adopting a philanthropic stance say, 'Well, nobody will object to this at least, because it's only doing good.' Doing good for free in a humble status is in itself a lower-middle-class position par excellence; and when you teach students this, you are also teaching them, for example, that there are certain things for which we don't *ask* to get paid or it isn't nice not to be willing to work, even though you don't get commensurate power with reference to it; or after all it isn't so bad that teen-agers don't have access to real economic opportunities. Look, we're teaching you that you're good enough to be able to really do this kind of work for which some people do get paid, and of course you aren't going to mind that you don't collect any pay. All of this is a part of the same instruction. I wouldn't say it was even so subliminal. What would happen in a program in a school in which a teacher did something quite different—in which he took the program you now have and said, 'Now we're going to use this as an example of community activity; and the question we're going to address ourselves to, if it is of interest to you, is why, when high school students participate in something in the community, they do so in this sort of second-class or halfhearted way. Why can't you go out and actually get the job, if in fact you are actually going to do it?' And this, it seems to me, would bring in quite a different set of learnings, some that would be no less valuable, and maybe more."

"No, no, I didn't mean that."

"Well, I misunderstood, then."

"My objections are made on the grounds that this is an experience for lower-status kids on middle-class terms in which they learned not to say, 'When I work, I get paid.' In my present research, I have pulled through the government an insistence that we get funds in our budget to pay high school kids two dollars a session for interviews. There's been some opposition to this in some of the schools that we work in, where kids would be so happy to do it free. In one of the schools, in fact, a girl, a community leader—I'm sorry to say also a Negro—came up with a proposal at the first group testing as to how wonderful it would be if the kids all put this into the scholarship fund or something else that the school had, and my assistant clobbered it. Here I was taking it on myself to teach something different; one of the attitudes in this study was that the kids were consultants for people and were to be treated with equal dignity because, in fact, they had it, and they were to get the two dollars a session and to use it as they saw fit. This is the reason for my concerns. This is what I mean."

Returning to the voluntary youth program, Operation Kindness, it was pointed out that the program included a very wide range of participants and could not be analyzed solely in terms of an exclusive lower-middle-class activity.

> "One of the complex phases of the program, Operation Kindness, is that it does include, according to our records and plans, kids from a wide range of social-class backgrounds, all the way from exclusive private secondary school youngsters, who are hardly lower-middle class, to those who are truly of lower-class origins, so that would make the job of applying this analysis much more complicated."

Concluding this discussion of the curriculum and the teacher, it may be well to recall the observations of the Educational Policies Commission in their consideration of the education of the disadvantaged Americans:

> The modern public school often bases its efforts on assumptions which are not valid for all children. The values of the teacher, the content of the program, and the very purposes of schooling may be appropriate for middle-class children, but not for disadvantaged children. These children's experiences at home and on the streets do not prepare them for a school established for another kind of child. If the school reinforces the sense of personal insignificance and inadequacy that life may already have imposed on a disadvantaged child, he is likely to benefit little from schooling. If the school insists on programs or standards that he regards as unrelated to his life or that

doom him to an unending succession of failures, he is likely to leave at the first opportunity.[11]

Limitations on the Role of the School

Throughout the four-day discussion, in general sessions and in small work groups, frequent comments could be heard concerning the extent to which the school program could actually make a dent on the Negro problem. Comments ranged from unlimited confidence and belief in the school as the one indispensable, central, and strategic agency to occasional pessimism that would relegate the school to a minor and circumscribed institutional role caught in a complicated social matrix. But more often, there was a pervasive feeling that schools could do much more than they were now doing and that the ceiling of the school's potential contribution could be raised considerably. One needs but to start somewhere. The schoolmen were urged to cut into the vicious circle of inaction. Even a small start to help the Negro students, if successful, could have a multiplier effect. The following excerpts present a representative, but brief, sampling of the discussion:

> "I think we'd all agree with you that education is only one institution among many in society, and that perhaps we are putting more stress on what it can do than can realistically be expected; but as soon as you started making your point, it hit me like a hammer over the head. For years I have worked with religious groups hoping with the power of religion to change society, and the ministerial crowd all talked in the exact same way. 'Sure, we have dogma that says this or that, but you know we're all very dependent on the fees we get from the membership,' and so on and so forth. If you talk to politicians, they say, 'Well, we can't do anything via the political system, because after all, we're dependent on the voters,' and so forth.
>
> "If you pick off any institution in American society or any other society, they can all make—and I think with some validity—the same points as you're making, the point that 'you cannot expect us to do it all.' I think in a sense this gets back to the point that someone made the first day, 'It's a vicious circle.' I think we *have* to remember there are severe limitations in public education, that it is only one institution among many; but at the same time, I'm not so sure that what we were doing earlier, before you made your comment, was necessarily a bad thing—that is, shooting for the moon and not prejudging the limitations of public education. I have a feeling that practically every institution and agency—I have more than a feeling; I have a conviction—feels the same. Perhaps educators are the last to think they have real power

through education. But the point is, unless every institution actually presses to the limits, we all will be standing back and looking at the other guy, so that the vicious circle of inaction cannot be broken at *my* point. The vicious circle has one nice feature to it: no matter where you break it, it becomes a benign circle and begins to go back in the opposite direction, in the sense we have a self-corrective system. If schools could only test the limits. . . . But in general, we haven't yet tested the limits in schools nor have we tested the limits in religion; and surely our politicians have come the least along the road to testing the limits of their real power. It's better that we shoot for the moon at least while we're brainstorming and not gear ourselves down too early with our limitations, which are real enough."

The school's dependency on community willingness and support in adapting its educational program to the Negro needs is pointed out by one educator, who fears that too much power is being attributed to this one agency:

"Many Negroes, to improve their status in society, place a very high emphasis on education, and as an educator, I hate to tell them they're sometimes wrong, for schools can only move so far in this direction; they only move so far as the community in which they are will let them. Personally, I think your Negro population in the Boston area will move forward much faster with your independent Freedom Schools than you will through any reform that you carry out in the public school system. After you move far enough via private institutions, the public schools will follow you; and this, I think, is something the Negro community must realize. I think we're in danger here of attributing to the school system a power that it doesn't have, and there are lots of reasons it doesn't have it. I'm not sure that it's a conspiracy that it doesn't have it, unless ignorance is a conspiracy; and there are many people both as historians and as school teachers who are ignorant of many phases and aspects of the development of their own country, and a lot of them are willing to learn."

Finally, a Negro teacher responds personally in terms of what she sees as she takes up her daily tasks in her slum-neighborhood classroom. Sadly and almost bitterly, she tells us:

"If you ever sit in an urban or ghetto classroom and you sit there through the year as a teacher and you see what happens and what doesn't happen, you know something drastic has to be done. If, likewise, you live in that community and don't go into the suburbs, it hits home to you every time you head for home at night. Sometimes I think maybe it wasn't such a good idea for one of these discussants to suggest that the teacher should live in the neighborhood school community, because she's so worn out at the end of the school day. You want to get away from this pressure and what you begin to feel as a sort of sickness. This is a heartfelt thing."

References

1. James B. Conant, *The Education of American Teachers,* New York, McGraw-Hill, Inc., 1963.
2. James D. Koerner, *The Miseducation of American Teachers,* Boston, Houghton Mifflin Company, 1963.
3. Bruno Bettelheim, "Class, Color and Prejudice," *The Nation,* October 19, 1963, p. 231–234.
4. George S. Counts, *Dare the School Build a New Social Order?* New York, The John Day Company, Inc., 1935.
5. James Baldwin, "A Talk to Teachers," *Saturday Review,* December 21, 1963, p. 42.
6. Robert J. Havighurst, "How Education Changes Society," *Confluence: An International Forum,* Spring, 1957, p. 86.
7. *Ibid.,* p. 88.
8. Educational Policies Commission, *Education and the Disadvantaged American,* Washington, D.C., National Education Association, 1962, pp. 15–16.
9. *Ibid.,* p. 7.
10. Eugene B. Brody, "Color and Identity Conflict in Young Boys: Observation of Negro Mothers and Sons in Urban Baltimore," *Psychiatry,* vol. 26, no. 201, May, 1963.
11. Educational Policies Commission, *op. cit.,* pp. 12–13.

section four CONFERENCE SUMMARY AND OUTCOMES

by The Staff of The Lincoln Filene Center for Citizenship and Public Affairs

The idea of a conference focused on Negro youth was supported by several representatives from the Coordinating Council of the Northeastern States Citizenship Project, who urged the Center to consider such a project as a part of its agenda. The Northeastern States Coordinating Council already had taken steps to focus the annual Youth Citizenship Conference, which was held in June, 1964, on the topic, *Equality: A Principle and a Dilemma.* The annual Lincoln Filene Center–Nine States Council workshop for teachers focused on the same subject in July, 1964, at the Lincoln Filene Center on the Tufts University campus. This workshop was the third in a series sponsored by the Commissioners of Education of the Northeastern States.

Attending the Conference were thirty-eight carefully chosen specialists who were knowledgeable and experienced in the problems of Negro youth and adults, with the schools, and with community programs aimed to help culturally deprived youth and families. Included in the educator group were representatives from eight of the nine states that make up the Northeastern States Citizenship Project, for which the Center serves as a clearinghouse and resource agency. A number of the participants were Negroes. (A roster of participants is found in the introductory statement.)

The variety of backgrounds of the participants enabled the Conference to pursue a wide set of objectives; these objectives were:

1. To draw together research knowledge of the existing condition of Negro youth
2. To assess the feasibility of changing that condition through innovation in the schools

3. To sense the goals and progress of other agencies in their programs directed at Negro youth
4. To become better acquainted with the substance and the emotional intensity of the Negro protest movement

The Conference was sponsored jointly by the Cooperative Research Branch, U.S. Office of Education (Project G-020-OE-410057) and the President's Committee on Juvenile Delinquency and Youth Crime. Dr. Ethel C. Dunham of Cambridge made a financial contribution to support the Conference.

The Conference was organized around three working papers, as follows:

1. *The Self-Concept: Basis for Reeducation of Negro Youth,* by Dr. Jean D. Grambs
2. *Political Socialization of Negroes: Image Development of Self and Polity,* by Dr. Bradbury Seasholes
3. *Negro Youth and Social Adaptation: The Role of the School as an Agent of Change,* by Dr. William C. Kvaraceus

One day was devoted to the presentation and discussion of each paper. The fourth day of the Conference involved a regrouping of participants into the three major categories of social scientists, community workers, and professional educators. Throughout the four days, a sustained effort was made to identify areas for needed research and for promising projects and programs which might be carried on by the Lincoln Filene Center. This report summarizes briefly the concrete suggestions and recommendations for research and/or practice that came out of the general discussion and the small-group sessions.

The Group Experience and Mood Orientation

Professional workers and experts are persons. Regardless of their sophistication, they have feelings, they suffer areas of ignorance, and they are frequently discipline-bound. The group of experts, Negro and white, who convened at the Lincoln Filene Center at Tufts University could boast a high degree of expertness in the behavioral sciences, in education, and in community development. But they were also human beings who underwent an intense and lasting learning experience. One group chairman summed it up in this fashion:

> "Strong feelings were expressed in the group, feelings of dissatisfaction, misunderstanding, confusion, and frustration. There was feeling in the group for even greater need for franker facing of the issues and problems of the Negro in our country. There was also the feeling that white Americans just don't know the full meaning of the present revolution, the significance of what is taking place, which is referred to as 'The Revolution.'

It seems to be ignored, even by some persons at this Conference. Continuing along more constructive lines, there was this item in regard to the contribution of education: education as a responsibility to bring to the American people and to all of its children an accurate and meaningful interpretation of the Negro in American life. It was agreed that there must be provision through education for further integration of the isolated groups in the mainstream of American life. Finally, there was a great deal of discussion of the group concept of this whole Conference. The group concept of the Conference might be expressed briefly as follows: members of the group came to look upon the Conference itself as a response to the current revolution; it was felt that this Conference should contribute to forceful response to the demands of today, recognizing that the Negro is a key issue, and response to this is essential."

Another group leader summed his observations up in these words:

"We finally decided that the major goal we were concerned about was the problem of providing the kids with a framework for understanding the world as they actually see it and with the skills to locate and utilize the knowledge that is available for dealing with that world; and that this was the central educational task, and not some of the other rather trite ones that are defined as the curriculum for these children at this time or for that matter for all children; and some of us accused the social scientists of stealing some of the tools of progressive education movement and deserting their academic colleagues who want us to move over in another direction. And finally as we began to work with implementation and we talked about rather eloquent experiences with teachers who really know how to do this sort of thing and who can move programs with kids, experiences were recounted where administratively they were not supported and where they could not follow through. Without a doubt the teachers who are successful are the ones who have the complete support of the power structure in the school system as well as community support. Now we spent a great deal of time on the strategy of getting this kind of thing moving, and of clearing the way for those people who are able to do this kind of reality education we're talking about. We even talked about some rather wonderful, but fantastic, techniques for getting communities going so that they would move action in school systems to create the kind of community support that will take the fearful educator off the hump and help get him moving in this direction. So there was a lot of strategy talk of a very imaginative kind about what might be done."

A third leader again recalled strong feelings in his group and suggests that, as the Negro community makes demands on the greater community, we had better listen and get ready to use their suggestions constructively and to help the Negro make his energy investment for personal and social-civic betterment.

"There was very strong feeling in our group that we must confront and come to grips with the problem of the tendency to level down the problems of the Negro to the general level of the problems of the underprivileged, deprived children, and to see this not simply as a process of the larger problem, which it also is, but to see it as a unique problem at this time and for a number of reasons. One is historical, and that is that things are happening right now that are very important to capitalize on, and which, as one member said, can very well precipitate a lot of gain in the total school structure at the same time that we meet specific needs and a specific moral crisis in our time. And the other is that the Negro problems *are* unique, but they have a special history, a special crisis, and that they are caste problems as well as multidimensional class problems and mobility problems and that therefore the Negro community is going to make certain kinds of demands on *their* community and we just better be ready to use it constructively and to help it along. And there was some conjecture about how the students who participated in the sit-ins and the marches may not be willing to sit passively in the kinds of classrooms they sat in before either, and that this calls for certain kinds of reconsideration of the picture. And it was pointed out that in the redevelopment programs that are going on, there would be tremendous opportunities for involving these youth and their parents in a kind of learning dimension which we have not utilized before, but we could now."

A recurring theme heard in all small-group sessions concerned Negro leadership. The problems could not be solved merely by doing things for Negro youth and their families. Many participants felt that the key that would open up more opportunities, lift levels of aspiration, and improve the Negro's lot would be found in the stimulation of Negro leadership.

"When we begin talking in terms of working with the schools, we keep thinking of the school as an isolated sort of resource and how we're going to do things for people. We begin thinking in terms of state departments of education and of public schools locally. 'How are we going to meet these problems? What are we going to do for these people?' Instead, we should begin to think in terms of 'Let's ask the people what it is they would like us to do.' We should begin with their cooperation in terms of 'What kinds of things can we help you in the community do? Or how can you help us?" And we need to identify and work with Negro leadership. I was working in Bucks County, where they're beginning to attack this problem. They told us, 'But we've already identified our Negro leaders.' And we asked, 'Who told you they were leaders?' and they said, 'That's a darn good question, because sometimes people who would like to be leaders don't look like leaders.' What I'm saying, then, is that we have to become totally involved in the community as it exists and involve the community in what it is we're doing. And we may not like some of the things that communities suggest or the way they criticize what it is we would like to do."

The identical note was struck by another Negro participant who recounts his experience with a comment on students as potential leaders:

"I remember a student in the field this summer saying, when we were talking about Negro leaders, 'They're not Negro leaders. They act like white people.' And the question was raised again, 'What is a Negro leader? What is a leader anyway? Is he a leader in a field or is he a leader for people, or is he a leader because someone appointed him to be your leader?' And they began to realize the difference in their community as to what leaders were. Sometimes I think if you left things more up to the students, it would be better, because often when adults get into it they just project all their fears. Kids just are much more open. I have a lot of faith in the children, even though I get disappointed at times."

Many of the Negro participants complained that very few of the white participants were listening. After the first day of the Conference, one of the chairmen made the following prophetic statement: "Perhaps by tomorrow we can actually start to work."

"It seems to me that yesterday we were very noisy. We talked because we were all busy trying to impress one another, and nobody really listened to the other person at all. This means that by this morning we were in a state of hard confusion; but in our group this afternoon we had a chance to shoot off all of our frustrations and come to grips with our own expectations so that by the time we got here this afternoon, we were ready to listen. I think this silence was not due so much to the fact that we weren't interested, but, first, we no longer felt the need to impress one another, and second, we felt we needed to listen. I now believe we're at the point to settle down and *do* something. We're ready to listen, we're ready to give, to take, to reorganize, and perhaps by tomorrow we can actually start to work."

With the noise of the Conference subsiding, the following sections will indicate the nature of the tasks before us, if we want to start to work.

Conference Outcomes

In the course of four days of discussion, a rich variety of concrete information and recommendations for action emerged. These are summarized in the paragraphs that follow. These Conference outcomes are grouped as follows: information learned and collated about the situation as it now exists, proposals for action designed to meet the problems of Negro youth, indications for research requirements, and specific opportunities in these areas of endeavor for the Lincoln Filene Center and the nine-states group.

Assessment of Current Knowledge

The following were among the most important statements discussed by participants about how the problem of Negroes, and particularly Negro youth, currently stands:

1. The central awareness that emerged from the Conference was that the problem that concerns us is both a general one of the disadvantaged youth and a specific racial one. Much of what is problematical about Negro youth can be cited for all youth of lower-class status. Delinquency, cynicism, or disillusionment about life chances, sense of personal inadequacy—all are to be found among teen-agers from families of low income. Negroes are only one of a number of groups in society which show signs of deprivation of the psychological and material benefits enjoyed by the majority in our society. Consequently, an attack on the general conditions that put people of lower socioeconomic status at a disadvantage would be expected to affect favorably the life opportunities of the great bulk of Negroes who presently fall in that class.

But the Negro problem also must be recognized as a uniquely racial or caste one. Lower-class Negroes are subjected daily to psychological injury above and beyond that which their economic standing incurs. And such injury extends to Negroes of *all* social classes. Job discrimination, housing segregation, the existence of all-Negro schools, undeniable tension in personal contacts with whites, and many other such events constantly remind the Negro that he is different and that the difference implies inferiority. No serious effort to meet the moral crisis that the life of Negroes in America poses can avoid dealing specifically with the racial character of the problem.

2. The Negro revolt and attendant social change are moving at high speed. Much of the research reflected in the working papers is fast becoming outdated. To lean on studies completed in 1960 is to run the risk of being out of touch in 1965. A major problem to be faced by schools and other community agencies is how to keep abreast of new developments and new knowledge. The Lincoln Filene Center might become a repository for new knowledge.

3. Schools are involved inescapably in a social revolution. However, social scientists aver that school people generally have not actually become a part of the movement. They say that professional educators have difficulty in accepting the changing situation as one in which school people bear a responsibility for initiating new solutions and as one in which their customary expectation of middle-class behavior on the part of children and youth may have to be modified. To social scientists at the Conference, it appeared that school people expected them to initiate new solutions. The social scientists agree that there is a good fund of information available to school people, but they say that it is up to the schools to absorb the information and to use it in solving school problems and in building new programs.

4. A basic dilemma facing the Negro as he moves up in the social structure involves the achievement of a sense of self and an identity without "selling out" to the white middle-class community. Increasing ambiguity among American Negroes about identifying with African events, past and present, about the social desirability of light skin, and about Black Muslim emphasis on race separation rather than integration were cited as prominent demonstrations of this dilemma.

Proposals for Action

The members of the Conference dealt on two levels with ways in which substantial movement toward the achievement of first-class citizenship by Negroes can be accomplished. Some quite specific suggestions for action through the schools and through other agencies were made, and these are discussed in detail below. The other level of recommendation dealt with improving the social-civic process by which Negroes can effectively define their objectives for themselves and see those objectives translated into policy within the American system.

Proposals for Changing Social-Civic Process

1. Effectiveness in politics was seen as a major method of improving Negroes' life chances through mutual efforts. And the schools were seen as offering a potentially influential source of future training of Negroes

for meaningful citizenship. At present, Negro youth learn to be skeptical about the utility of exercising the responsibilities of citizenship while they are of school age; but this seems more to be because the schools make little or no impact on their thinking about politics, rather than making a negative impact. In a number of ways, the schools can contribute to a greater sense of how much can be realistically expected from political participation as an instrument for individual and group betterment; and they can also contribute to the development of more effective skills and strategies in politics so that those new expectations can be fulfilled.

2. Ways need to be explored in which the school can make use of such community events as boycotts, marches, and sit-ins to advance the educational understanding and growth of both white and Negro youth, particularly within social studies programs.

3. Continuous dialogue should be maintained by the school and Negro parents concerning the aims, purposes, and procedures of the school agency. These conversations should begin long before the child enters school. This may involve a parent-education program in which cultural encouragement is given to the home by the school and other agencies.

4. Negro families and youth frequently have many direct contacts and involvements with municipal, county, and state government units, such as welfare offices, employment and unemployment services units, police, courts, and other agencies. This kind of experience and competency can possibly be used constructively to help the social-civic development of Negroes.

Proposed Direct Changes

1. Psychological and social differentiation among Negro youngsters must be made to break the common stereotype. It may be helpful for the school authorities to consider three of the following overlapping categories within the spectrum of Negro youth: *(a)* the Negro students who are already "well on their way" and who may even try to out-middle-class the middle-class academic white students; *(b)* those students who have upward aspirations, but who are blocked and for whom there appear no legitimate means to chosen goals; and *(c)* those Negroes who are stable and are staying in the submilieu representing often the hard core of the defeated, the paralyzed, and the unmotivated. Negroes are like white youngsters in intelligence, aptitude, and achievement. Hence, different approaches and programs will be required to meet the needs of all Negro youth.

2. Opportunities should be provided for "role playing" and "role taking" in the daily school life of Negro and white youth. These techniques should be used with teachers as well as pupils as a means of improving mutual understanding of each group's positions and of systematically breaking down racial stereotypes.

3. Identification problems and opportunities of Negro youth need careful attention with particular reference to role and hero models in the school and neighborhood. Preparation of visual, auditory, and printed materials showing Negroes who have moved along in the social, economic, and educational scene should be prepared and tried out experimentally with both white and Negro youth.

4. Special training of teachers working with culturally deprived Negroes should be available in both teacher-preparation institutions and in-service training programs.

5. The experimental use of a modified social worker trained in group dynamics to assist teachers in the classroom in an effort to improve interpersonal relationships among pupils and among teachers and to modify aspects of the school culture or way of life has been recommended as a fruitful area for research.

6. It was also suggested that the quality of human relationships that are engendered among all pupils through current school practices needs to be reexamined carefully. Rules, regulations, and rituals of many schools often tend to block communication and to have a dehumanizing effect on all youngsters, including Negro youth. Development of close ties and friendships by pupils can do much to improve human relationships.

7. What support can be obtained for strengthening Negro self-concept by using the traditions to be found in African history? In using these sources, a check should be made to see whether youth feel first Negro, then American, or whether they feel American first and then Negro. It was suggested that the darker Negro may tend to show more positive orientation to Africa as a source of social and psychological uplift or locally to such groups as the Black Muslims.

8. Caution was expressed concerning the use and interpretation of standardized tests and measures with youngsters who have been culturally deprived and who often do not meet the conditions set by tests of intelligence, achievement, and aptitude. The development of "culture-fair" tests and testing practices was urged. Particular attention needs to be placed on the "cut-off" points that are established in selecting and grouping pupils for remediation and special educational treatment and which often induce either further segregation or deprivation of special services, such as remedial reading.

9. As a means of closing the informational gap between social scientists and educators who confront the problems of Negro young people directly, a publication was strongly urged that would indicate what the research on the Negro and other culturally disadvantaged youngsters implies for school practices.

10. Greater attention in classroom learning and textbook material needs to be devoted to the "Negro problem" in its various forms—e.g., segregation, discrimination, poverty, politics, delinquency, and dropouts—as a central political and moral issue in American life.

Proposals for Research

1. The psycho-social-political developmental processes of Negro children and youth should be studied with reference to the accumulated effect of low self-concept, inferior schools, and sterile environment on failure in school. Special note must be taken of aggressive behavior resulting from constant frustration with a view toward turning aggression into a positive force.

2. A study of Negro self-concept and education should also focus on the white population, whose concepts, projections, and stereotypes are an integral part of the Negro's problem. Replicative studies might also be made of slow-acculturating white groups whose problems of cultural disadvantage resemble those of the Negro, such as French Canadians, Puerto Ricans, and "poor (Anglo-Saxon) whites" from the South. Emphasis on the "Negro problem" should include an orientation that it is also a "white man's problem." This would call for programs aimed at white youth and adults in addition to supportive programs for the Negro.

3. A study of the evasion and stalling tactics that enable school personnel to sidestep or gloss over the harsh realities of the Negro youngsters who come from depressed and repressed Negro neighborhoods should be explored. This study may inquire as to how schools change and how teachers modify their attitudes and programs to help the culturally deprived Negro. The effect of Negro teachers on Negro youngsters and the question of male teachers as models and supports for Negro boys need to be investigated.

4. The subliminal, or hidden, curriculum of the school dictating a way of life by establishing norms as to how to behave and how not to behave should be studied at both the elementary and secondary school levels. The cultural imperatives of the school as powerful and pervasive forces for improving the educational and social development of the Negro need to be investigated.

5. A study of the cognitive style of Negro youngsters and educational strategies to engage them in the learning process is required in an effort to solve the school-failure problem. Particular attention to intrinsic and extrinsic motivations within the reward-punishment systems of the primary reference group versus the system in the school needs careful exploration.

6. The school must reach out to the Negro community in different ways. The need to establish and test out various models for bridge building between the school and the Negro family and community was cited.

7. Negro attacks on *de facto* school segregation in the North have raised important questions about the concept of the "neighborhood school." We need to study the nature and extent of parents' commitment to this concept. Special consideration needs to be given to the effects on pupils and schools of moving new youngsters, Negro or white, into or out of the neighborhood to achieve racial balance.

8. The development over time of discouragement among Negro young people about their chances for success in life—their prospects for effectiveness as citizens, as job holders, and as members of society at large—needs to be traced over the entire span of the school years. The specific contributions of schools, through formal or informal experiences, to reinforcing or mitigating such discouragement needs to be determined.

"An Opportune Precedent"

Dr. Bernard Kramer summarized the feelings of many participants on the final day of the work conference, saying:

> "For me, here is the key concept in this whole Conference: I believe it is absolutely true that if we face up to the problem of the Negro in American education then we shall face up to education and we shall face up to finances and we shall face up to sanitation and we shall face up to reading and we shall face up to science and to everything else that goes directly to the heart of the problem of education and the problem of America. So I would say it's not enough merely to bring this problem to the attention of the administration—this problem is one of many problems. I believe it must be forcefully brought to the attention of the school administrators that the Negro in America is a central problem of America—of all America—that the basic, key need is to bring to the American public an accurate and meaningful interpretation of the Negro in American life, both in educational content and in educational practice. I view content not merely in terms of textbooks filled with heroes, but textbooks dealing with the Negro in American life in the fullest sense—historically, politically, socially, and artistically; and this also applies to educational content as well as educational practice. This means facing up to the question of segregation—it can't be looked away from. If you look away from it, you will not be facing up to the problem of the Negro in American life and you will not be facing up to *American* life. So this calls for what I've put down in bold letters—*the willingness to take risks, the willingness to face events current—the willingness to adopt a position of moral leadership*. These things are required. If we don't adopt these positions then we will accept, in fact, that this is a dangerous precedent—I believe those words were used and the question was raised—'Isn't it a dangerous precedent to introduce materials specifically relating to Negroes?' We will adopt materials that refer to Negroes *if* we are interested in America. We will take the risk of a dangerous precedent. To me, it's not a dangerous precedent—it's an opportune precedent."

INDEX